The Rise of Ethnic Politics in Latin America

The Rise of Ethnic Politics in Latin America explores why indigenous movements have recently won elections for the first time in the history of the region. Raúl L. Madrid argues that indigenous parties have won by using a combination of inclusive ethnic and populist appeals to reach out to whites and mestizos as well as indigenous people. Indigenous parties have managed to win support across ethnic lines because the long history of racial mixing in Latin America blurred ethnic boundaries and reduced ethnic polarization. The ethnopopulist appeals of the indigenous parties have especially resonated in the Andean countries because of widespread disenchantment with the region's traditional parties and growing ethnic consciousness and mobilization. This book contains up-to-date qualitative and quantitative analyses of parties and elections in seven countries, including detailed case studies of Bolivia, Ecuador, and Peru.

Raúl L. Madrid is an associate professor in the Department of Government at the University of Texas at Austin. He is the author of *Retiring the State: The Politics of Pension Privatization in Latin America and Beyond* (2003) and is a co-editor of *Leftist Governments in Latin America: Successes and Shortcomings* (Cambridge, 2010). His articles have appeared in *Comparative Politics*, *Electoral Studies*, the *Journal of Latin American Studies*, *Latin American Politics and Society*, *Latin American Research Review*, *Political Science Quarterly*, and *World Politics*.

The Rise of Ethnic Politics
in Latin America

RAÚL L. MADRID

The University of Texas at Austin

CAMBRIDGE UNIVERSITY PRESS
Cambridge, New York, Melbourne, Madrid, Cape Town,
Singapore, São Paulo, Delhi, Mexico City

Cambridge University Press
32 Avenue of the Americas, New York, NY 10013-2473, USA

www.cambridge.org
Information on this title: www.cambridge.org/9780521153256

First published 2012

Printed in the United States of America

A catalog record for this publication is available from the British Library.

Library of Congress Cataloging in Publication data
Madrid, Raúl L.
    The rise of ethnic politics in Latin America / Raúl L. Madrid,
    University of Texas, Austin.
        p. cm.
    Includes bibliographical references and index.
    ISBN 978-0-521-19559-1 (hardback) – ISBN 978-0-521-15325-6 (paperback)
    1. Indians of Central America – Politics and government. 2. Indians of
    South America – Politics and government. 3. Political parties – Central America.
    4. Political parties – South America. 5. Central America – Ethnic relations – Political
    aspects. 6. South America – Ethnic relations – Political aspects I. Title.
    F1434.2.P76M34 2012
    305.80098–dc23   2012000053

ISBN 978-0-521-19559-1 Hardback
ISBN 978-0-521-15325-6 Paperback

For my parents

Contents

Figures

Tables

Acknowledgments

I have acquired numerous debts in the time that it took to complete this book, and many of them are owed to my home institution. The University of Texas at Austin awarded me a faculty research assignment that provided me with a semester off during the early stages of this project. The Teresa Lozano Long Institute for Latin American Studies at UT Austin provided me with various Mellon Faculty Fellowships that enabled me to carry out the field research for this book. A University of Texas at Austin Subvention Grant awarded by President William C. Powers, Jr., paid for the compilation of the index and the rights to the cover photo.

This study has benefited from the careful research assistance of various students at the University of Texas, especially Jin Seok Bae, Fred Cady, Danilo Contreras, Leonardo Correa, Eduardo Dargent, Scott Garrison, and Matt Johnson. The Department of Government and the College of Liberal Arts at the University of Texas at Austin provided the funding that made it possible to hire them.

I am fortunate to have a terrific group of faculty colleagues here at the University of Texas at Austin. Dan Brinks, Henry Dietz, Zach Elkins, Ken Greene, Juliet Hooker, Wendy Hunter, and Rob Moser provided insightful comments on one or more chapters. Kurt Weyland has gone way beyond the call of duty by reading and critiquing virtually the entire manuscript. A number of other people both inside and outside of the University of Texas also commented on one or more chapters, including Robert Barr, Luis Camacho, Carlos de la Torre, Eduardo Dargent, Christina Ewig, Austin Hart, Mala Htun, Fabrice Lehoucq, Steve Levitsky, Robin Madrid, Paula Muñoz, and Maritza Paredes. Of course, none of these people are responsible for the contents of this book.

I presented parts of this book at conferences or symposiums of the American Political Science Association, the Latin American Studies Association, the Center for Strategic and International Studies, Cornell University, Harvard University, Texas A&M University, Trinity University, the University of North Texas, the University of Notre Dame, and the Woodrow Wilson Center. I have received many helpful comments during these presentations. In particular, I thank Matthew Cleary, Merilee Grindle, María Inclán, Scott Mainwaring, Arturo Valenzuela, and the late Donna Van Cott, all of whom provided thoughtful criticisms and suggestions in their capacity as discussants.

Dozens of politicians, indigenous movement leaders, and academics in Bolivia, Ecuador, Peru, and Guatemala agreed to be interviewed for this study, and their insights considerably enriched my understanding of their countries. I am particularly grateful to Salvador Romero Ballivián, Diego Tello, Eduardo Dargent, Aldo Panfichi, and Dinorah Azpuru for providing me with data, helping set up interviews, and facilitating my field research in numerous ways.

I am also very grateful to Eric Crahan, my editor at Cambridge University Press, for shepherding this book through the review process so efficiently. This book benefited a great deal from Cambridge's review process and particularly from the detailed and helpful comments provided by Jóhanna Birnir and an anonymous reader.

Chapters 1 and 2 draw on material from my article "The Rise of Ethnopopulism in Latin America," which was published in *World Politics* Vol. 60, No. 3, April 2008: 475–508. Chapter 4 includes material from another of my articles, titled "Ethnic Proximity and Ethnic Voting in Peru," which appeared in the *Journal of Latin American Studies* Vol. 43, No. 2, May 2011: 267–97. Chapter 6 draws on selected material from my article "Indigenous Parties and Democracy in Latin America," which was published in *Latin American Politics and Society* Vol. 47, No. 4, Winter 2005: 161–79. I am grateful to the publishers of those journals, the Johns Hopkins University Press, Cambridge University Press, and Wiley-Blackwell, for granting me permission to use those materials.

My greatest debts are to family. Various members of my family, including Carlos Madrid, Marisa Madrid, Concha Madrid, Mia Madrid, and Antonia Castañeda, provided support, encouragement, and diversions that made writing this book easier. I am also grateful to my sister, Marisa Madrid of Aquacarta, for producing the map of Bolivia included in Chapter 2.

My wife, Paloma Díaz, and children, Nico and Bela Madrid, have been with me from the beginning to the end of this book. They accompanied me on field research trips to Bolivia, Ecuador, Guatemala, and Peru, and they tolerated the inevitable mood swings and weekend absences that come with writing a book. Most of all, they brought loads of joy and laughter (and no small amount of chaos) into my life, and for that I am very grateful.

My parents, Arturo Madrid and Robin Madrid, supported my strange interests from the beginning and were a never-ending source of intellectual stimulation. They encouraged me to travel the world, to obtain my Ph.D., and to enter academia. Most important, both in their own ways have served as role models for me. Their diverse interests and political commitments as well as their generosity and humor have inspired me as a scholar and as a human being. It is with great love and appreciation that I dedicate this book to them.

Abbreviations

ADN	Acción Democrática Nacionalista (Nationalist Democratic Action)
AICO	Movimiento de Autoridades Indígenas de Colombia (Movement of Indigenous Authorities of Colombia)
AIDESEP	Asociación Interétnica de Desarrollo de la Selva Peruana (Interethnic Association for the Development of the Peruvian Rainforest)
AP	Acción Popular (Popular Action)
APHU	Alianza para la Alternativa de la Humanidad (Alliance for an Alternative for Humanity)
APRA	Partido Aprista Peruano (Peruvian Aprista Party)
ASI	Alianza Social Indígena (Indigenous Social Alliance)
ASP	Asamblea de la Soberanía de los Pueblos (Assembly for the Sovereignty of the Peoples)
CAOI	Coordinadora Andina de Organizaciones Indígenas (Andean Coordinator of Indigenous Organizations)
CCP	Confederación Campesina del Perú (Peasant Confederation of Peru)
CEPAL	Comisión Económica para América Latina y el Caribe (Economic Commission for Latin America and the Caribbean)
CFP	Concentración de Fuerzas Populares (Concentration of Popular Forces)
CIDOB	Confederación Indígena del Oriente Boliviano (Indigenous Confederation of Eastern Bolivia)
CMS	Coordinadora de Movimientos Sociales (Coordinator of Social Movements)
CNA	Confederación Nacional Agraria (National Agrarian Confederation)
CNE	Corte Nacional Electoral (National Electoral Court)
CNOC	Coordinadora Nacional de Organizaciones Campesinas (National Coordinator of Peasant Organizations)

CONACAMI	Confederación Nacional de Comunidades del Perú Afectados por la Minería (National Confederation of Peruvian Communities Affected by Mining)
CONAIE	Confederación de Nacionalidades Indígenas del Ecuador (Confederation of Indigenous Nationalities of Ecuador)
CONALCAM	Coordinadora Nacional para el Cambio (National Coordinator for Change)
CONAP	Confederación de Nacionalidades Amazónicas del Perú (Confederation of Amazonian Nationalities of Peru)
CONAPA	Comisión Nacional de Pueblos Andinos, Amazónicos y Afroperuanos (National Commission of Andean, Amazonian, and Afro-Peruvian Peoples)
CONDEPA	Conciencia de Patria (Conscience of the Fatherland)
CONFENAIE	Confederación de Nacionalidades Indígenas de la Amazonía Ecuatoriana (Confederation of Indigenous Nationalities of the Ecuadorian Amazon)
CONIVE	Consejo Nacional Indio de Venezuela (National Indian Council of Venezuela)
COPPIP	Conferencia Permanente de Pueblos Indígenas del Perú (Permanent Conference of Indigenous Peoples of Peru)
CSUTCB	Confederación Sindical Única de Trabajadores Campesinos de Bolivia (Unique Confederation of Peasant Workers of Bolivia)
DP	Democracia Popular (Popular Democracy)
ECUARUNARI	Ecuador Runacunapac Riccharimui (Awakening of Ecuadorian People)
EG	Encuentro por Guatemala (Gathering for Guatemala)
EGTK	Ejército Guerrillero Tupak Katari (Tupak Katari Guerrilla Army)
EJE	Eje Pachakuti (Axis of Pachakuti)
FEINE	Federación Ecuatoriana de Iglesias Evangélicas (Ecuadorian Federation of Evangelical Churches)
FENOC	Federación Nacional de Organizaciones Campesinas (National Federation of Peasant Organizations)
FENOCIN	Federación Nacional de Organizaciones Campesinas, Indígenas y Negras (National Federation of Peasant, Indigenous, and Black Organizations)
FIN	Frente Integración Nacional (National Integration Front)
FRENATRACA	Frente Nacional de Trabajadores y Campesinos (National Front of Workers and Peasants)
FULKA	Frente Único de Liberación Katarista (Unique Front of Katarista Liberation)
ID	Izquierda Democrática (Democratic Left)
IMF	International Monetary Fund

INE	Instituto Nacional de Estadística (National Institute of Statistics)
IPSP	Instrumento Político para la Soberanía de los Pueblos (Political Instrument for the Sovereignty of the Peoples)
IU	Izquierda Unida (United Left)
LAPOP	Latin American Public Opinion Project
MAS	Movimiento al Socialismo (Movement Toward Socialism)
MBL	Movimiento Bolivia Libre (Movement Free Bolivia)
MCNP	Movimiento Ciudadano Nuevo País (Citizen's Movement for a New Country)
MIAJ	Movimiento Independiente Amauta Jatari (Amauta Jatari Independent Movement)
MIAP	Movimiento Indígena Amazónico del Perú (Amazonian Indigenous Movement of Peru)
MINCAP	Movimiento Independiente de Campesinos y Profesionales (Independent Movement of Peasants and Professionals)
MIP	Movimiento Indígena Pachakuti (Pachakuti Indigenous Movement)
MIR	Movimiento de Izquierda Revolucionaria (Movement of the Revolutionary Left)
MITKA	Movimiento Indio Tupak Katari (Tupak Katari Indigenous Movement)
MKN	Movimiento Katarista Nacional (National Katarista Movement)
MNR	Movimiento Nacionalista Revolucionario (Revolutionary Nationalist Movement)
MRTK	Movimiento Revolucionario Tupak Katari (Tupak Katari Revolutionary Movement)
MRTKL	Movimiento Revolucionario Tupak Katari de Liberación (Tupak Katari Revolutionary Movement of Liberation)
MSM	Movimiento Sin Miedo (Movement Without Fear)
MUPI	Movimiento Unido de Pueblos Indígenas (United Movement of Indigenous Peoples)
MUPP-NP	Movimiento Unidad Plurinacional Pachakutik – Nuevo País (Pachakutik Plurinational Unity Movement – New Country)
NFR	Nueva Fuerza Republicana (New Republican Force)
ONIC	Organización Nacional Indígena de Colombia (National Indigenous Organization of Colombia)
ONPE	Oficina Nacional de Procesos Electorales (National Office of Electoral Processes)
PDC	Partido Demócrata Cristiano (Christian Democratic Party)
PLC	Partido Liberal Constitucionalista (Liberal Constitutionalist Party)
PNP	Partido Nacionalista Peruano (Peruvian Nationalist Party)

PODEMOS	Poder Democrático y Social (Social and Democratic Power)
PPB-CN	Plan Progreso para Bolivia – Concertación Nacional (Plan Progress for Bolivia – National Concertation)
PPC	Partido Popular Cristiano (Popular Christian Party)
PRE	Partido Roldosista Ecuatoriano (Ecuadorian Roldosist Party)
PRIAN	Partido Renovador Institucional Acción Nacional (Institutional Renewal Party of National Action)
PSC	Partido Social Cristiano (Social Christian Party)
PSP	Partido Sociedad Patriótica, 21 de Enero (Patriotic Society Party, 21st of January)
PS-FA	Partido Socialista – Frente Amplio (Socialist Party – Broad Front)
PUAMA	Pueblos Unidos Multiétnicos de Amazonas (United Multiethnic Peoples of Amazonas)
RAAN	Región Autónoma del Atlántico Norte (North Atlantic Autonomous Region)
RAAS	Región Autónoma del Atlántico Sur (South Atlantic Autonomous Region)
TSE	Tribunal Supremo Electoral (Supreme Electoral Tribunal)
UCS	Unidad Cívica Solidaridad (Civic Solidarity Union)
UDP	Unión Democrática y Popular (Democratic and Popular Union)
UN	Unidad Nacional (National Unity)
UNO	Unidad Nicaragüense Opositora (United Nicaraguan Opposition)
UPP	Unión por el Perú (Union for Peru)
URNG	Unidad Revolucionario Nacional Guatemalteca (Guatemalan National Revolutionary Unity)
YATAMA	Yapti Tasba Masraka Nanih Asla Takanka (Organization of the Children of the Mother Earth)

I

Ethnicity and Ethnopopulism in Latin America

It is almost an axiom of politics that ethnicity shapes political participation. In most countries, individuals join political parties, evaluate policies, and vote based in part on their ethnic identification. Political parties, meanwhile, choose candidates, forge alliances, design platforms, and employ certain types of rhetoric and symbols in efforts to attract voters of particular ethnicities.

Latin American countries were traditionally the exception to this rule. Not only were there no important ethnic parties in Latin America, but the dominant non-ethnic parties largely avoided ethnic themes in their campaigns and platforms. Latin American citizens, meanwhile, generally did not vote along ethnic lines. Indigenous people, for example, often split their votes among various parties or voted in ways that were indistinguishable from the rest of the population (Birnir and Van Cott 2007; Madrid 2005a, 2005c; Van Cott 2005).[1]

In the last couple of decades, however, the region has begun to change. Indigenous people have taken to the streets to protest government policy, topple presidents, and demand economic, political, and social reforms. Non-ethnic parties, especially populist parties, have increasingly embraced indigenous peoples' demands, recruited indigenous candidates, and employed indigenous symbols. Perhaps most important, in a number of countries, the indigenous movement has formed parties aimed specifically at representing indigenous interests.

Some of these indigenous parties have been quite successful. In this study, I define success as winning at least ten percent of the vote in presidential or legislative elections. Obtaining ten percent or more of the vote is a significant achievement in Latin America's often fragmented party systems, and it frequently leads to appreciable policy influence. Parties that gain ten percent or more of the vote typically have considerable legislative representation and at

---

[1] There were exceptions. In the 1950s and early 1960s, for example, the indigenous population in Bolivia voted overwhelmingly for the ruling Movimiento Nacionalista Revolucionario (MNR). Similarly, in Mexico, indigenous voters traditionally voted en masse for the ruling Partido Revolucionario Institucional. Neither of these parties were indigenous parties, however, and their leadership was almost exclusively white or mestizo.

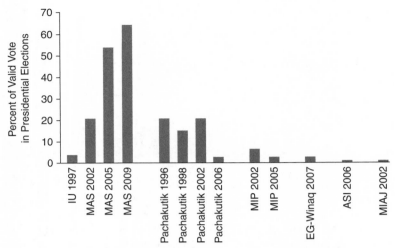

FIGURE I.I. The performance of indigenous parties, 1996–2009.

times are asked to join the government and granted control of certain ministries. They also are usually guaranteed state funding and a place on the ballot in subsequent legislative elections.

As Figure 1.1 indicates, the most successful indigenous party in Latin America to date has been the Movimiento al Socialismo (MAS), which won a majority of the vote and captured the presidency in Bolivia in 2005 and again in 2009. The Movimiento Unidad Plurinacional Pachakutik – Nuevo País (MUPP-NP), which I will refer to as Pachakutik, was also initially successful: In alliance with other parties and movements it won fifteen to twenty percent of the presidential vote and approximately ten percent of the legislative vote in the 1996, 1998, and 2002 elections in Ecuador. Other indigenous parties have fared poorly, however. Only one of the numerous Indianista and Katarista parties that emerged in Bolivia won more than three percent of the vote, and that party, the Movimiento Indígena Pachakuti (MIP), did so only once, obtaining six percent of the vote in 2002. Nobel Prize winner Rigoberta Menchú and her party, Winaq, won a mere three percent of the vote in Guatemala in 2007 and 2011, and the Alianza Social Indígena (ASI) in Colombia fared even worse.

What explains the recent emergence of indigenous parties in Latin America? Why have some of these parties been successful while others have failed?

This study examines indigenous parties in seven countries – Bolivia, Ecuador, Peru, Guatemala, Nicaragua, Colombia, and Venezuela – focusing mostly on the first three countries. It discusses how these parties arose and explains why some indigenous parties, such as the MAS and Pachakutik, have been successful, while others, like the MIP, Winaq, and the ASI, have fared poorly. It also shows how some mestizo-led parties and politicians, especially in the case of Peru, have employed ethnic appeals to win the support of indigenous voters.

Finally, the book explores what impact indigenous parties, particularly in Bolivia and Ecuador, have had on democracy in the region. These analyses are carried out using a variety of quantitative and qualitative data, including surveys, elite interviews, newspapers and other archival sources, and municipal and provincial electoral and census data.

Understanding the rise of indigenous parties in Latin America is important because these parties have had an important impact on policy, especially in Bolivia, where an indigenous party has governed at the national level since 2006. Indigenous parties have pushed for the revision of their countries' constitutions to recognize indigenous peoples' cultures and rights, and they have helped enact a variety of laws that have benefited the indigenous population, from affirmative action programs to bilingual education. As Chapter 6 discusses, however, some indigenous parties also have taken steps that have undermined democracy. The MAS, in particular, has weakened democracy in Bolivia by concentrating power, undermining horizontal accountability, and harassing the opposition.

The rise of indigenous parties in Latin America is also interesting from a theoretical perspective. We still know relatively little about why some ethnic parties flourish while others do not. Nor is there much consensus about why ethnic parties vary significantly in terms of the types of appeals that they employ and the impact they have on democracy. This study seeks to contribute to theories of ethnic parties by shedding light on these important questions.

THE ARGUMENT IN BRIEF

Existing studies have provided several different explanations for the rise of indigenous parties in Latin America (Beck and Mijeski 2001, 2006; Collins 2006; Durand Guevara 2006; Huber 2008; Laurent 2009; Madrid 2008; Marenghi and Alcántara Sáez 2007; Muñoz-Pogossian 2008; Rice 2006; Van Cott 2005, 2003c). Some studies have attributed the emergence of indigenous parties to institutional reforms that Latin American countries carried out during the 1990s, which made it easier to create new parties. Other studies have attributed their rise to the decline of the traditional parties, particularly left-of-center parties, which opened space in the political system for new parties. Finally, some scholars have suggested that powerful indigenous social movements have played a key role in fostering indigenous parties.

Although these arguments are quite helpful in explaining why and how indigenous parties were formed, they are less useful in explaining their electoral performance. In particular, they cannot easily explain why, within the same countries, some indigenous parties were successful while others were not. Nor can they readily explain why some of these parties have managed to win the support of many white and mestizo as well as indigenous voters.

This study argues that the type of appeals used by indigenous parties explains to a large degree their electoral performance. Indigenous parties – and some mestizo-led parties – have succeeded where they have used a combination of inclusive ethnic and populist appeals. The astounding rise of Evo Morales and the MAS in Bolivia, for example, was due in large part to the party's decision to embrace populist strategies and reach out to non-indigenous organizations and leaders, while still maintaining its close ties to the indigenous movement. Similarly, Pachakutik in Ecuador enjoyed success in the late 1990s and early 2000s by maintaining cross-ethnic alliances and balancing ethnic and traditional populist appeals.

Indigenous parties have used a variety of ethnic appeals to woo indigenous voters. They have nominated numerous indigenous candidates, maintained close links with indigenous organizations, invoked traditional indigenous symbols, and embraced many of the longstanding demands of the indigenous movement. In contrast to traditional ethnic parties, however, the successful indigenous parties in Latin America have also sought to attract non-indigenous voters. Thus, they have eschewed exclusionary rhetoric; developed a broad and inclusive platform; and recruited many white and mestizo candidates, leaders, and organizations to their side.

Populist strategies have been a key component of the efforts of the successful indigenous parties to attract voters of all ethnic backgrounds. Both the MAS and Pachakutik have focused their campaigns on the poorer sectors of the population, relentlessly attacked the political establishment, and used a variety of personalistic appeals. Like traditional populist parties, they also have denounced foreign intervention in their countries and called for income redistribution and a greater role for the state in the economy.

Indigenous parties are not the only parties that have successfully employed ethnopopulist appeals. Some mestizo-led parties, such as Conciencia de Patria (CONDEPA) in Bolivia, and Perú Posible and the Partido Nacionalista Peruano (PNP) in Peru, have also used a combination of inclusive ethnic and populist appeals to assemble broad multi-ethnic coalitions. These mestizo-led parties have focused mostly on populist appeals, but they have recruited indigenous candidates and organizations and embraced ethnic demands and symbols in order to reach out to voters in indigenous areas.

These inclusive ethnic appeals have been successful in large part because of the long history of *mestizaje* (ethnic or racial mixing) in the region. *Mestizaje* has not eliminated ethnic attachments or ethnic discrimination, but it has blurred ethnic boundaries and reduced ethnic polarization. The fluidity of ethnic boundaries and the low level of ethnic polarization in the region have enabled indigenous parties to win the support of many whites and mestizos. Nevertheless, ethnic proximity has shaped voting patterns in the region. People who self-identify as indigenous or who come from an indigenous background have supported the indigenous parties in the greatest numbers because they have sympathized with their ethnic demands and proposals to combat ethnic discrimination and marginalization.

This study has important implications for the literature on ethnic parties. The literature on ethnic parties would not expect such parties to be inclusive or to win support across ethnic lines (Horowitz 1985; Rabushka and Shepsle

1972; Reilly 2001; Sisk 1996). Much of the existing literature on ethnic parties has argued that such parties will use exclusionary appeals to mobilize co-ethnics, which will promote ethnic conflict and undermine democracy. This study, however, shows that where ethnic identities are fluid and ethnic polarization is low, as in ethnically mixed societies, ethnic parties are much more likely to employ inclusive appeals and to woo support across ethnic lines. Inclusive ethnic appeals, moreover, are unlikely to promote ethnic conflict in the way that exclusionary ethnic appeals often do. These findings suggest that the literature on ethnic parties needs to take into account the nature of ethnic identification and inter-ethnic relations in order to predict what sorts of appeals ethnic parties are likely to use and what their impact will be.

This study also has important implications for the literature on populism. The Latin American literature on populism would hardly expect populist parties to embrace ethnic appeals or to emerge from rural indigenous movements (Conniff 1982; Kaufman and Stallings 1991; Weyland 1999). This book, however, demonstrates that ethnic and populist appeals can be effectively combined to win the support of members of marginalized ethnic groups.

This study focuses on Latin America, but the arguments made in it should apply more broadly. Specifically, I would expect inclusive ethnic appeals to be effective anywhere ethnic identities are relatively fluid and ethnic polarization is low, but especially in those societies that have undergone considerable ethnic mixing. Populist appeals, meanwhile, should attract voters in those countries where parties are weak, political disenchantment is high, and large sectors of the population suffer from marginality and exclusion.

This chapter begins by defining the key terms that are employed in this book. It then evaluates the strengths and weaknesses of some existing explanations for the rise of indigenous parties in the region. It also examines the literature on ethnic parties in other regions and shows how, contrary to the expectations of this literature, indigenous parties in Latin America have won votes across ethnic lines by using inclusive appeals. Ethnic mixing in Latin America, it argues, has encouraged this inclusive approach. The chapter subsequently examines the literature on populism. It demonstrates that contrary to the expectations of the Latin America literature, ethnic and populist appeals may be effectively combined to win support from the marginalized sectors of the population. It shows how those parties that have combined ethnic and populist appeals have fared much better than those parties that have focused mostly on ethnic appeals or that have ignored ethnic demands altogether. The concluding sections of this chapter lay out the research design, methods, and organization of the book.

DEFINITIONS

Following Chandra and Wilkinson (2008, 517), this book defines *ethnicity* and *ethnic groups* as categories "in which descent-based attributes are necessary for membership." Ethnic groups are typically organized around characteristics that are identifiable and difficult to change, such as race, phenotypes, and language (Birnir 2007, 3–4; Chandra 2006). Nevertheless, this book employs constructivist assumptions about ethnicity and ethnic identification. It assumes that people often belong to multiple ethnic categories, and that the category they choose to identify with may vary over time depending on the circumstances.

Following Van Cott (2005, 2), I employ the definition of *indigenous peoples* developed by the United Nations Subcommission on the Prevention of Discrimination and Protection of Minorities:

> Indigenous communities, peoples and nations are those which, having a historical continuity with pre-invasion and pre-colonial societies that developed on their territories, considered themselves distinct from other sectors of the societies now prevailing in those territories, or parts of them (United Nations 1986, para. 379).

As discussed later in this chapter, I define the *indigenous population* to include not just those people who self-identify as indigenous (or with some indigenous category such as Aymara or Quechua), but all people who grew up speaking an indigenous language, regardless of how they self-identify. I employ the term *Indian* as a synonym for indigenous.

I use the term *mestizo* to refer to people of mixed European and indigenous ancestry. An *indigenous mestizo* is someone who self-identifies as mestizo, but who comes from an indigenous background and typically maintains some indigenous customs (de la Cadena 2000; Programa de las Naciones Unidas para el Desarrollo 2004). In the Andean nations, people of mostly indigenous descent and appearance who have adopted mestizo identities are often popularly referred to as *cholos*, but relatively few people self-identify as cholo in part because the term sometimes has pejorative connotations.

Throughout this book I use the term *party* to refer to any movements or organizations that participate in elections, regardless of how they describe themselves or their degree of organization and institutionalization. I define an *ethnic party* as an organization that prioritizes the interests of a particular ethnic group or set of ethnic groups and seeks to appeal to them as members of that ethnic group. A non-ethnic party, by contrast, does not prioritize the interests of any single ethnic group. Ethnic parties may be inclusive or exclusionary and in this sense my definition differs from those of other scholars such as Horowitz (1985, 291–3) and Chandra (2004, 2011).[2] Inclusive ethnic parties prioritize the interests of a particular ethnic group or cluster of ethnic groups, but they seek to appeal across ethnic lines and do not exclude any groups. Exclusionary ethnic parties, by contrast, do not seek to appeal across ethnic lines.

---

[2] Horowitz (1985, 291) defines *ethnic parties* as organizations that receive their support exclusively from a single ethnic group (or cluster of ethnic groups) and serve the interests of that group, and Chandra (2011, 155) defines ethnic parties as organizations that champion the interests of certain ethnic groups while seeking to exclude others. Their definitions of an ethnic party thus resemble what I refer to as an *exclusionary ethnic party*, and their definitions of a *multiethnic party* correspond more closely to what I refer to as an *inclusive ethnic party*.

I use the term *indigenous party* to refer to those electoral organizations that prioritize the interests of the indigenous population regardless of whether they are inclusive or exclusionary. Indigenous parties are therefore a particular type of ethnic party.

I define *mestizo-led parties* as parties whose leadership is mostly mestizo.[3] This includes the vast majority of parties in Latin America. Mestizo-led parties in Latin America do not explicitly prioritize the interests of the mestizo population, the indigenous population, or any other ethnic group and they are therefore not ethnic parties. As noted, however, some mestizo-led parties such as CONDEPA, Perú Posible, and the PNP, have made ethnic appeals to indigenous people in order to try to win their support.

Populism is a notoriously slippery concept and its meaning has been the subject of a great deal of debate. Some scholars have identified it as a set of economic policies, specifically deficit spending, income redistribution, and widespread state intervention in the economy (Dornbusch and Edwards 1991; Sachs 1989). Other scholars have focused on the social base of populism, identifying it as a multi-class movement rooted in the urban popular sectors (Conniff 1982; Ianni 1975). Still other scholars have focused on populism as a discourse that presents politics as a Manichean struggle between the masses and the corrupt elites (de la Torre 2000; Hawkins 2010; Laclau 2005; Panizza 2005). Finally, some scholars have characterized populism as a form of personalistic rule involving mass mobilization. Weyland (2001, 14), for example, defines it as "a political strategy through which a personalistic leader seeks or exercises government power based on direct, unmediated, uninstitutionalized support from large numbers of mostly unorganized followers."

In this study, I opt for a multidimensional definition that combines several of the attributes of populism stressed by different scholars. I define *populism* as a campaign and governing strategy in which a personalistic leader seeks to mobilize the masses in opposition to the elites. This implies three core attributes. First, populist movements are personalistic. They revolve around a dominant personality or *caudillo*, and these leaders tend to concentrate power in themselves rather than in a party bureaucracy. Second, populist leaders campaign and govern in the name of the masses and they seek to mobilize them to achieve their electoral and policy aims. The leaders of populist movements may come from the middle classes or elites and they may enjoy broad multi-class support, but they nevertheless focus their appeals on the common people and they typically employ popular language, style, and dress in their efforts to mobilize them. Third and finally, populist movements are anti-establishment. Populist leaders frequently criticize the political and economic elites and employ often incendiary language in doing so.

---

[3] It is often difficult to distinguish between whites and mestizos in Latin America and I make no effort to do so with respect to the leadership of parties.

TABLE 1.1. *Key Distinguishing Characteristics of Different Types of Populism*

	Ethnopopulism	Traditional populism	Neoliberal populism
Employs personalistic appeals?	Yes	Yes	Yes
Focuses appeals on lower classes?	Yes	Yes	Yes
Makes anti-establishment appeals?	Yes	Yes	Yes
Makes extensive ethnic appeals?	Yes	No	No
Adopts nationalist and state interventionist rhetoric and policies?	Sometimes	Yes	No
Advocates neoliberal policies?	Sometimes	No	Yes

I also identify several secondary or subordinate categories of populism, namely traditional populism, neoliberal populism, and ethnopopulism.[4] As Table 1.1 indicates, these secondary categories have the core properties of populism, plus one or more additional characteristics. *Traditional populism* I define as a campaign and governing strategy that includes nationalist, state interventionist, and redistributive policies and appeals in addition to the aforementioned characteristics. *Neoliberal populism*, by contrast, is a strategy that eschews statist and nationalist appeals and policies in favor of market-oriented measures.

Ethnopopulism refers to a campaign and governing strategy in which politicians or parties combine ethnic and populist appeals or policies. Ethnopopulism can be exclusionary as well as inclusive. In Latin America, the parties that have employed widespread ethnopopulist appeals have been inclusive, but in Europe the most prominent parties that have employed ethnopopulist appeals have been exclusionary, right-wing, anti-immigrant parties (Betz 2001, 1994; Mudde 2007; Mudde and Rovira Kaltwasser 2010). Ethnopopulism can also involve different types of economic policies and appeals. In Latin America, indigenous parties have typically employed the nationalist and state interventionist appeals that are characteristic of traditional populism, but some populist politicians, such as Alberto Fujimori and Alejandro Toledo, have combined ethnic and neoliberal populist appeals.

As mentioned previously, a variety of politicians and parties has successfully employed ethnopopulist appeals in Latin America in recent decades, including indigenous parties such as the MAS and Pachakutik and mestizo-led movements such as CONDEPA, Perú Posible, and the PNP. This study classifies both of these types of parties as ethnopopulist. Nevertheless, as we shall see, there are important differences between these two types of parties. The indigenous parties, unlike the mestizo-led parties, have prioritized the demands of the indigenous population and they have had a much greater percentage of

---

[4] On categories and concepts, see Sartori (1970), Collier and Mahon (1993), and Weyland (2001).

indigenous people in leadership positions. The indigenous parties also have focused to a greater extent on ethnic appeals than have the mestizo-led parties, whereas the mestizo-led parties have focused on populist appeals to a larger degree than have the indigenous parties. Finally, the two types of parties also differ in terms of their organization. Whereas the mestizo-led parties that I focus on are top-down, personalistic organizations, most of the indigenous parties have important social movement bases.[5]

EXISTING EXPLANATIONS

To date, most of the literature on indigenous politics in Latin America has focused on indigenous movements rather than indigenous parties per se (Albó 1991; Andolina 1999; Becker 2008; Brysk 2000; Dary 1998; Lucero 2008; Maybury-Lewis 2002; Pajuelo Teves 2007; Postero and Zamosc 2004; Selverston-Scher 2001; Van Cott 2000; Yashar 2005). Nevertheless, a growing number of studies has examined indigenous parties in the region (Beck and Mijeski 2001, 2006; Collins 2006; Durand Guevara 2006; Huber 2008; Laurent 2009; Madrid 2008; Marenghi and Alcántara Sáez 2007; Mijeski and Beck 2011; Muñoz-Pogossian 2008; Rice 2006; Rice and Van Cott 2006; Van Cott 2005, 2003c). The literature on indigenous parties has typically sought to explain how these parties were formed as well as why some of them have enjoyed a great deal of success. In this study, however, I focus mostly on performance, rather than formation, because the indigenous parties have only had an important impact to the extent that they have been successful. Moreover, it is the success of some of these parties that is truly surprising. In most Latin American countries, it is relatively easy to create a new party, but it is quite difficult to build a successful one. Indeed in the last couple of decades, numerous indigenous groups have formed parties, but the vast majority of these parties have fared poorly.

The emerging literature on indigenous parties has concentrated on three types of explanatory variables: institutional factors; social movement variables; and party system factors. Some studies have ascribed explanatory weight to all three types of variables. Indeed, the most prominent study of indigenous parties to date, Van Cott's (2005, 48) book, argues that: "[I]nstitutional changes, party system changes, and social movement factors were important in encouraging or discouraging the formation of ethnic parties, and in influencing their relative success, in all six countries [that the book examines]."

---

[5] Some scholars would not characterize either the MAS or Pachakutik as populist parties on the grounds that they have important social movement bases and are not purely personalistic movements (Levitsky and Roberts 2011; Roberts 2007). My definition of populism, however, focuses on the types of appeals that the parties make rather than on their organizational structure. Both the MAS (beginning in 2002) and Pachakutik (between 1996 and 2002) made extensive populist appeals, including personalistic appeals, in their presidential campaigns.

Perhaps the most common approach attributes the rise of indigenous parties to various institutional reforms that Latin American countries carried out in the 1990s (Birnir 2004; Collins 2006; Marenghi and Alcántara Sáez 2007; Muñoz-Pogossian 2008; Rice 2006; Van Cott 2003c, 2005). These arguments build on a large literature that has found that the formation of new parties is favored by certain institutional factors (Grofman and Lijphart 1986; Harmel and Robertson 1985; Ordeshook and Shvetsova 1994; Shugart and Carey 1992). This literature suggests that new parties are more likely to form and succeed where there are few barriers to having them on the ballot, where electoral rules grant legislative representation to small parties, and where such parties may gain access to important local-level offices before seeking power at the national level. Other scholars have argued that certain types of electoral rules, such as proportional representation and high district magnitude, encourage the formation of ethnic parties, in particular, by allowing ethnic groups to gain representation without reaching across ethnic lines (Horowitz 1991; Lijphart 1977; Norris 2004; Reilly 2001; Sisk 1996).[6]

The literature on indigenous parties maintains that institutional reforms not only facilitated the formation of these parties, but also helped lead to their success in some countries. According to this literature, a number of different types of reforms have played a role in the rise of these parties. In the case of Bolivia, scholars have focused on two main reforms: the 1994 law that created municipalities throughout the country and called for the direct election of their mayors and councilors, and the 1994 constitutional reform that established single-member districts for electing more than half of the members of the Bolivian Chamber of Deputies (Collins 2006; Muñoz-Pogossian 2008; Stefanoni 2004; Urioste 2004; Van Cott 2005). In the case of Ecuador, scholars have focused on changes in ballot access requirements, specifically a 1995 law that allowed independent movements to participate in national elections (Birnir 2004; Macdonald Jr. 2002; Van Cott 2005). Some analysts have also argued that the creation of national legislative seats reserved for indigenous people spurred the rise of indigenous parties in Colombia and Venezuela (Rice 2006; Van Cott 2005). Conversely, the case has been made that other institutional factors, namely strict ballot access requirements and the centralization of political power, have impeded the emergence of indigenous parties in Peru (Rice 2006; Van Cott 2005, 163–6).

Institutional explanations are not without merit. Registration requirements clearly have impeded the formation of indigenous parties in some instances, and the loosening of those requirements may have played a role in the creation of Pachakutik in Ecuador. The 1994 decentralization law in Bolivia, meanwhile, stimulated the formation of the predecessor of the MAS, the Asamblea Soberanía de los Pueblos, which was created in part to compete in the 1995

---

[6] Conversely, some studies have argued that single-member districts can favor ethnic parties where these parties draw their support from geographically concentrated minority groups (Meguid 2008; Rae 1971; Sartori 1976).

municipal elections in Bolivia.[7] And the establishment of reserved legislative seats encouraged indigenous organizations in Colombia and Venezuela to form parties in order to compete for those seats.

Although institutional reforms can help explain the *formation* of indigenous parties in some countries, they are less useful in explaining the *success* of these parties. Because these reforms are national-level measures that affect all parties, institutional reforms are ill-suited to explaining the varying performance of different parties within the same countries. For example, they cannot easily explain why the MAS succeeded in Bolivia, while other indigenous parties that emerged in Bolivia about the same time, such as the MIP, failed. Moreover, some of the institutional reforms, such as changes in registration requirements, are only said to explain party formation, not party success.

In addition, there is only limited empirical evidence linking the success of indigenous parties to institutional reforms.[8] Van Cott (2003c, 16; 2005, 23–32) examined how various types of institutional reforms affected indigenous party formation and success in six countries, but she found only mixed support for her hypotheses. Indeed, she concludes that "Given the multiplicity and diversity of institutional changes in the six cases studied, it is difficult to discern a systematic causal effect attributable to any one particular law or regulation" (Van Cott 2005, 31). In a valuable study of voting at the district level in six Latin American countries, Rice and Van Cott (2006, 724–5) did find that district magnitude was positively correlated with indigenous party formation and indigenous parties' share of the total vote. This interesting finding, however, would seem to contradict Van Cott's own claims that the creation of single-member districts in Bolivia stimulated the rise of the MAS.

Institutional theorists have also misinterpreted the significance of some of the reforms. Party registration requirements in Peru, for example, have not traditionally been very demanding, nor were they particularly strict in Ecuador prior to the 1995 law. Moreover, contrary to the arguments of institutional theorists, the creation of single-member districts in Bolivia did not lead to the election of significantly more indigenous party legislators than would have been elected under the previous system. And the establishment of a few reserved seats was not enough to bring about the success of indigenous parties in Colombia and Venezuela. Indeed, indigenous parties in these countries never managed to win more than a tiny fraction of the national vote.

Thus, the jury is still out on what role institutional factors have played in the rise of indigenous parties in the region. Certain institutional reforms, such as the establishment of reserved seats and the loosening of registration

---

[7] Nevertheless, some prominent leaders of the indigenous parties in Bolivia and Ecuador have questioned whether the institutional reforms played a key role in the formation of indigenous parties, arguing that they would have created the parties even in the absence of the reforms (interviews with Cabascango 2005 and Pacari 2005). See also the 2001 interview with Bolivian indigenous leader Alejo Véliz, cited in Van Cott (2003c, 22).

[8] Institutional theorists tend to focus on different types of reforms in different countries, which complicates any effort to test these explanations cross-nationally.

requirements, appear to have stimulated the creation of indigenous parties, but there is not much hard evidence to suggest that these reforms have played a major role in the performance of indigenous parties in elections.

Changes in Latin American party systems represent another potential explanation for the recent emergence and success of some indigenous parties. The parties literature has long argued that the nature of the existing party system may encourage or discourage the formation of new parties. Various scholars have argued that new parties are more likely to emerge and thrive in weakly institutionalized or decaying party systems in which voters do not have strong attachments to the existing parties (Bruhn 1997; Dalton et al. 1984; Kitschelt 1988; Lago and Martínez 2011; López 2005). Other scholars have argued that new parties are more likely to rise in party systems that have important unoccupied areas of issue or policy space (Hug 2001; Kitschelt 1988; Lawson and Merkl 1988). According to this logic, new parties fare well where they are able to stake out unclaimed policy territory, exploit untapped social cleavages, or embrace important demands of the electorate that the traditional parties have failed to address.[9]

Studies of indigenous parties have argued that the decay and fragmentation of party systems in the region helped give birth to the indigenous parties (Rice 2006; Rice and Van Cott 2006; Van Cott 2005). According to these scholars, indigenous parties were able to win the support of many of the voters who had become disaffected with the traditional parties. Van Cott (2005, 37) argues that the decline of the left, in particular, helped indigenous parties because it "opened space in the political system for indigenous movements accustomed to participating in politics through leftist parties."[10] She maintains that the decline of the left enabled indigenous parties to draw on "cadres from defunct or diminished leftist parties, organized labor, and leftist intellectuals searching for a viable alternative political project ..." (Van Cott 2005, 38).

There is some truth to the argument that the decline of traditional and leftist parties facilitated the rise of indigenous parties in the region. As we shall see, the traditional parties did encounter problems beginning in the 1990s in part because of corruption scandals and failures of governance, but also because voters became increasingly disenchanted with the market-oriented economic policies that they had embraced. The decline of the traditional parties and in some cases, leftist parties, freed up many voters and activists, and some of these individuals ended up supporting indigenous parties.

---

[9] Mustillo (2007) points out that this logic applies mostly to programmatic party systems, not systems in which people cast their votes based on clientelist or personal linkages.

[10] In some cases, leftist parties, such as the Movimiento de Izquierda Revolucionario in Bolivia, did not decline as much as shift to the center. In the wake of the debt crisis, many leftist, as well as populist, parties embraced market-oriented policies, abandoning the nationalist and state interventionist policies they had traditionally advocated (Madrid 2010). This shift created opportunities for indigenous parties because many traditionally leftist voters and activists grew increasingly disenchanted with the market-oriented policies.

Nevertheless, this explanation, too, has a number of shortcomings. To begin with, there is a limited amount of statistical evidence in support of it.[11] Van Cott (2005, 34–5) finds no correlation between low levels of party system institutionalization or fragmentation and the emergence of indigenous parties in the six countries she examines. Similarly, Rice and Van Cott's (2006) subnational analysis finds that neither party system fragmentation nor the left's share of the vote is a statistically significant predictor of indigenous party emergence, although their analysis does find that the left's share of the vote is negatively associated with the share of the vote won by indigenous parties in each district. In addition, a party systems explanation raises troubling issues of endogeneity. There is ample evidence to suggest that the rise of indigenous parties is a cause, not just a consequence, of the decline of the traditional parties, including left-of-center parties.

Moreover, a party systems explanation is necessarily incomplete because it cannot explain why the voters and cadres that had formerly supported the traditional parties shifted their support to the indigenous parties instead of other parties or movements. Nor can it explain why some indigenous parties succeeded in winning the support of these voters and activists while other indigenous parties failed to do so. To explain this, we must turn our attention away from the characteristics of the existing party systems and toward the indigenous parties themselves. As we shall see, some indigenous parties were able to win the support of large numbers of voters and activists because of the content of their appeals. Although the decline of the traditional parties, especially leftist parties, created the conditions that enabled some indigenous parties to flourish, only those indigenous parties that embraced inclusive ethnopopulist appeals were able to take full advantage of this decline. The indigenous parties that fared best not only put new issues, such as ethnic demands, on the agenda, they also occupied the nationalist and state interventionist policy space that had been largely abandoned by the traditional parties, including many left-of-center parties.

Another explanation for the rise of indigenous parties has focused on the role played by the indigenous movement. As a variety of studies have shown, social movements may provide crucial human and material resources to incipient parties (Kalyvas 1996; Keck 1992; Mainwaring and Scully 2003). According to some scholars, indigenous parties thrived in Bolivia and Ecuador because of the support that these parties received from the countries' powerful indigenous movements (Andolina 1999; Collins 2006; Marenghi and Alcántara Sáez 2007; Van Cott 2005). Conversely, indigenous parties failed to emerge in Peru owing to the weakness of the indigenous movement in that country (Rice 2006; Van Cott 2005).

As we shall see, this explanation has a great deal of merit. Indigenous movements have played a key role in the formation of indigenous parties throughout

---

[11] The low level of statistical support for these variables may stem from the fact that party system decay and fragmentation was widespread in Latin America during the 1990s.

Latin America. They have also contributed to their electoral success. Powerful indigenous movements in Bolivia and Ecuador, for example, have supplied a variety of resources to these parties' campaigns, including activists, candidates, and even some material contributions. Perhaps even more important, Bolivian and Ecuadorian indigenous movements provided legitimacy to the parties they founded and used their considerable influence in indigenous areas to help the parties build ties to voters.

Indigenous parties have fared less well outside of Bolivia and Ecuador in part because they have received less assistance from indigenous movements elsewhere. The weakness and fragmentation of indigenous movements in Guatemala and Peru have meant that they had limited organizational resources to supply to indigenous parties in those countries. Partly as a result, no national-level indigenous parties have emerged in Peru, and the only national-level indigenous party that has risen in Guatemala to date has fared poorly. Similarly, the poor performance of indigenous parties in Colombia, Nicaragua, and Venezuela stems partly from the small size and limited influence of the indigenous movements in those countries. Thus, the strength of the indigenous movement helps explain the varying performance of indigenous parties across Latin America.

Nevertheless, an explanation that focuses on the indigenous movement also has its shortcomings. To begin with, the strength of the indigenous movement cannot account for the sharp variation in support for indigenous parties over time since the strength of the indigenous movement has not varied dramatically from election to election. Nor can it explain why certain parties, such as the MIP in Bolivia or the Movimiento Independiente Amauta Jatari (MIAJ) in Ecuador, failed in spite of being backed by important sectors of the indigenous movement. Finally, this approach does not explain why some indigenous parties, such as the MAS and Pachakutik, have won large numbers of votes in urban areas where the indigenous movement has little influence.

This study argues that the most important indigenous parties have succeeded by going beyond the indigenous movement. It shows how the MAS and Pachakutik forged ties with numerous non-indigenous leaders and organizations and developed an inclusive populist platform that took advantage of growing disenchantment with the traditional parties and their market-oriented policies. This approach enabled these parties to fuse traditional populist constituencies – lower and middle class urban mestizos – to their rural, largely indigenous bases. This book also shows how some parties that originated outside of the indigenous movement, such as CONDEPA, Cambio 90, Perú Posible, and the Partido Nacionalista Peruano, used a similar strategy to forge coalitions of indigenous and non-indigenous voters.

THEORIES OF ETHNIC PARTIES

The general literature on ethnic parties cannot easily explain the success of some indigenous parties in Latin America either. Much of this literature suggests that such parties win by mobilizing co-ethnics.[12] A central claim of these studies is that ethnic parties do not behave according to standard Downsian electoral logic (Downs 1957). Instead of moderating their platforms and rhetoric in order to pursue the support of the median voter, leaders of ethnic parties focus their campaigns on one segment of the electorate: members of their own ethnic group (Gunther and Diamond 2003; Horowitz 1985; Rabushka and Shepsle 1972; Reilly 2001; Sisk 1996).[13] Leaders of ethnic parties are typically interested in maximizing the number of votes they receive, but they recognize that reaching out to members of other ethnic groups would be futile. Horowitz (1985, 346) writes that "because ethnicity is a largely ascriptive affiliation, the boundaries of party support stop at the boundaries of ethnic groups. ... In an ascriptive system, it is far more important to take effective steps to reassure ethnic supporters than to pursue will-o'-the-wisps by courting imaginary voters across ethnic lines."[14] Similarly, Reilly (2001, 9–10) argues that "political parties in divided societies are normally ethnic parties, and voters are normally ethnic voters, who are no more likely to cast their vote for a member of a rival group than rival ethnic parties are to court their support."

According to this literature, leaders of ethnic parties mobilize members of their own group by exaggerating the threat posed by members of other ethnic groups and adopting exclusionary rhetoric and platforms. Party leaders have little incentive to moderate their pronouncements on ethnic issues since they have few prospects of winning support from members of other ethnic groups (Horowitz 1985, 346). Instead, they denounce conspiracies against their own ethnic group while systematically excluding members of other ethnic groups. As ethnic tensions worsen, more moderate leaders of ethnic parties are frequently replaced by radicals in a process that has become known as *outbidding*. Sisk (1996, 17) writes that "extremist leaders, seeking to capitalize on mass resentment, outbid moderates by decrying acts of accommodation as a sellout of group interests, citing collective betrayal and humiliation." Similarly, Rabushka and Shepsle (1972, 86) suggest that:

Moderation on the ethnic issue is a viable strategy only if ethnicity is not salient. Once ethnicity becomes salient and as a consequence, all issues are interpreted in communal terms, the rhetoric of cooperation and mutual trust sounds painfully weak.

---

[12] As we have seen, some of this literature defines *ethnic parties* as exclusionary or as organizations that draw their support from a single ethnic group or cluster of ethnic groups (Chandra 2004, 2011; Gunther and Diamond 2003, 183; Horowitz 1985, 291).

[13] As Downs (1957) and others have made clear, the expectation that parties will move toward the center in pursuit of the median voter depends on various assumptions that often do not hold in the real world, including the assumptions that there are only two parties and that there is only one dimension of party competition.

[14] Horowitz (1985, 318) also writes that an ethnic party "recognizing that it cannot count on defections from members of the other ethnic group, has the incentive to solidify the support of its own group."

More importantly, it is strategically vulnerable to flame fanning and the politics of outbidding.[15]

The ethnic polarization of the electoral campaign often leads to an ethnic polarization of the vote. Indeed, elections may become so polarized that they resemble an ethnic census in which each party's share of the vote is roughly the same as the corresponding ethnic group's share of the population (Horowitz 1985, 326–30). Under these circumstances, ethnic parties will be successful only if the targeted ethnic group represents a significant percentage of the electorate. Surprisingly, however, ethnic parties may limit their appeals to members of their own ethnic group even when this group represents a small minority of the population. Horowitz (1985, 307–8) acknowledges that it may seem irrational for a party leader to "pursue a course foreseeably leading to a permanent minority position for his party," but he maintains there is an electoral logic to doing so.[16] In ethnically polarized societies, he suggests, leaders of minority ethnic groups that try to reach out to members of other ethnic groups will not succeed and will potentially alienate members of their own ethnic group, leaving them with no support whatsoever (Horowitz 1985, 306–11).

The dominant literature on ethnic parties would therefore not expect indigenous parties to be inclusive, and it would predict that any efforts to reach out to members of other ethnic groups would fail. This literature, however, focuses on ethnically divided countries. In these societies, politics, in the words of Horowitz (1985, 304), are "unidimensional – along an ethnic axis." In societies that are not ethnically polarized, ethnic issues would typically be of lesser salience, and ethnicity would presumably be only one of a number of dimensions that shape voting behavior. Thus, a party based in one ethnic group might be able to attract support from members of other ethnic groups by appealing to them on these other dimensions. As a result, ethnic parties in nonpolarized societies have greater incentives to eschew exclusionary appeals and instead reach out to members of other ethnic groups, as some indigenous parties in Latin America have done.

The arguments of Horowitz and others assume that individuals have a single ethnic identity and that the boundaries dividing ethnic groups are clear and relatively stable. These assumptions, which are typically referred to as _primordialist assumptions_, are deeply problematic, however (Chandra 2001, 2004). Indeed, most scholars of ethnic politics now subscribe to what has become known as a _constructivist approach_. Constructivists maintain that individuals

---

[15] Nonetheless, Horowitz (1991) maintains that certain electoral systems do provide ethnic parties with incentives to moderate and court support across ethnic lines. Specifically, he advocates the adoption of preferential voting systems in which voters rank order candidates, thereby providing parties with incentives to seek second-place (or third-place) votes. See also Reilly (2001).

[16] Horowitz (1985, 308) notes that leaders may occasionally be motivated by "a conviction that the political cause of the ethnic group is so just that it is worth risking permanent opposition for its sake," but in most cases, he suggests, the actions of politicians are driven by an electoral logic.

typically have multiple and fluid ethnic identities (Barth 1969; Chandra 2001, 2004; Laitin 1998; Posner 2005; Wilkinson 2006).[17] Multiple identities, especially where they crosscut each other, can reduce the salience of any single identity and defuse social and political conflict (Goodin 1975; Lipset 1959; Powell 1976). When individuals have multiple, crosscutting identities, their interests stemming from one identity may conflict with their interests stemming from another, thereby leading them to compromise or moderate their views. Parties and politicians in societies with crosscutting cleavages, meanwhile, may be forced to moderate their positions in order not to alienate any of their constituencies. Thus, where the population has multiple, crosscutting identities, ethnic parties may be less likely to engage in exclusionary appeals and voters may be less likely to respond favorably to such appeals (Chandra 2005; Dunning and Harrison 2010; Lipset and Rokkan 1967).

Constructivist scholars have offered their own theories about the performance of ethnic parties, of which perhaps the most prominent is by Chandra (2004). Chandra maintains that in developing democracies with large public sectors, parties and politicians woo support by delivering clientelistic benefits, such as jobs and state resources, to citizens. Voters, meanwhile, cast their votes for whichever parties or politicians they believe will deliver the most patronage to them. Given the limited information available to them, voters typically assume that politicians will favor co-ethnics in the delivery of goods and services. Voters will therefore tend to support the party that has the most leaders of their same ethnicity as long as the party has a reasonable chance of winning the election or at least gaining representation. Ethnic parties, meanwhile, will seek to attract the leading politicians of the targeted ethnic group, but Chandra argues they will only be able to do so if they have rules that enable these elites to advance through the party hierarchy. Ethnic parties will therefore tend to succeed where they have competitive rules for intraparty advancement and the groups they seek to mobilize are of sufficient size.

Chandra's theory cannot account for the success of some indigenous parties in Latin America, however. To begin with, it does not explain why successful indigenous parties in Latin America reached out to whites and mestizos, even in those countries, such as Bolivia, where they could have won significant legislative seats, and perhaps even the presidency, with indigenous votes alone. Moreover, there is little evidence to suggest that indigenous voters have supported indigenous parties in order to obtain access to state patronage. Indeed, the most successful indigenous parties, the MAS and Pachakutik, denounced the clientelistic tendencies of the traditional parties and vowed to create more transparent and honest governments, although they, too, have engaged in patronage politics once in power (Van Cott 2005, 2009). Nor is there much

---

[17] Van Evera (2001) argues that primordialist assumptions may be tenable in ethnically polarized societies since ethnic conflict can harden ethnic identities and elevate certain identities to the exclusion of others. Where ethnic polarization is low, however, it is more reasonable to assume that individuals have multiple ethnic identities and that these identities can change.

evidence to suggest that successful indigenous parties have employed competitive rules for intraparty advancement. Indigenous parties have recruited indigenous elites as candidates in order to attract indigenous voters, but these candidates have typically been chosen by the social movements, the party hierarchy, or, in the case of the MAS, often by Morales himself, rather than through party primaries. Thus, neither the traditional literature on ethnic parties nor the most prominent constructivist alternative offers an adequate explanation for the performance of indigenous parties in the region.

ETHNIC MIXING AND ETHNIC PARTIES

Constructivists nevertheless provide many insights that can help us understand the behavior and performance of indigenous parties in the region. Constructivists point out not only that ethnic identification is often fluid and multiple, but also that the degree of ethnic identification and ethnic polarization varies cross-nationally and that all of these factors have important implications for ethnic politics. This study draws on these insights in developing an explanation for the performance of indigenous parties in Latin America. It argues that the kinds of appeals that ethnic parties can use effectively will vary depending on the nature of ethnic identification and polarization in a society. In societies in which ethnic polarization is high and ethnic identification is singular and stable, ethnic parties are more likely to succeed with exclusionary appeals. But where ethnic polarization is low and ethnic identification is fluid, inclusive appeals are more likely to be effective. Latin American countries, as we shall see, fall in the latter category.

This study argues that ethnic mixing reduces ethnic polarization and increases ethnic fluidity. Ethnic mixing is commonplace throughout much of the world, but it is particularly prevalent in Latin America. Nevertheless, it has received insufficient attention in the comparative ethnic politics literature to date. Constructivists often discuss how people have multiple ethnic identities, but they are typically referring to the fact that people have identities that correspond to different cleavages or category sets, such as language, religion, or race (Chandra and Wilkinson 2008; Posner 2005). For example, an individual may be black, Catholic, and Spanish-speaking. Where ethnic mixing occurs, however, people may identify with both sides of the *same* cleavage or category set or at least have sympathies toward both groups. Thus an individual of mixed ancestry may identify as Serb and Croat, Hindu and Muslim, or indigenous and Spanish, although he or she will frequently have stronger attachments to one group than another.[18] Ethnically mixed individuals may also identify partly or solely with a mixed category, such as mestizo.

---

[18] In some countries the state has encouraged people of mixed origin to identify with a particular group. In the United States, for example, the government traditionally classified people who had only a small amount of African ancestry as black and encouraged them to identify as such. In twentieth-century Latin America, the state encouraged people who were mostly or even completely of indigenous ancestry to classify themselves as mestizo.

Other things beings equal, individuals who have roots on both sides of an ethnic cleavage are more likely to have sympathies toward both sides than are individuals who only have roots on one side of a cleavage. Ethnic mixing should thus reduce ethnic polarization even more than the existence of cross-cutting ethnic cleavages. Ethnic mixing will also increase the potential costs for parties of being exclusionary and increase the potential gains of being inclusive. Where considerable ethnic mixing has taken place, it would be counter-productive for ethnic parties to use exclusionary appeals because many people will identify with both sides of any given cleavage or at least empathize with people on both sides. Exclusionary appeals would alienate those people whose ethnic identities or sympathies comprise the included as well as the excluded group. A party that adopts an inclusive strategy, by contrast, might appeal to all people who share a given ethnic identity without alienating those who also have other ethnic identities. Thus, where considerable ethnic mixing has taken place, even ethnic parties have incentives to try to appeal across ethnic lines.

Ethnic mixing does not eliminate ethnic attachments, however. Nor does it bring an end to ethnic prejudice and discrimination.[19] Nevertheless, wide-spread ethnic mixing blurs the boundaries between ethnic groups and often produces a plethora of intermediate ethnic categories used to describe ethnically mixed individuals. Ethnicity may thus come to represent a continuum rather than a small number of discrete categories, and the precise ethnicity of individuals may become ambiguous.[20]

By blurring the boundaries between ethnic groups and multiplying the number of ethnic categories and attachments, ethnic mixing makes ethnic voting much more complex. Voters may be uncertain as to the precise ethnic identity of the candidates or parties because of the uncertainty over where ethnic boundaries begin and end in ethnically mixed societies. Nevertheless, voters will typically recognize certain candidates or parties as being more ethnically proximate than others. Members of ethnically proximate groups share certain phenotypes or have a similar language, religion, or culture. These cultural and phenotypical similarities may lead voters to identify with and feel a sense of ethnic solidarity with candidates or parties from ethnically proximate groups. They may also believe that ethnically proximate candidates or parties are more likely to support their interests and demands.

To be sure, ethnic proximity does not always lead to ethnic or political solidarity. In some cases, high levels of antagonism have existed between ethnically proximate groups, such as that experienced by Serbs and Croats in the wake of the dissolution of the former Yugoslavia. The argument here is only that voters are *more likely* to feel ethnic solidarity toward ethnically proximate

[19] If ethnic mixing eliminated ethnic attachments and ethnic discrimination altogether, ethnic appeals would be ineffective and ethnic parties would disappear.

[20] It is important to remember, however, that ethnic identification is shaped not just by genetics, but also by culture and society. Individuals may identify with an ethnic group, not just because of their genetic inheritance, but also because of their cultural backgrounds and the social, economic, and political pressures they face.

groups, not that they will *always* do so. Although one would expect voters to have lower levels of ethnic attachment to candidates and parties of proximate ethnic groups than to their own ethnic group, we would still expect them to feel a greater sense of ethnic solidarity with proximate ethnic groups than with distant ones. In addition, people might also be more likely to vote for parties or candidates of ethnically proximate groups because they know or assume that these parties or candidates have policy positions closer to their own preferences than do the parties or candidates identified with ethnically distant groups. Thus, in ethnically mixed societies, ethnic proximity will frequently shape ethnic voting behavior (Madrid 2011).

MESTIZAJE AND INDIGENOUS PARTIES IN LATIN AMERICA

Since the colonial era, Latin America has experienced widespread *mestizaje* or ethnic/racial mixing, which has profoundly shaped ethnic relations in the region. *Mestizaje* refers to two related phenomena: a process of biological mixing in which people of indigenous and European descent (and sometimes people of African descent or other backgrounds) produce children of mixed race or ancestry; and a process of cultural assimilation in which indigenous people abandon many of their traditional customs and begin to identify as mestizos.

Mestizaje has had important consequences for ethnic politics in Latin America. First, as a result of *mestizaje*, mestizos gradually came to represent a large majority of the population in most Latin American countries. This has meant that in order to win national-level elections, political parties, including indigenous parties, must typically obtain mestizo votes. Second, *mestizaje* has blurred ethnic boundaries and reduced ethnic polarization in the region. As a result, there have been far fewer incidents of ethnic conflict in Latin America in recent decades than in most other regions of the world (Cleary 2000; Gurr 1993). Rather than hardening ethnic identities and dividing ethnic groups into opposing camps, *mestizaje* has softened the boundaries between members of different ethnic groups. This has made it easier for parties, including indigenous parties, to win support across ethnic lines.

Nevertheless, *mestizaje* has not eliminated ethnic attachments altogether, nor has it gotten rid of ethnic discrimination. Indigenous parties have used these lingering ethnic attachments and grievances to establish strong ties to indigenous voters. Indeed, ethnic consciousness and prejudice have enabled indigenous parties to be successful in Latin America. If *mestizaje* had gradually brought an end to ethnic identification and discrimination in Latin America as some proponents of the racial democracy thesis suggest, then ethnic parties and ethnic appeals would not have resonated among sectors of the population (Degler 1971; Freyre 1959; Tannenbaum 1947).

Mestizaje took place from the earliest days of the Spanish conquest and accelerated over time. By the end of the colonial period, mestizos already represented more than one quarter of the population of Spanish America, and their numbers continued to grow after independence (Mörner 1967, 98; Rosenblat

1954).[21] Esteva Fabregat (1995, 38) reports that in 1810 there were three times as many Indians as mestizos in Mexico, but by 1900, there were twice as many mestizos as Indians.

From the outset, the *mestizaje* process in Latin America was characterized by a great deal of prejudice and exploitation. *Mestizaje* was driven initially by the shortage of Spanish women in the Americas and the privileged position of the Spaniards and the *criollo* in the economic and social hierarchy of the Americas (Mörner 1967; Esteva-Fabregat 1995, 33).[22] This encouraged often exploitative sexual relationships between men of Spanish descent and indigenous women. Both the church and the state actively discouraged interracial marriage during the colonial era and, as a result, it was relatively rare. Interracial concubinage was widespread, but the church and the state disapproved of it as well, and the mestizo (and mulatto) offspring of these relationships had only limited rights.

After independence, the state adopted a more tolerant view of *mestizaje* and it eliminated legal restrictions on mestizos but not initially on indigenous people and Afro-Latinos. In some Latin American countries, the state actually encouraged *mestizaje* as part of its efforts to whiten the population and build more unified nations. Nevertheless, widespread social discrimination against indigenous people and Afro-Latinos and, to a lesser extent, mestizos remained. Far from being a racial democracy, Latin America after independence continued to resemble a pigmentocracy in which light-skinned individuals occupied the highest rungs of the socioeconomic ladder and dark-skinned people clustered at the bottom (Hanchard 1999; Mörner 1967; Nobles 2000; Sidanius et al. 2001; Wade 1997).

In the twentieth century, many Latin American governments implemented assimilationist projects intended to promote Spanish literacy among the indigenous population, to develop indigenous communities, and to bring indigenous people into the mainstream. Some Latin American governments also sought to recast the rural indigenous population as peasants, even banning the use of the term *Indian* in official discourse (Dary 1998; Yashar 2005). Widespread social discrimination, meanwhile, led many indigenous people to seek to assimilate, abandoning indigenous names, dress, and customs. Numerous people of indigenous descent opted to identify themselves as mestizos rather than as Indian or indigenous because they viewed the latter terms as pejorative and associated them with backwardness. Pressures to assimilate were particularly intense in the cities to which many indigenous people migrated in search of economic opportunities. In urban areas, indigenous people came into contact and intermarried with members of other ethnic groups, and many of the indigenous

---

[21] These population shifts stemmed not just from *mestizaje*, but also from the dramatic decline in the size of indigenous population owing to the spread of diseases and other factors associated with the conquest.

[22] During the colonial era, the term *criollo* referred to a person of European descent born in the Americas.

migrants and their children embraced mestizo identities. People of indigenous descent also had to use Spanish to a much greater extent in urban areas and, partly as a result, the percentage of indigenous language speakers in Latin America declined steadily in the latter half of the twentieth century.

Nevertheless, the assimilation process was far from complete. Ethnic inequality and prejudice remained deeply entrenched, and much of the indigenous population remained mired in poverty. Recent surveys and censuses show that self-identified indigenous people and indigenous language speakers continue to be much poorer and less educated than non-indigenous people on average, and they typically have much less access to quality housing and health care (Buvinić and Mazza 2004; Hall and Patrinos 2006; Psacharopoulos and Patrinos 1994).

Particularly in rural areas, many indigenous people continued to speak indigenous languages, maintain traditional customs, and identify with their indigenous communities. According to recent census data, thirty-five percent of the population in Bolivia, thirty-one percent of the population in Guatemala, and eighteen percent of the population in Peru reported that an indigenous tongue was the first language they learned in their childhood. Many indigenous language speakers self-identify as mestizo rather than as indigenous, but they often retain some indigenous practices and traditions. These people, whom some scholars call indigenous mestizos, outnumber the population who openly self-identify as indigenous in some areas (de la Cadena 2000; Programa de las Naciones Unidas para el Desarrollo 2004).[23] Regardless of how they self-identify, people of indigenous descent are often perceived by others as Indians and they frequently experience discrimination and marginalization. As a result, many of these so-called indigenous mestizos have been sympathetic to the ethnic demands and symbols of the indigenous movement and its efforts to redress inequality and discrimination.

Although *mestizaje* has not eliminated ethnic differences, it has blurred the boundaries between members of different racial and ethnic groups, creating multiple, fluid, and ambiguous ethnic identities. Numerous surveys in the region have found that which ethnic group people identify with depends in part on what choices they are offered. In Bolivia, for example, the percentage of the population that self-identifies as indigenous has varied from less than

---

[23] Numerous other terms have been used to describe people of different skin colors, phenotypes, or admixtures of Indian, black, and white heritage, although some of these terms are no longer common currency. Mörner (1967, 58–9) provides a list of racial terminology used in Peru during the eighteenth century: "1. Spaniard and Indian woman beget mestizo; 2. Spaniard and mestizo woman beget cuarterón de mestizo; 3. Spaniard and cuarterona de mestizo beget quinterón; 4. Spaniard and quinterona de mestizo beget Spaniard or requinterón de mestizo; 5. Spaniard and Negress beget mulatto; 6. Spaniard and mulatto woman beget quarterón de mulato; 7. Spaniard and cuarterona de mulato beget quinterón; 8. Spaniard and quinterona de mulato beget requinterón; 9. Spaniard and requinterona de mulato beget white people; 10. Mestizo and Indian woman beget cholo; 11. Mulatto and Indian woman beget chino; 12. Spaniard and china beget cuarterón de chino; 13. Negro and Indian woman beget sambo de Indio; 14 Negro and mulatto woman beget zambo."

twenty percent in some surveys to more than sixty percent in others, depending on the precise phrasing of the question.[24] Surveys in Peru also have identified dramatic variation in the percentage of people willing to identify as indigenous from approximately six percent in a 2006 survey by the Latin American Public Opinion Project to more than twenty-five percent in the 2006 census. Similar variation exists in the willingness of people to identify with other ethnic or racial categories, such as white. These fluctuations occur in large part because many Latin Americans have multiple ethnic attachments and feel considerable ethnic ambiguity. How people identify themselves ethnically (and are identified by others) depends not just on their ancestry, but also on various other factors such as their name, skin color, phenotypes, and social class, as well as their cultural traditions. Indeed, it is frequently argued that culture rather than ancestry is what distinguishes Indians from non-Indians in Latin American society (de la Cadena 2000 and 2001).

Some scholars have described Latin America as having an ethnic or racial continuum, ranging from indigenous (or black) on one side to white on the other, with mestizos in the middle (Mörner 1967; Wade 1997).[25] The continuum model has been criticized on the grounds that it does not adequately represent how certain minority ethnic or racial groups, such as Asians, Jews, and Arabs, are incorporated in Latin American societies (Sue 2009, 1062). Moreover, as some scholars have pointed out, in many communities in Latin America, race or ethnicity is fundamentally binary: there are whites and non-whites, Indians and non-Indians (Sheriff 2001; Weismantel 2001). Nevertheless, the continuum model is useful in that it highlights the importance of intermediate or mixed ethnic categories and the low level of ethnic polarization. Indeed, repeated surveys have found that in most countries the majority of the population will identify themselves as mestizo when provided with that option. The continuum model is also helpful in that it indicates that certain individuals and groups are more ethnically proximate than others. Although some mestizos identify more with whites and European traditions, others identify more with indigenous people and customs. As we shall see, these ethnic sympathies often affect voting behavior.

Ethnic mixing in Latin America has traditionally made it an inhospitable environment for ethnic parties and exclusionary appeals. Prior to the 1990s, only a few ethnic parties emerged in the region, and these parties failed to win many votes. As Chapter 2 discusses, the exclusionary rhetoric and platforms of so-called Indianista parties, which rose in Bolivia during the 1970s and 1980s, not only alienated whites, but many indigenous people and mestizos as well. Even the less radical Katarista parties, which generally avoided exclusionary

---

[24] In surveys Latin Americans are typically more willing to identify with an indigenous ethno-linguistic group such as Aymara or Quechua than they are with the term *indigenous*.

[25] In the Andean countries, Mexico, and Guatemala, the dominant racial/ethnic cleavage is between whites and indigenous people with mestizos in the middle. In Brazil and many of the Caribbean countries, the dominant racial/ethnic cleavage is between blacks and whites with mulattos in the middle.

rhetoric, fared poorly in part because of their failure to reach out beyond their base in the Aymara population. None of these parties ever won more than three percent of the national vote, although they fared somewhat better in Aymara areas.

During the late 1970s and 1980s, the indigenous population typically supported white- and mestizo-led parties, such as the Movimiento Nacionalista Revolucionario and the Unión Democrática y Popular in Bolivia; the Concentración de Fuerzas Populares and Izquierda Democrática in Ecuador; Acción Popular, the Partido Aprista Peruano, and Izquierda Unida in Peru; and the Democracia Cristiana Guatemalteca in Guatemala.[26] These parties wooed indigenous voters through a combination of programmatic, personalistic, and clientelist strategies, but they largely eschewed ethnic appeals. The parties did not recruit many indigenous leaders as candidates, nor did they establish close ties to indigenous organizations or embrace many of their traditional demands. Leftist parties, which had a long history of organizing among the indigenous peasantry, were often more willing to espouse indigenous demands. Nevertheless, even these parties focused mostly on economic issues and class-based themes and their leadership was almost exclusively white or mestizo.

Beginning in the mid-1990s, a new, much broader, wave of indigenous parties emerged. This new wave of indigenous parties was a direct outgrowth of the resurgence of indigenous movements and identities in the region. Indigenous movements grew increasingly active during the 1990s, particularly in Bolivia and Ecuador, and they carried out numerous marches and protests in order to try to influence government policies. The indigenous movements also stepped up their grassroots organizing during this period, and expanded and strengthened their membership base. The growing strength and influence of the indigenous movements encouraged them to venture into the electoral arena. As a result, various indigenous organizations founded parties during this period and devoted substantial human and material resources to their campaigns (Van Cott 2005; Yashar 2005). Indigenous movements in Bolivia and Ecuador, for example, used their dense networks of organizational affiliates in the rural highlands to support the new parties they created.

Indigenous movements also helped the indigenous parties by contributing to the process of reindigenization in the region. Indigenous organizations have encouraged Latin Americans to embrace their indigenous heritage by promoting indigenous pride and traditions. In their book on the Ecuadorean indigenous movement, Guerrero Cazar and Ospina Peralta (2003, 164) discuss how a talk by Ecuadorean indigenous leader Luis Macas led one young man to reclaim his indigenous identity and join the indigenous movement:

---

[26] In the Andean countries, indigenous people did not participate extensively in electoral politics until the return to democracy in the region. Much of the indigenous population in Ecuador and Peru could not vote until the late 1970s owing to literacy restrictions on the franchise. Illiterates gained the right to vote in Bolivia following the 1952 Bolivian revolution, but Bolivia was governed by a series of military regimes throughout most of the 1960s and 1970s. As a result, even Bolivia's indigenous population had limited experience with voting prior to the late 1970s.

In his speech, Macas had mentioned that it wasn't possible to cease to be an Indian. You could cut off your braid and change your dress, but you would continue to be indigenous inside. And furthermore, to try to abandon what you were and what your parents had been was a mistake. You had to be proud of your origins, of your culture, of your way of living.

The reindigenization process has provided indigenous parties with a growing base of potential supporters on which they can draw. According to LAPOP surveys, the percentage of the population that self-identifies as indigenous in Bolivia climbed by more than ten percentage points between 2000 and 2008 (Moreno Morales et al. 2008, xxxiii).[27] Indigenous parties have benefited considerably from the increase in indigenous identification in Latin America because indigenous people with a strong ethnic consciousness are more likely to embrace the parties' ethnic claims, more inclined to identify with the parties' indigenous leadership and symbols, and more likely to have ties to the parties' organizational allies.

The new indigenous parties have won support among indigenous voters in part by prioritizing the interests of the indigenous population. They have recruited numerous indigenous candidates, they have maintained close ties to indigenous organizations, and they have invoked numerous indigenous symbols in their campaigns. They have also embraced many of the traditional demands of the indigenous movement from agrarian reform to indigenous autonomy. And they have vowed to combat discrimination against indigenous people and to address ethnic inequalities.

The most successful of the indigenous parties, the Movimiento al Socialismo in Bolivia and the Movimiento Unidad Plurinacional Pachakutik in Ecuador, have also made great efforts to be inclusive. They have sought not just to win the support of indigenous people, but to capture the votes of whites and mestizos as well. Thus, they have recruited numerous whites and mestizos as candidates or for leadership positions within the parties. They have forged close ties with numerous urban mestizo-dominated organizations and middle class groups. And they have adopted broad and inclusive platforms.

The inclusive strategies of some indigenous parties have paid off because of the region's fluid ethnic boundaries and low levels of ethnic polarization. Indigenous parties have won the support not only of self-identified indigenous people, but also of many self-identified mestizos who are of indigenous descent and identify with indigenous culture. Some indigenous parties have even won support from whites and non-indigenous mestizos thanks in part to the low level of ethnic polarization prevailing in the region. As we shall see, whites and non-indigenous mestizos have supported the indigenous parties at times because

---

[27] A similar increase has occurred in Brazil and a recent study by Perz, Warren, and Kennedy (2008) found that reclassifying as indigenous played a more important role than demographic trends in explaining the increase in the size of the self-identified indigenous population in that country.

they have sympathized with their ethnic demands, but, even more important, because they have supported the parties' populist rhetoric and policies.

The inclusive appeals of some indigenous parties have also helped unify the indigenous population. Throughout much of the region, indigenous people are divided into communities with distinct languages, traditions, leaders, and organizations. The inclusive strategies adopted by some indigenous parties, like the MAS and Pachakutik, have helped overcome intra-indigenous divisions and unite these disparate communities behind a single party. By contrast, the exclusionary rhetoric adopted by some other indigenous parties, such as the MIP in Bolivia, divided the indigenous population in addition to alienating whites and mestizos. Thus, the ethnic landscape in Latin America has helped make inclusive ethnic appeals more effective than exclusionary ones.

Support for indigenous parties has not been distributed evenly across the ethnic spectrum, however. Rather, individuals who self-identify as indigenous or are ethnically proximate to the indigenous population, such as indigenous mestizos or cholos, have been most likely to vote for indigenous parties. Many of these people have suffered from ethnic discrimination and marginalization and they are more likely to sympathize with the indigenous parties' ethnic demands. Ethnically distant groups, such as whites and non-indigenous mestizos, have been the least likely to support indigenous parties in Latin America, although even members of these groups have voted for them in large numbers in some cases. The indigenous parties have therefore tended to fare better in countries such as Bolivia and Ecuador where the indigenous and indigenous mestizo population is relatively large. They have performed less well in countries such as Colombia, Nicaragua, and Venezuela where only a small portion of the population self-identifies as indigenous or speaks an indigenous language. Within each country, the indigenous parties also have had the most success in the more indigenous departments, provinces, and municipalities. The MAS and Pachakutik, for example, have fared much better in the largely indigenous highlands of their countries than in the largely white and mestizo lowlands. Thus, in spite of the inclusive nature of these parties, ethnicity has profoundly shaped their electoral performance.

POPULIST APPEALS

Populist appeals have been a crucial part of the efforts of some indigenous parties to win support from voters of all ethnic backgrounds in recent elections. As noted previously, I define *populism* as a personalistic campaign and governing strategy that seeks to mobilize the masses in opposition to the elites. Some indigenous parties have been populist in that they have adopted a highly personalistic and anti-establishment campaign strategy that has focused on mobilizing the lower classes. They have also employed the nationalist and state interventionist rhetoric and proposals typical of traditional populism.

These appeals have worked well in recent years because of the high levels of political disenchantment that have gripped the region. Many Latin American governments implemented market-oriented reforms beginning in the late 1980s and these policies initially generated some positive results, bringing down inflation and for a time producing strong economic growth as well. In the late 1990s, however, the economies of many Latin American nations began to stagnate, which undermined support for the traditional parties and their market-oriented policies (Madrid 2010). High levels of crime, corruption, and other governance failures also exacerbated political disenchantment in the region (Mainwaring 2006; Mainwaring et al. 2006). Populist leaders from Argentina to Venezuela have fed on this disenchantment by attacking the political establishment, denouncing neoliberal policies, and portraying themselves as the saviors of their countries.

Not all indigenous parties have used populist appeals, however. Many indigenous parties such as the Pueblo Unido Multiétnico de Amazonas in Venezuela, the Alianza Social Indígena in Colombia, Winaq in Guatemala, the Movimiento Independiente Amauta Jatari in Ecuador, and the MIP in Bolivia, have focused mostly on ethnic appeals and have largely eschewed populist strategies. As a consequence, these parties have held little attraction for self-identified mestizo and white voters, who constitute a large majority of the electorate in most of these countries. Moreover, some of these parties, like the MIP in Bolivia, have used exclusionary appeals, which have antagonized not only whites and mestizos, but many self-identified indigenous people as well.

By contrast, the successful indigenous parties, namely the MAS and Pachakutik, have wooed voters with a combination of ethnic and traditional populist appeals. As we have seen, the MAS and Pachakutik have used ethnic appeals to establish identity-based ties with indigenous voters. They have invoked indigenous symbols, they have recruited numerous indigenous leaders as candidates, they have made ethnic demands a centerpiece of their campaigns, and they have maintained strong ties to the indigenous movement. But the MAS and Pachakutik have also reached out to whites and mestizos through populist strategies, including personalistic, anti-establishment, and lower class focused appeals. Neither the MAS nor Pachakutik are personalistic parties to the same degree as many other populist movements. Indeed, they both have strong grassroots bases that help shape the parties' platforms and policies. Nevertheless, they have both run personalistic electoral campaigns that have revolved around the charismatic personalities of their presidential candidates. The MAS and Pachakutik also have employed extensive anti-establishment rhetoric, aggressively criticizing the traditional parties and politicians. Finally, the MAS and Pachakutik have employed nationalist and state interventionist appeals. They have staunchly opposed market-oriented policies and U.S. intervention in their countries, and they have vowed to assert greater control over their countries' natural resources.

The degree to which the MAS and Pachakutik have combined ethnic and populist appeals has evolved, however, and this evolution helps explain variation in support for the two parties over time. In its early days the MAS was composed almost entirely of indigenous people and it focused largely on indigenous issues, particularly coca cultivation. As a result, it won few votes outside of the rural, largely indigenous areas of Cochabamba where it originated. Beginning in 2002, however, the MAS recruited numerous white and mestizo candidates, formed alliances throughout the country with non-indigenous as well as indigenous organizations, and developed a more inclusive and populist discourse. It broadened its anti-establishment and nationalist rhetoric and began to take the forefront in the struggle against market-oriented policies in Bolivia. It also started to center its campaigns on its charismatic leader, Evo Morales, who consolidated his control of the party. This shift helped the MAS win a significantly greater share of the vote beginning in 2002, particularly in urban, mestizo-dominated areas. Indigenous people have continued to represent the most dependable core of the MAS's support, but since 2002 the MAS has had considerable backing across all ethnic groups. The MAS's populist rhetoric has helped it fare particularly well among poor, leftist, nationalist, and politically disenchanted voters of all ethnicities.

The Movimiento Unidad Plurinacional Pachakutik in Ecuador similarly enjoyed success in the late 1990s and early 2000s by combining inclusive ethnic and traditional populist appeals, but it became less inclusive and populist beginning in 2006, which had a negative effect on the party's fortunes. During its first decade, Pachakutik recruited numerous white and mestizo leaders and candidates, and it established close alliances with mestizo-dominated organizations. Indeed, the party declined to put forward its own presidential candidate in the 1996, 1998, and 2002 elections, preferring to support the white or mestizo leaders of allied movements. Pachakutik centered its campaigns on these leaders, Freddy Ehlers and Lucio Gutiérrez, who were both charismatic political outsiders. Pachakutik also employed a great deal of populist discourse in its campaigns between 1996 and 2002. It emphasized its opposition to foreign intervention and market-oriented policies, and it denounced the traditional parties and elites. Partly as a result, the party attracted many politically disenchanted, leftist, and nationalist voters and fared well in mestizo-dominated urban areas as well as in rural indigenous communities.

Pachakutik, however, was hurt by its participation in the government of Lucio Gutiérrez (2003–5), which adopted neoliberal policies and was accused of corruption. Moreover, beginning in 2006, the party increasingly emphasized indigenous issues, abandoning its populist strategy. In the 2006 elections, Pachakutik declined to form alliances with other parties for the first time and opted to run its own candidate, indigenous leader Luis Macas, for president. It also awarded most of the other key candidacies to indigenous leaders rather than whites or mestizos. Many of the mestizo leaders and mestizo-dominated organizations that had supported the party in the past abandoned it because of their concerns about the party's increasingly ethnonationalist rhetoric and actions. Partly as a result, Pachakutik fared poorly in the 2006 elections, especially in mestizo areas, and it has not been able to recover since.

The MAS and Pachakutik are not the only parties that have successfully combined ethnic and populist appeals. Some mestizo-led parties, such as

Conciencia de Patria in Bolivia, and Perú Posible and the Partido Nacionalista Peruano in Peru, have also used ethnopopulist appeals with considerable success. These parties have not prioritized the demands of the indigenous population in the way that the indigenous parties have, but they have made numerous ethnic appeals. They have invoked indigenous symbols and recruited many indigenous and indigenous mestizos as high-profile candidates, particularly in indigenous areas. They also have forged ties with indigenous organizations and embraced many of the traditional demands of these organizations. As a result, these mestizo-led parties have fared quite well in indigenous areas. CONDEPA, for example, dominated many indigenous areas in the department of La Paz during the 1990s. Perú Posible and the PNP, meanwhile, have swept the indigenous highlands in recent presidential elections in Peru. By contrast, mestizo-led parties that have not embraced ethnic appeals, such as Poder Democrático y Social in Bolivia, Partido Renovador Institucional Acción Nacional in Ecuador, and the Partido Aprista Peruano in Peru, have fared poorly in indigenous areas in recent elections.

CONDEPA, Perú Posible, and the PNP have employed populist appeals to an even greater extent than ethnic appeals. They have run campaigns centered on the personal characteristics of their leaders, rather than on the parties or their programs. They have employed anti-establishment messages, presenting their leaders as political outsiders and as honest and grassroots alternatives to the corrupt traditional politicians. And they have focused their appeals primarily on the lower classes. They have forged alliances with numerous working class groups from peasant associations to unions, informal sector organizations, and neighborhood groups. The leaders of these parties have adopted a popular, at times folksy, style of campaigning, and much of their discourse has centered on meeting the needs of disadvantaged and neglected sectors of the population. Some of the mestizo-led parties, such as CONDEPA and the PNP, have also made nationalist and state interventionist appeals, denouncing neoliberal policies and U.S. intervention. Others, such as Perú Posible, have largely avoided this type of rhetoric, however, and have embraced some market-oriented policies.

The Latin American literature on populism would not have predicted that populist parties would employ ethnic appeals.[28] Populist movements in Latin America have not traditionally had an important ethnic component and Weyland (1999, 383) goes so far as to suggest that ethnic appeals might not go together well with populism because populists tend to appeal to "undifferentiated 'people.'" There is nothing incompatible about populist and ethnic appeals, however. Populism has traditionally been ideologically flexible, and

---

[28] Studies of populism in other regions have noted the compatibility of ethnic and populist appeals. Subramanian (1999), for example, argues that Dravidian parties in South India have combined populist and ethnic appeals in a fruitful manner. Various scholars, meanwhile, have shown that right-wing populist parties in Europe have frequently used exclusionary ethnic appeals, employing extensive anti-immigrant rhetoric (Betz 2001, 1994; Mudde 2007; Mudde and Rovira Kaltwasser 2010).

thus it is not surprising that populist leaders would incorporate ethnic appeals into their repertoire. Moreover, in regions such as Latin America where ethnic polarization is low and ethnic identification is multiple and fluid, ethnic appeals need not be divisive. To the contrary, in countries with large socioeconomically disadvantaged ethnic groups, parties may more effectively woo lower class voters through a combination of populist and ethnic appeals than with populist or ethnic appeals alone. Indeed, indigenous people, who have traditionally been economically and politically marginalized, have been attracted to populism because of its anti-establishment rhetoric, its focus on the poor, and its nationalist and redistributive agenda. By combining populist and ethnic appeals, indigenous and mestizo-led parties and politicians have stitched together broad coalitions of indigenous people and politically disenchanted whites and mestizos, particularly from the lower classes.

RESEARCH DESIGN AND METHODS

This book examines indigenous parties in seven Latin American countries – Bolivia, Ecuador, Peru, Guatemala, Colombia, Venezuela, and Nicaragua – focusing mostly on the first three countries. These countries were chosen in part because they have reasonably well-known indigenous parties, but also because these parties have varied considerably in terms of their degree of success. They therefore offer a range of variation on the principal dependent variable in this study, which is indigenous party performance. Various chapters, especially Chapter 4 on Peru, also examine the performance of mestizo-led parties that have employed ethnopopulist appeals.

The book examines the varying performance of these parties over time and across space. I analyze not just how the parties fared on the national level in aggregate, but how they performed in different kinds of provinces and municipalities as well as with various types of individual voters. This strategy enables me to dramatically expand the number of observations under analysis.

This study employs two principal research methods. First, I use qualitative methods to carry out case studies of individual parties. These case studies examine how the appeals of parties, including their platforms, rhetoric, candidate profiles, and campaign strategies, changed over time and how these changes affected their electoral results. Second, I use quantitative methods to examine the determinants of individual-level, municipal-level, and provincial-level voting behavior. I explore what types of individuals, municipalities, and provinces tended to support the parties and under what circumstances they did so.

This study utilizes a range of different types of data. This book is based on extensive field research in Bolivia (2003, 2004, and 2007), Ecuador (2003, 2005, and 2007), Peru (2006 and 2008), and Guatemala (2002 and 2008) that included dozens of interviews with indigenous leaders and government and party officials as well as academics and other political analysts. These interviews have been crucial to identifying the evolving political strategies of the parties and movements in each country. I also conducted extensive archival research that included examination of newspapers, party documents, and governmental publications as well as the secondary literature on this topic. This research enabled me to trace the content of the appeals that these parties have made over the course of various elections. In addition, I acquired numerous surveys of public opinion in these countries and I use these surveys, particularly those carried out by the Latin American Public Opinion Project (LAPOP), to examine who voted for the parties and why they did so. Finally, I have compiled and merged municipal- and provincial-level census and electoral data from Bolivia, Ecuador, and Peru. These original data sets include a couple of censuses for each country and all presidential and legislative elections held in these countries between 1980 and 2011. I use the data sets to examine shifts in voting patterns across time and space.

Any study that focuses on ethnicity must deal with some tricky measurement issues and this study is no exception. As noted earlier, individuals frequently have fluid, multiple, and/or ambiguous ethnic identities, which complicate the task of identifying ethnicity. The LAPOP survey data fortunately provided a number of questions that can be used to identify ethnicity or indigenous status, including self-identification questions and linguistic questions. (The LAPOP surveys were also useful because they used a national sample and were conducted in indigenous languages as well as in Spanish.) These questions enabled me to pinpoint those individuals who self-identified as indigenous as well as people who had more ambiguous identities, such as those individuals who did not self-identify as indigenous but who had grown up speaking an indigenous language. This was crucial because I expected the latter as well as the former people to respond favorably to ethnopopulist appeals. The LAPOP surveys also at times contained other questions that helped identify the ethnicity of individuals, including questions that allowed individuals to rank the degree to which they felt Aymara or Quechua (on a scale from one to seven) as well as queries about the ethnic identification or linguistic status of an individual's parents. In the quantitative analyses that employ survey data, I include variables on self-identification as well as variables on linguistic background to measure the independent effects of both of these variables.

For the analyses of municipal- and provincial-level electoral data, I relied mostly on census data on the maternal language of the population to measure the proportion of the population that is indigenous in each province or municipality. The most recent round of censuses in the Andes also contained questions about ethnic self-identification, but the linguistic and ethnic self-identification variables are highly correlated across provinces and municipalities, which precludes including both variables in the quantitative analyses. I opted to use the linguistic variable for Bolivia and Peru because it has been used in previous censuses and it is more consistently worded (and less controversial) than the ethnic self-identification variable. Using the ethnic self-identification variable, however, would not have appreciably changed the results. In the case of

Ecuador, however, I used the ethnic self-identification variable in large part because the percentage of people who speak indigenous languages in Ecuador is quite low. Chapters 2 through 4 discuss both the linguistic and the ethnic self-identification data for each country at some length.

ORGANIZATION OF THE BOOK

The ensuing chapters are organized as follows. Chapter 2 examines the rapid ascent of the MAS in Bolivia. It argues that the MAS has done surprisingly well in Bolivia because it has wooed not only indigenous voters, but also whites and mestizos. It shows how the MAS started out with limited appeal, winning support only in its base in the Quechua-speaking, coca-growing areas of rural Cochabamba. Beginning in the early 2000s, however, the party reached out to members of other ethnic groups, recruiting white and mestizo candidates, forging alliances with numerous urban and mestizo-dominated organizations, and employing traditional populist rhetoric and proposals. These strategies largely succeeded. The MAS finished second in the 2002 presidential and legislative elections, and then triumphed in 2005 and 2009. By contrast, other indigenous parties in Bolivia fared poorly largely because they focused mostly on ethnic appeals and failed to build a base outside of the Aymara population.

Chapter 3 analyzes the rise and decline of Pachakutik in Ecuador. It argues that Pachakutik fared well in the initial elections (1996–2002) in which it competed largely because it combined inclusive ethnic appeals with traditional populist strategies. From the outset, the party forged alliances with non-indigenous parties, recruited charismatic white and mestizo candidates, and developed an anti-establishment and anti-neoliberal platform. These strategies helped the party win the support of numerous politically disenchanted whites and mestizos as well as indigenous voters. In 2006, however, the party began to move in a more ethnonationalist direction, focusing more on ethnic issues and allocating most of the party's key candidacies to indigenous leaders. In response, a lot of white and mestizo leaders abandoned the party, as did many of the mestizo-dominated unions and civil society organizations that had supported it in the past. As a result, the party fared poorly in the 2006 elections and it has yet to recover.

Chapter 4 explores ethnic politics in Peru. It argues that a national-level indigenous party has failed to emerge in Peru in large part because the country's indigenous movement is weak and fragmented. Nevertheless, various politicians, especially Alberto Fujimori, Alejandro Toledo, and Ollanta Humala, have employed ethnic appeals to win the support of a disproportionate percentage of the country's indigenous voters. All three of these politicians have embraced some ethnic demands, invoked indigenous symbols, recruited various indigenous candidates, and presented themselves as ethnic outsiders. Ethnic appeals have been less central to their campaigns than populist appeals, however. Fujimori, Toledo, and Humala have all denounced the political establishment, presented themselves as Peru's savior, and directed their appeals largely at the poorest sectors of the population, but they have differed in the degree to which they have employed nationalist and state interventionist rhetoric. Whereas Humala has extensively criticized neoliberal policies and foreign intervention, Fujimori and Toledo implemented numerous market-oriented reforms and largely avoided nationalistic discourse and proposals.

Chapter 5 examines the failure of indigenous parties in Guatemala, Colombia, Venezuela, and Nicaragua. It argues that indigenous parties have had meager results in these countries in part because they have failed to employ many populist appeals. Some of these parties, such as YATAMA in Nicaragua and PUAMA in Venezuela, have focused mostly on ethnic demands and have failed to reach out to the non-indigenous population. Other parties, such as Winaq in Guatemala and ASI in Colombia, have reached out to whites and mestizos, but have failed to adopt the populist strategies that proved successful in the central Andes. Indigenous parties in these countries have also fared poorly because of the relative weakness of the indigenous movement in all four countries. Indigenous people only represent a small portion of the population in Colombia, Nicaragua, and Venezuela, and the indigenous movement's influence in these countries is largely limited to indigenous areas. The indigenous population is considerably larger in Guatemala, but the country's indigenous movement is fragmented and demobilized and did not play a major role in Winaq's campaign.

Chapter 6 analyzes the impact of indigenous parties on democracy, focusing on the MAS because it is the only indigenous party with much governing experience at the national level. The chapter argues that the parties' ethnic policies have deepened democracy in some ways. The indigenous parties have increased indigenous representation in the legislature and government ministries, they have boosted voter turnout and satisfaction with democracy in indigenous communities, and they have helped enact policies to improve the socioeconomic standing of indigenous people, which should make the Andean democracies more inclusive. By contrast, the populist tendencies of some indigenous parties, particularly the MAS, have weakened democracy. The chapter shows how the MAS's efforts to concentrate power and its aggressive attacks on the political opposition, the media, and the church have undermined horizontal accountability and weakened the rule of law. As a result, in many respects, democracy in Bolivia is more fragile now than when the MAS took power in 2005.

The conclusion to this book examines the implications of my arguments for theories of ethnic parties and populism. It argues that the literature on ethnic parties needs to take into account the nature of ethnic identification and inter-ethnic relations in developing theories about what sorts of appeals ethnic parties can make effectively. More specifically, it suggests that theories of ethnic parties must consider the level of ethnic polarization and ethnic fluidity, which in turn are shaped by the degree of ethnic mixing in a society. The conclusion also argues that the Latin American literature on populism needs to recognize the compatibility of populist and ethnic appeals. Populist and ethnic appeals can be effectively combined in part because populism is ideologically flexible, but also because its anti-establishment rhetoric and focus on the lower classes will attract members of marginalized ethnic minorities. The conclusion ends by identifying some promising areas for future research.

2

The Ascent of the MAS in Bolivia

> We respect, we admire all sectors, professionals and non-professionals, intellectuals and non-intellectuals, businessmen and non-businessmen; we all have the right to live in this land. ... There you can see that the indigenous movement is not exclusionary; it is inclusive.
>
> Evo Morales in his 2006 inaugural address
> (Stefanoni and Do Alto 2006, 133)

The Movimiento al Socialismo (MAS), an indigenous party founded in the mid-1990s, has dominated Bolivian politics in recent years. The MAS has won every single election held in Bolivia since 2004 by a large margin. In the 2009 general elections, for example, the MAS and its leader, Evo Morales, captured sixty-four percent of the valid votes, almost forty percentage points ahead of its closest rival. The MAS currently controls not only the presidency of Bolivia, but approximately two-thirds of the seats in the legislature, and many important departmental and municipal offices as well. The traditional parties, meanwhile, have crumbled and the political opposition is in disarray.

The MAS's rise to dominance is surprising given that indigenous parties had traditionally fared poorly in Bolivia. A number of indigenous parties emerged in the late 1970s and early 1980s, but none of these parties won more than a small fraction of the vote. The MAS initially gave little indication that it would enjoy any more success than previous indigenous parties. Indeed, it won only three percent of the vote in the initial elections in which it competed. In the 2002 general elections, however, the MAS finished a close second, and it has won every election held in Bolivia since.

What explains the dramatic ascent of the MAS? Why has it come to dominate Bolivia's traditionally fragmented party system in such a short period of time?

Existing studies have attributed the rise of the MAS in large part to institutional reforms that Bolivia carried out in the 1990s, notably decentralization and the adoption of a mixed electoral system (Marenghi and Alcántara Sáez 2007; Muñoz-Pogossian 2008; Rice 2006; Van Cott 2005). This chapter, by contrast, argues that the success of the MAS was due in large part to its inclusive ethnic and populist appeals. The MAS won the support of Bolivia's indigenous population in part because, unlike the traditional parties, it established close ties with indigenous organizations, ran numerous indigenous candidates, and embraced a broad range of indigenous demands. Beginning in the early 2000s, however, it also aggressively wooed whites and mestizos, recruiting many of them to serve as candidates, and forging alliances with many urban organizations in which they predominated. This inclusive strategy worked in part because Bolivia has traditionally had a high level of ethnic fluidity and a low level of ethnic polarization.

The MAS also has used traditional populist strategies to woo voters of all ethnic backgrounds. By the 1990s, many Bolivians, especially the poor and lower middle class, had become disenchanted with the governing parties and the market-oriented economic policies they had implemented. The MAS capitalized on this disaffection. It denounced the traditional parties and elites, and vigorously opposed neoliberal policies and U.S. intervention in Bolivia. It focused its campaign on the lower classes, relying to a large degree on the charismatic and down-to-earth personality of the party's unquestioned leader, Evo Morales. These appeals helped the party win high levels of support among poorer and less educated voters, as well as people with nationalist and anti-establishment views.

This chapter is organized as follows. The first section explains why institutional factors cannot account for the surprising rise of the MAS, although they help explain the MAS's creation. The second section discusses Bolivia's complex ethnic landscape and how the MAS took advantage of it. Sections three through five provide a sketch of Bolivia's recent electoral history, analyzing the failure of previous indigenous parties, the gradual decline of the traditional parties, and the rise of the MAS. The sixth section examines the MAS's inclusive ethnic appeals in detail, and shows how they were effective in winning the support of self-identified indigenous voters without alienating whites and mestizos. The seventh section discusses the MAS's use of classical populist strategies and their contribution to the MAS's electoral success. The conclusion summarizes the central arguments of this chapter and speculates on the future of the MAS.

INSTITUTIONAL EXPLANATIONS

Some studies have attributed the rapid rise of the MAS in part to the institutional reforms that Bolivia carried out in the 1990s. Van Cott (2003c, 756), for example, maintains that Bolivia's PR system, which used large, multimember districts, "made it difficult for geographically-concentrated indigenous movements to win enough votes nationwide to gain national office." She and others have argued that Bolivia's constitutional reform of 1994 facilitated the rise of the MAS by creating smaller single-member districts for elections to one tier of the lower chamber of the legislature (Collins 2006; Stefanoni 2004,

22; Van Cott 2005, 2003c) (interview with Lazarte 2004). Indeed, all four of the legislators elected by the Izquierda Unida, the MAS's predecessor, in 1997 were elected from single-member districts in the department of Cochabamba.

This explanation is unconvincing, however, because the MAS or its predecessor would have won approximately the same number of seats in 1997 and 2002 if Bolivia had retained the previous proportional representation system. For example, the vote that the MAS earned in the 1997 elections would have earned it three legislative seats under the old system, as opposed to the four seats that it won under the new system. Indeed, the German-style mixed system that Bolivia adopted was designed to achieve proportionality by using the PR tier to offset any disproportionality created by the outcomes of the races in the single-member districts. Moreover, under the old system the MAS did not need to win a significant share of the national vote to gain seats in the legislature because the old proportional representation system used nine departmental districts to award seats rather than a single national district. Thus, the MAS only needed to fare well in a single department, such as Cochabamba, to win seats under the old system.

Another institutional explanation for the rise of the MAS has focused on the decentralization process Bolivia underwent in the mid-1990s. The 1994 Law of Popular Participation created 311 municipalities nationwide and called for elections to be held for mayoral and council member positions throughout the country. The MAS was formed in the wake of the passage of this law, and some scholars have argued that the municipal elections enabled the MAS to gain a foothold at the local level, which its members used as a stepping stone for national offices (Andolina 1999, 240; Collins 2006; Urioste 2004, 345–6; Van Cott 2003c) (interviews with García Linera 2004; Rivera 2004; and Torrico 2004).

The decentralization law does help explain the formation of the MAS since its precursor was created specifically to compete in the municipal elections. This reform is less helpful in explaining the subsequent success of the MAS, however. To begin with, the municipal electoral victories of the MAS and its predecessor in 1995 and 1999 were confined largely to the department of Cochabamba (Rojas Ortuste 2000). It therefore seems unlikely that the MAS's strong electoral performance outside of Cochabamba in the 2002 elections could be explained by the resources, experience, or reputations won by the party's mayors in Cochabamba. Moreover, there is no evidence that the MAS has performed better in those municipalities where it has elected mayors or council members. To the contrary, between 1997 and 2002, the MAS increased its share of the total vote by a much smaller margin in those municipalities where it had elected mayors in 1995 than in those municipalities where it did not control the mayoralty – the MAS boosted its vote by thirteen percentage points in the former municipalities and nineteen percentage points in the latter. Similarly, the MAS increased its share of the vote by one percentage point less in those municipalities where it had elected council members in 1995 than in those where it had no municipal council members.

Thus, there is little evidence to suggest that either the decentralization law or the shift to a mixed electoral system played a major role in the success of the MAS, although the decentralization law clearly did contribute to the formation of the MAS. As we shall see, much of the explanation for the success of the MAS lies in the specific demands and strategies of the party itself.

ETHNICITY AND ETHNOPOPULISM IN BOLIVIA

This chapter argues that the MAS's inclusive ethnopopulist appeals have fueled its ascent. To be sure, other factors, such as the strengthening of indigenous consciousness and organization and growing disenchantment with the traditional parties and their record of governance, played a role in the rise of the MAS, but the MAS's ethnopopulist rhetoric and platform helped the party take advantage of these developments.

Several features of the ethnic landscape in Bolivia helped make these appeals successful. To begin with, a relatively large percentage of the population in Bolivia comes from an indigenous background. By some estimates, Bolivia is the Latin American country with the largest proportion of indigenous people. According to the census, 49.4 percent of the Bolivian population above the age of six spoke an indigenous language in 2001, more than in any other country (Instituto Nacional de Estadística 2003a, 142). Moreover, indigenous Bolivians are poorer, less educated, and have much less access to public health facilities than their non-indigenous counterparts. In 2002, for example, 73.9 percent of indigenous language speakers in Bolivia lived in poverty, as opposed to 52.5 percent of non-indigenous language speakers (Jiménez Pozo et al. 2006, 48–9). Indigenous people in Bolivia are also the subject of frequent discrimination. According to one recent survey, fifty-nine percent of the population asserted that there is a lot of discrimination in Bolivia and that skin color is the most important cause of discrimination ("7 de cada 10 bolivianos se ven mestizos" 2009). As a result, indigenous parties have a sizable base of indigenous voters on which they can draw, and these voters have numerous grievances that parties can use to mobilize them.

The indigenous population in Bolivia is highly fragmented, however. According to the 2001 census, 27.6 percent of the total population speaks Quechua, 18.4 percent of the population speaks Aymara, and 1.2 percent of the population speaks lowlands indigenous dialects. Moreover, there are considerable differences within these ethno-linguistic groups as well as across them. The various indigenous communities in Bolivia have different organizations that represent them and they often have sharply varying interests and demands. To win support from these disparate groups, indigenous leaders and parties have needed to be inclusive. As we shall see, parties that have focused on the Aymara population and that have been identified with Aymara nationalism, such as the Katarista parties, have understandably failed to win much support among Quechua speakers and lowlands indigenous groups. But the

MAS's inclusive approach has drawn extensive support from all of the major indigenous categories.

The low level of ethnic polarization in Bolivia and the ambiguity and fluidity of ethnic identification in Bolivia also favor an inclusive approach. The fluidity and ambiguity and the low level of ethnic polarization is due in part to widespread *mestizaje*, which has blurred the lines between different ethnic groups and created a large intermediate ethnic category. The process of *mestizaje* dates to the Spanish conquest, but it accelerated in the twentieth century (Sanjinés C. 2004; Yashar 2005). In the wake of the 1952 Bolivian revolution, the Bolivian government organized indigenous people around their class rather than their ethnic identities and began to refer to Indians almost exclusively as peasants (Yashar 2005).[1] The use of indigenous languages was actively discouraged in Bolivian schools and other public places, and the percentage of people who spoke indigenous languages declined.[2] Many indigenous people ceased to wear traditional indigenous clothing and some indigenous people adopted Spanish names (Patzi Paco 1999, 27–34). This assimilation process was particularly common in the cities, to which many indigenous people migrated.

In recent decades, the indigenous movement has sought to increase ethnic consciousness among the indigenous population, but widespread discrimination against indigenous people remains, and many people of indigenous descent have internalized this discrimination. As a result, a significant proportion of Bolivians from indigenous backgrounds identify themselves, at least some of the time, as mestizo rather than as indigenous. Surveys by the Ministry of Human Development (Rojas Ortuste and Verdesoto Custode 1997), the United Nations Development Program (Programa de las Naciones Unidas para el Desarrollo 2004), and the Latin American Public Opinion Project (Seligson et al. 2006, 13–21) have found that between sixty and seventy percent of the Bolivian population self-identifies as mestizo and less than twenty percent of the population self-identifies as indigenous.[3] Nevertheless, many of these self-identified mestizos speak indigenous languages and identify to some degree with indigenous culture. Indeed, in a recent survey conducted by LAPOP,

[1] Emblematic of this was the decision to change the name of the Ministry of Indian and Peasant Affairs to the Ministry of Peasant Affairs (Yashar 2005, 159).

[2] According to the census, the percentage of Bolivians who reported that an indigenous language was their principal or maternal language fell from 63.5 percent in 1950 to 35.4 percent in 2001 (Dirección General de Estadística y Censos 1950; Instituto Nacional de Estadística 2003a, 151). The percentage of Bolivians who spoke an indigenous language (whether or not it was their principal or maternal language) declined from 65.6 percent in 1976 to 55.0 percent in 1992 and 49.4 percent in 2001 (Instituto Nacional de Estadística 2003a, 142). Molina and Albó (2006, 102) present slightly different figures based on their analyses of census data. They report that 49.3 percent of the Bolivian population spoke an indigenous language in 2001, 58.3 percent in 1992, and 63.7 percent in 1976. These figures refer to the entire population in 1976 and the population above six years of age in 1992 and 2001.

[3] The surveys have posed some variation of the following question: "Do you consider yourself white, mestizo, or indigenous?" In some cases, additional categories such as cholo, black, or other are included.

fifty-five percent of the people who self-identified as mestizo spoke an indigenous language, and seventy percent of the people who self-identified as mestizo stated that they belonged to an indigenous ethno-linguistic category, mostly Quechua or Aymara.[4]

In this ethnic environment, inclusive appeals have been much more effective than exclusionary appeals. As we shall see, the MAS's inclusive ethnic appeals have attracted not only those people who self-identify as indigenous, but also the numerically much larger group of people who self-identify as mestizo but come from an indigenous background. These indigenous mestizos typically have some degree of ethnic consciousness and have felt more ethnically proximate to Morales and the MAS than to the other main candidates and parties. The MAS has even been able to win the support of some whites and mestizos who do not identify as indigenous at all, thanks in part to the low level of ethnic polarization in Bolivia. By contrast, parties that have engaged in exclusionary appeals or that have focused their appeals almost exclusively on the indigenous population have not fared nearly as well. Indeed, these parties have not only alienated self-identified whites and mestizos, but many indigenous people as well.

INDIGENOUS VOTERS AND PARTIES IN TWENTIETH-CENTURY BOLIVIA

The indigenous population in Bolivia, unlike its counterparts in Ecuador and Peru, has been an important actor in electoral politics since the 1950s. In the wake of the 1952 revolution in Bolivia, the ruling Movimiento Nacionalista Revolucionario (MNR) removed literacy restrictions on suffrage, thereby enfranchising the country's largely illiterate indigenous population. The MNR also carried out a sweeping land reform program, expanded education and social services in rural areas, and established peasant unions, which it used to control the rural population as well as distribute benefits. Partly as a result of these initiatives, the rural indigenous population initially voted overwhelmingly for the MNR.[5] In the 1958 elections, for example, the MNR won ninety-five percent of the vote in provincial areas where the indigenous population predominated, but only fifty-one percent of the vote in the more ethnically mixed departmental capitals (Corte Nacional Electoral 1958).[6] The unrivaled

---

[4] The 2006 LAPOP survey included a question about indigenous identity modeled on a question from the 2001 census. It asked: "Do you consider yourself to belong to one of the following native or indigenous peoples? Quechua; Aymara; Guaraní; Chiquitano; Mojeño; other native; none of the above." In the 2001 census, sixty-two percent of the population chose one of these indigenous ethno-linguistic categories, and in the 2006 LAPOP survey seventy-one percent of the population selected one of the indigenous categories. This question was widely criticized, however, in part because it did not include the option of self-identifying as mestizo. See Seligson et al. (2006).

[5] The MNR also used fraud, intimidation, and clientelist practices to ensure its electoral victories (Ticona Alejo et al. 1995).

[6] These figures exclude the departments of Santa Cruz, Chuquisaca, and Potosí for which data were not available.

dominance of the MNR lasted only until 1964, however, when the Bolivian military overthrew the government, ushering in eighteen years of almost uninterrupted military rule.

Indigenous parties did not emerge in Bolivia until the transition to democracy began in the late 1970s. The first wave of indigenous parties rose from the Aymara-based Katarista movement, which also gave birth to an independent confederation of indigenous peasant unions, the Confederación Sindical Unica de Trabajadores Campesinos de Bolivia (CSUTCB).[7] The Katarista parties varied somewhat in ideology as well as leadership, but they all sought to increase ethnic consciousness among the Aymara population and to promote its political and economic advancement. None of the Katarista parties registered much electoral success, although they did fare somewhat better in Aymara-speaking areas in the department of La Paz.[8]

The first indigenous party to compete independently in a general election was the Movimiento Indio Tupak Katari (MITKA), which participated in the 1978 elections. These elections were annulled because of massive fraud, and in new elections held the following year, the MITKA earned only 1.9 percent of the valid vote. The MITKA subsequently split in two as the result of leadership divisions and both the splinter group, MITKA-1, and the remainder of the original party, MITKA, participated in the 1980 elections, winning a combined total of 2.5 percent of the valid vote and one seat each in the legislature.[9]

The entrance of other Katarista parties into the electoral arena did not appreciably improve these results. In 1978, leaders of an Aymara peasant confederation founded the Movimiento Revolucionario Tupak Katari (MRTK). This party disintegrated into several factions, however, and none of these factions competed in the elections in 1978, 1979, or 1980, preferring to throw their support to mestizo-led parties, especially the Movimiento Nacionalista Revolucionario (MNR) and the Unión Democrática y Popular (UDP) (Pacheco 1992, 177–217; Rivera Cusicanqui 1986, 142–3; Rocha 1992, 255; Van Cott 2005, 83). In the 1985 elections, two of the factions of the MRTK opted to compete on their own, but they did not fare much better than previous Katarista parties. The Movimiento Revolucionario Tupak Katari de Liberación (MRTKL) led by Genaro Flores earned 2.1 percent of the valid vote and won two congressional seats, while the rump MRTK led by Macabeo Chila won a mere 1.1 percent. The MRTKL competed again in the 1989 elections, but this time its ticket was headed by Victor Hugo Cárdenas. Flores, meanwhile, founded a new party, the Frente Único de Liberación Katarista (FULKA), after a falling out with Cárdenas and other leaders of the MRTKL. These parties

---

[7] The Katarista movement took its name from Tupak Katari, who led an indigenous uprising in what is now Bolivia during the eighteenth century. On the Katarista movement see: Hurtado 1986; Pacheco 1992; Patzi Paco 1999; Rivera Cusicanqui 1986; Rocha 1992; Romero Ballivián 2003; Tapia 1995; Ticona Alejo et al. 1995; Van Cott 2005; Yashar 2005.

[8] According to the 2001 census, seventy-seven percent of the Aymara-speaking population lives in the department of La Paz (Instituto Nacional de Estadística 2003a, 66).

[9] New elections were held in 1980 because of an intervening military coup.

also fared poorly, however, with the MRTKL winning 1.6 percent of the valid vote and FULKA earning 1.2 percent.

Two new Katarista parties – the Movimiento Katarista Nacional (MKN) and the Eje Pachakuti (EJE) – competed in the 1993 elections, but neither of these parties managed to obtain even the modest level of support enjoyed by previous Katarista parties.[10] EJE won 1.1 percent of the valid vote and the MKN won a mere 0.8 percent. The MRTKL, meanwhile, opted to ally with the MNR, and Cárdenas ran as the vice president on the MNR-MRTKL ticket.[11] This alliance won the 1993 elections thanks in large part to the continuing strength of the MNR. Cárdenas thus became the country's first indigenous vice president, but many indigenous leaders criticized him for allying with the MNR. They also argued that the MNR gave the MRTKL little in exchange for its electoral support.[12] Embroiled in controversy, the MRTKL disintegrated in the years that followed.

No Aymara-based party competed in the 1997 elections, but in the 2002 elections a new party, the Movimiento Indígena Pachakuti (MIP), registered the best showing of a Katarista party to date.[13] The MIP was created by Felipe Quispe, a radical Aymara leader who had a long trajectory in the Katarista movement, having served as a leader of MITKA in the 1970s and early 1980s. In the late 1980s, he helped form the Ejército Guerrillero Tupak Katari (EGTK) and he was subsequently arrested and imprisoned for his participation in this group's guerrilla activities. A few years after his release, he was elected secretary general of the CSUTCB, and in 2000 he founded the MIP and ran as its presidential candidate in the 2002 elections. In those elections, Quispe and the MIP won 6.1 percent of the valid vote, more than twice as much as any previous Katarista party. The relative success of Quispe's MIP was short-lived, however. The party won approximately two percent of the total vote in the 2004 municipal and the 2005 general elections – a share of the vote that roughly corresponded to previous Katarista parties – and the party has since disappeared. Thus, more than three decades after their inception, the Katarista parties have yet to demonstrate significant electoral clout.

Van Cott (2005, 82–5) attributes the poor electoral performance of the Katarista parties to institutional barriers, internal leadership disunity, low levels of voter registration in indigenous areas, and strong clientelist and

---

[10] Some scholars have claimed that the ruling ADN-MIR coalition helped create the MKN in order to counter the appeal among indigenous people of the MNR-MRTKL ticket (Albó 1993, 31; Van Cott 2005, 82).

[11] Another Aymara leader, Genaro Flores, ran as the vice presidential candidate of Izquierda Unida, a left-wing party, in 1993.

[12] The alliance helped the MNR win twenty-eight percent of the vote in majority Aymara-speaking provinces in 1993, as opposed to only 17.4 percent in 1989.

[13] A precursor of the MAS, the IU/ASP, competed in the 1997 elections, but this was not a Katarista party. A successor of Eje Pachakuti, Eje de Convergencia Patriótica, also participated in the 1997 elections, but after most of its indigenous leaders had left the party. Many of the indigenous leaders of Eje Pachakuti, such as Evo Morales, ended up in the MAS (Van Cott 2005, 67).

TABLE 2.1. *Vote for Katarista Parties, 1979–2002 (as a percent of the valid vote)*

	1979	1980	1985	1989	1993	1997	2002
MITKA	1.9%	1.2%					
MITKA-1		1.3					
MRTK			1.1%				
MRTKL			2.1	1.6%			
FULKA				1.2			
MKN					0.8%		
EJE					1.1		
MIP							6.1%
National vote for all Katarista parties	1.9	2.5	3.2	2.8	1.9	0%	6.1
Mean in majority Spanish provinces	NA	NA	1.5	1.0	1.8	0	1.4
Mean in majority Quechua provinces	NA	NA	3.2	3.3	2.1	0	2.4
Mean in majority Aymara provinces	NA	NA	11.4	12.2	8.5	0	25.7

Source: Corte Nacional Electoral

programmatic ties between the traditional parties and indigenous voters, but none of these factors provides an entirely satisfactory explanation. Institutional rules, which obliged parties that did not receive at least fifty thousand votes to reimburse the National Electoral Court for the costs of printing their ballots, led Katarista parties to lose their party registration, but such rules cannot explain why they fared poorly in the first place. Moreover, there is no evidence to suggest that the Katarista parties would have done better had they maintained their registration. As Table 2.1 shows, each Katarista party tended to fare worse over time, not better. Nor can the lack of unity among the Katarista parties explain why they fared poorly. Indeed, even if we sum the votes of the different Katarista parties together, they never won more than 3.2 percent of the vote in any single election until 2002. The clientelist and programmatic ties that the traditional parties had established with the indigenous population did initially represent an obstacle for the Katarista parties, but the strength of these ties diminished over time. Indeed, by 1993, the traditional parties had already lost a great deal of ground in indigenous areas, but the Katarista parties were unable to take advantage of their decline. Nor can differences in voter registration or turnout account for the poor electoral performance of the Katarista parties. Voter registration and turnout was typically lower in indigenous areas than in non-indigenous areas in the 1980s and 1990s, but this was not the case in Aymara areas where support for Katarista parties was concentrated.[14]

---

[14] The percentage of the voting age population who cast ballots was significantly lower in majority Aymara provinces than in other areas in 1985 but not in 1989. In 1993, turnout and registration

What then explains the failure of the Katarista parties to win a larger percentage of the vote? One crucial factor was their failure to reach out to the non-Aymara population. Some of the Katarista parties alienated voters, especially whites and mestizos, with their exclusionary rhetoric. The more radical ethnonationalist Katarista parties, sometimes referred to as Indianista parties, drew inspiration from Fausto Reynaga's Partido Indio de Bolivia, which rejected *mestizaje* and called for a war against white culture (Hurtado 1986; Pacheco 1992).[15] According to the manifesto of the party, this would not be "a simple war, a war just to kill whites, no; it is a war without pity, without truce, without rest against all that signifies their religion, their culture, their economy, their morality, their life, everything" (Pacheco 1992, 37). The leaders of MITKA, the MITKA-1, and the MIP at times used exclusionary rhetoric. Quispe, for example, has frequently denounced the *q'aras* (a pejorative term for whites), saying that "they want to bathe themselves in indigenous blood" (interview with author 2004).[16] He has often spoken of creating an Aymara homeland in which whites and others would not be entirely welcome. In an interview with Canessa (2006, 251), Quispe was characteristically blunt:

Those lying q'aras. When the Pachamama walks again in Qullasuyu, when her laws reign, then we will be able to judge them. Those who want to leave can go; but those who stay will eat what we eat; they will work the way we work, dripping with sweat; they will have blisters on their hands; they will suffer like we do. Then truly the Aymara nation, what people call the indigenous [nation], what we call Qullasuyu, will come forth.

This sort of Aymara nationalism alienated not only whites and mestizos, but also Quechuas and even many Aymaras.

Other Katarista parties, such as the MRTKL, MRTK, and FULKA, adopted more moderate and inclusive stances, and the leaders of these parties have typically avoided such rhetoric. Even these parties, however, have failed to take many steps to win non-Aymara voters. In an interview with the author, Dionisio Núñez, an Aymara congressman from the MAS, argued that:

Katarismo was important in consciousness raising. It created schools that trained leaders. The problem with those parties was that they only brought together a group of Aymaras.... Those who were not Kataristas or Aymara could not participate. (Interview with author 2004)

---

were actually higher in majority Aymara provinces than in other areas, perhaps because of the MNR-MRTKL alliance. Moreover, even in 1985, lower registration and turnout in Aymara areas did not significantly depress votes for the Katarista parties. Indeed, if turnout rates in majority Aymara provinces had been identical to those in other areas in 1985, the Katarista parties' share of the national vote would have increased by less than one percentage point.

[15] The Partido Indio de Bolivia never participated in elections, nor did it develop much of a following.

[16] Quispe's commitment to democratic institutions remains limited. In an interview with the author (2004), he remarked, "I continue to think that it is possible to capture [the state] through armed struggle, but the masses prefer the legal path."

The Katarista parties did not recruit many white, mestizo, and Quechua leaders to their organizations, and as a result, the leadership and the base of the Katarista parties were overwhelmingly Aymara.[17] Nor did the Katarista parties establish ties to many organizations outside of the Aymara heartland. Some of the Katarista parties, such as the MRTKL and FULKA, had strong roots in the Aymara peasant unions, particularly in the department of La Paz, but they failed to build close ties to Quechua-dominated peasant associations in other departments or to urban mestizo-dominated groups. In some cases, the Katarista parties did establish alliances with traditional parties such as the UDP and the MNR, but these were unequal alliances, which typically resulted in the subordination and cooptation of the indigenous parties and leaders (Hurtado 1986, 112–18; Ticona Alejo et al. 1995, 121–56). The MRTK, for example, received little in exchange for its support of the UDP in 1978, and its candidates were placed at the bottom of the alliance's list, which ensured that they would not be elected (Hurtado 1986, 115).

The Katarista parties' use of exclusionary rhetoric and their failure to recruit many non-Aymara candidates or to establish ties with many non-Aymara organizations limited the appeal of these parties outside of the Aymara heartland. The Katarista parties fared poorly in majority Quechua-speaking areas and even worse in areas that were predominantly Spanish-speaking. In no year did the Katarista parties win more than 3.3 percent of the vote in majority Quechua-speaking provinces or more than 1.8 percent of the vote in majority Spanish-speaking provinces. They fared much better in Aymara-speaking areas. In 1985, for example, the MRTK and the MRTKL together won 11.4 percent of the vote in majority Aymara-speaking provinces, and in 2002, the MIP alone won 25.7 percent of the vote in majority Aymara-speaking provinces. A large majority of these votes were won in the department of La Paz, even though La Paz accounted for only about one-third of the electorate. Indeed, the MRTK and the MRTKL earned 54.7 percent of their votes in La Paz in 1985 and the MIP won an astounding ninety-two percent of its votes in La Paz. Even within the Aymara heartland, however, most voters opted for non-Katarista parties in part because of these parties' overriding emphasis on ethnic issues and their insular, often exclusionary, strategies.

THE DECLINE OF THE TRADITIONAL PARTIES

In the 1980s and 1990s, indigenous as well as non-indigenous voters mostly supported the traditional parties. Although the Movimiento Nacionalista Revolucionario's ties to the indigenous population had weakened considerably under military rule, it continued to enjoy support in many indigenous areas. The left, especially the Movimiento de Izquierda Revolucionaria (MIR) and

---

[17] There were some exceptions. The MRTKL, for example, recruited Filemón Escobar, a mestizo union leader, as its vice presidential candidate in 1985, and it elected Walter Reinaga, a Quechua leader, as a deputy from Potosí that same year.

its precursor, the UDP, also had a lot of support in indigenous areas thanks in part to the extensive organizing it carried out in these communities in the 1970s and 1980s and the ties it had developed to indigenous organizations and leaders (Hurtado 1986, 133–5; Ticona Alejo et al. 1995, 130–3).[18] The UDP or the MIR won a plurality of the vote in indigenous areas in the 1980, 1989, and 1997 elections, but the MNR triumphed in these areas in the 1985 and 1993 elections. The right-wing Acción Democrática Nacionalista (ADN), founded by former military ruler Hugo Banzer, also won a fair number of votes in indigenous areas, but it typically finished third behind the MNR and the MIR (or the UDP).

In the late 1990s and early 2000s, however, the traditional parties began to weaken. Disaffection with the traditional parties was particularly high in indigenous areas. Whereas in 1989 the MNR, the ADN, and the MIR together won 64.6 percent of the valid vote in provinces where a majority of the population reported growing up in a home where an indigenous language was spoken, these three parties accounted for only 49.5 percent of the vote in these provinces in 1997, and by 2002, their share had fallen to 31.5 percent.[19] The growing levels of disenchantment with the traditional parties stemmed in part from their clientelist methods and their involvement in various corruption scandals (Calderón and Gamarra 2004; Mainwaring 2006; Mayorga 2005). The market-oriented policies these parties implemented also gradually undermined their popularity because these policies failed to generate steady economic growth or significantly reduce poverty and inequality. Some of these policies, such as the elimination of agricultural subsidies and price controls, the reduction of barriers to agricultural imports, and cuts in social spending, generated particularly high levels of resentment in indigenous areas, as did the government's United States-sponsored coca eradication programs.

The failure of the traditional parties to embrace many of the demands of the indigenous movement or to field prominent indigenous candidates also undermined their support in indigenous areas. In the 1980s, the traditional parties wooed indigenous voters largely through clientelist methods and their standard programmatic offerings, rather than by making ethnic appeals. Beginning in the 1990s, the traditional parties did embrace some ethnically oriented legislation. The MIR-led government of Jaime Paz Zamora (1989–93), for example, recognized two and a half million hectares of indigenous territories and ratified the International Labor Organization's Convention 169 on indigenous and tribal peoples. The MNR-led government of Gonzalo Sánchez de Lozada (1993–7),

---

[18] The UDP was a broad left-wing alliance that included the MIR, the Movimiento Nacionalista Revolucionario de la Izquierda, and the Partido Comunista de Bolivia. The UDP disintegrated during the disastrous government of Hernán Siles (1982–5), and the MIR was the only one of its members that remained an electoral force.

[19] The data on provinces that have a majority of indigenous language speakers is from the 2001 census. Using data from the 1992 census does not appreciably change the results. According to the census, fifty-seven of Bolivia's 112 provinces had an indigenous language speaking majority in 2001.

meanwhile, carried out an agrarian reform law (Ley de Servicio Nacional de Reforma Agraria), a political decentralization measure (Ley de Participación Popular), a multicultural education reform (Ley de Reforma Educativa), and a constitutional amendment that recognized Bolivia's multi-ethnic and pluri-cultural nature. Nevertheless, these measures were typically implemented in a top-down fashion, and they did not go nearly as far as the indigenous organizations and leaders would have liked (Van Cott 2000; Yashar 2005).

Moreover, although the traditional parties did sometimes recruit indigenous candidates for local offices, they rarely recruited indigenous people for more prestigious positions, and they often placed indigenous candidates low on the ballot, which reduced the likelihood they would gain office.[20] As a result, very few indigenous people served in the legislature as representatives of the traditional parties in the 1980s and 1990s. The traditional parties, for example, had no indigenous senators and only one indigenous deputy in the 1997–2002 congress, nor did they have any indigenous people on their executive committees (Albó 2002, 95; Madrid 2005a, 12) (interview with Carvajal 2004).[21]

Populist parties, especially Conciencia de Patria (CONDEPA), the Unidad Cívica Solidaridad (UCS), and the Nueva Fuerza Republicana (NFR), initially took advantage of the political vacuum created by the decline of the traditional parties. CONDEPA first emerged in the 1989 elections when it won 12.2 percent of the valid vote, but it grew steadily in the 1990s, winning 14.3 percent of the vote in 1993 and 17.2 percent in 1997. The UCS participated for the first time in general elections in 1993, winning 13.8 percent of the valid vote. It then expanded its share to 16.1 percent in 1997. The NFR, meanwhile, did not compete in general elections until 2002 when it captured 20.9 percent of the valid vote. Although both the UCS and NFR won a sizable number of indigenous votes, neither of these parties fared any better in indigenous areas than in non-indigenous areas.[22] CONDEPA, by contrast, won the vast majority of its votes in Aymara-speaking areas of La Paz. In 1997, for example, it won 32.9 percent of the vote in majority Aymara-speaking provinces, but only 4.2 percent of the vote in other areas.

The success of these parties was due in large part to their anti-establishment rhetoric, personality focused campaigns, and other classical populist strategies, but they also used ethnic appeals to win votes. For example, Max Fernández, the leader of the UCS, spoke Quechua on the campaign trail and was often referred to as a cholo entrepreneur, although he generally eschewed identity politics. The leader of the NFR, Manfred Reyes Villa, recruited Alejo Véliz and

---

[20] The most notable exception was the MNR's decision to forge an alliance with the MRTKL and name Victor Hugo Cárdenas as its vice presidential candidate in the 1993 elections, but even this pact did not translate into many important positions for indigenous leaders.

[21] The traditional parties did elect more indigenous candidates in the 2002 elections, but even then their numbers were relatively modest (Rivero Pinto 2002, 36; Van Cott 2005, 94–5).

[22] The UCS did fare somewhat better in majority indigenous provinces than in other areas in 1993, but this dynamic was reversed in 1997. The NFR fared slightly worse in majority indigenous provinces than in majority non-indigenous provinces in 2002.

various other indigenous candidates, and ended up placing eight indigenous people in the national legislature in the 2002 elections.[23] CONDEPA made the most explicit ethnic appeals of the three parties, however. The leader of CONDEPA, Carlos Palenque, was mestizo, but he was a popular television and radio personality in the Aymara community and he often invoked Aymara sayings and traditions (Alenda Mary 2002; Romero 2003; San Martín Arzabe 1991). Palenque also incorporated the *wiphala*, an indigenous flag, and other indigenous symbols into his party's campaign propaganda and he recruited indigenous candidates for some important positions. For example, he placed an Aymara woman, Remedios Loza, at the top of the list of candidates for the Chamber of Deputies in La Paz in 1989, and the party nominated her as its presidential candidate in 1997 after Palenque's death. CONDEPA also embraced some traditional indigenous demands, such as agrarian reform, the creation of an indigenous university, and the recognition of Aymara as an official language.

The success of the populist parties was relatively short-lived, however. CONDEPA and the UCS fell apart in the 2002 elections, with the UCS earning only 5.5 percent of the valid vote and CONDEPA winning less than 0.4 percent. Neither party even competed in the 2005 or 2009 general elections. The NFR, meanwhile, disintegrated after its strong showing in 2002, winning less than 0.7 percent of the valid vote in 2005. The collapse of the populist parties stemmed in part from their dependence on charismatic leaders who failed to build strong party institutions (Alenda Mary 2002; Romero Ballivián 1999; San Martín Arzabe 1991). Both Palenque and Fernández died unexpectedly in the mid-1990s, depriving their parties of the leadership and affective ties to voters that they provided. The NFR, meanwhile, was hurt by Manfred Reyes Villa's decision not to compete in the 2005 presidential elections and to distance himself from his own party's presidential candidate (Romero Ballivián 2006, 30). The populist parties were also hurt by their association with the traditional parties and the unpopular policies these parties implemented. All three of these parties joined governments led by the traditional parties at some point during the 1990s and 2000s, which undermined their anti-establishment image.

The collapse of the populist parties, along with the decline of the traditional parties, created a highly propitious environment for the rise of the MAS. By the early 2000s, a substantial portion of the electorate, especially the indigenous electorate, had become unmoored. Disenchanted with the political establishment and increasingly ethnically conscious, many of these voters proved receptive to the MAS's ethnopopulist appeals.

---

[23] Populist and leftist parties have also recruited significant numbers of indigenous candidates for municipal elections. In the 1995 municipal elections, the Movimiento Bolivia Libre elected ninety indigenous municipal council members, more than any other party. See Albó (2002, 84). UCS and CONDEPA, meanwhile, elected thirty-four and twenty-four indigenous council members in these elections, which placed them in third and fourth place respectively in this category.

THE RISE OF THE MAS

The MAS initially provided little indication that it would fare any better than previous indigenous parties, although it had a very different base from the outset. The precursor of the MAS, the Izquierda Unida (IU), also known as the Asamblea de la Soberanía de los Pueblos (ASP), won only three percent of the valid vote nationally in the 1995 municipal elections and 3.7 percent in the 1997 general elections. The vast majority of those votes came from rural Cochabamba where the IU/ASP was based. Indeed, in the 1997 elections, the IU/ASP won nearly three-quarters of its total votes in Cochabamba, where it finished third overall with 17.5 percent of the vote.[24] As Figure 2.1 indicates, outside of Cochabamba, the party fared poorly, winning only 1.2 percent of the total vote. This situation changed only marginally in the 1999 municipal elections, by which time Evo Morales and his allies had left the IU/ASP and taken over the MAS.[25] In 1999, the MAS won nine mayoralties and eighty councilmember positions, with half of the latter positions coming from outside of Cochabamba (Rojas Ortuste 2000, 103–12). Nevertheless, the MAS's share of the vote in Cochabamba, 7.8 percent, and the nation as a whole, 3.3 percent, in 1999 was less than that of the IU/ASP in 1997.[26]

In 2002, however, the MAS surprised most observers by winning 20.9 percent of the valid vote nationwide. Morales, who ran as the party's presidential candidate in 2002 for the first time, surged in the polls in the last weeks of the campaign, and on election day he finished second, less than two percentage points behind the winner, Gonzalo Sánchez de Lozada of the MNR.[27] Manfred Reyes Villa of the NFR, who had led most preelection surveys, finished third, a mere 800 votes behind Morales.[28] The MAS's strong performance in 2002 gave it twenty-seven seats in the Chamber of Deputies and eight seats in the senate, making it the largest opposition party. Equally important, the MAS ceased to be a regional party in 2002 by expanding its base of support beyond Cochabamba

[24] The IU/ASP accounted for an even larger share of the vote (thirty percent) in rural areas and small towns in the department of Cochabamba (i.e., outside the departmental capital).

[25] The MAS was initially known as the Instrumento Político para la Soberanía de los Pueblos (IPSP) and is still frequently referred to as the MAS-IPSP.

[26] The other faction of the IU/ASP, headed by Alejo Véliz, ran under the inscription of the Communist Party of Bolivia in 1999. It fared reasonably well in the department of Cochabamba, winning 5.5 percent of the vote and twenty-two councilmember positions, but it failed to make much of a showing elsewhere. In many areas it was not even on the ballot.

[27] There are several reasons the surveys may have underestimated the vote for Morales and the MAS. First, the surveys typically did not include the dispersed rural population, which voted disproportionately for Morales (Gálvez Vera 2002) (interviews with Garay 2004 and Quiroga 2004). Second, many of the respondents who refused to answer or said that they had not made up their mind may have voted for Morales. Third, some voters who reported that they would vote for other parties may have changed their minds during the week between the final preelection surveys and the actual election.

[28] Because no one won more than fifty percent of the vote, it fell to the Bolivian congress to choose the new president, and after some negotiations, the legislators chose Sánchez de Lozada to serve a second term.

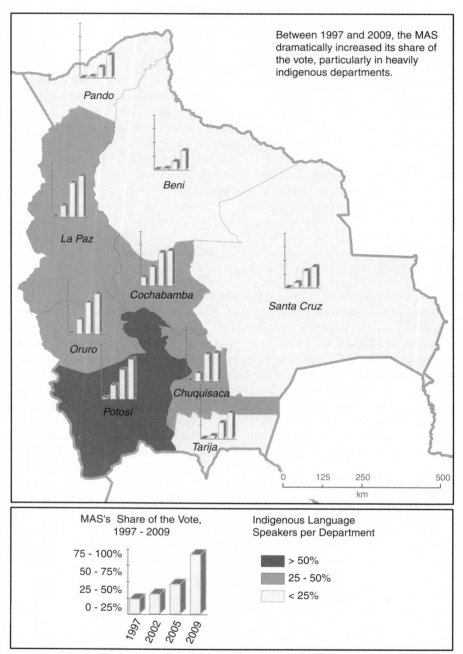

FIGURE 2.1. Indigenous language speakers and the vote for the MAS in Bolivia, 1997–2009.
Source: CNE and INE. Mapping by Aquacarta

to the western highlands of Bolivia. The MAS finished in first place not only in the department of Cochabamba where it won 37.6 percent of the valid vote, but also in the highlands departments of Oruro with 29.2 percent of the vote, Potosí with 27.0 percent, and La Paz with 22.5 percent. It fared less well in the eastern, less indigenous departments, but it still managed to finish third in Chuquisaca with 17.1 percent of the valid vote, and fourth in Santa Cruz and Tarija, with 10.2 percent and 6.2 percent of the vote respectively.[29]

The MAS consolidated its gains in the 2004 municipal elections. The vote in the 2004 municipal elections was highly fragmented in part because citizen and indigenous groupings, and not just parties, were allowed to field their own candidates for the first time. Although the MAS won only 17.1 percent of the total vote, this was twice as much as any other party and represented fourteen percentage points more than the MAS had received in the previous municipal elections (Romero Ballivián 2005, 47). As in 2002, the MAS fared much better in the highly indigenous western departments than it did in the eastern departments.

In the 2005 general elections, the performance of the MAS exceeded even its own lofty expectations. Morales not only finished first, he won 53.7 percent of the valid vote, by far the largest share any candidate had won since the return to democracy in the 1980s. By contrast, the second-place finisher, Jorge Quiroga of Poder Democrático y Social (PODEMOS), won only 28.6 percent of the vote. As previously, the MAS finished first in the western departments of La Paz, Cochabamba, Oruro, and Potosí, but this time it triumphed there by impressive margins, winning between fifty-seven and sixty-seven percent of the valid votes in each one of them. Moreover, the MAS also fared relatively well in the eastern departments. It finished first in Chuquisaca with 54.2 percent of the vote, and second in Santa Cruz and Tarija, with 33.2 percent and 31.6 percent of the vote respectively.[30] The MAS's resounding victory gave it control not only of the presidency, but also of the Chamber of Deputies, where it gained fifty-five percent of the seats (seventy-two out of 130). The MAS won only twelve out of twenty-seven seats in the senate, however, and it gained the governorships (prefectures) of only four of the nine departments (Cochabamba, Oruro, Potosí, and Chuquisaca).

Shortly after taking office, Morales called for the election of a constituent assembly in order to rewrite Bolivia's constitution. Elections for the constituent assembly were held in July of 2006 and the results cemented the MAS's status as Bolivia's dominant party. The MAS won 50.3 percent of the valid vote in these elections, far ahead of PODEMOS, which finished in second place with 15.3 percent of the valid vote. The MAS again dominated in the

---

[29] The MAS fared quite poorly in 2002 in Beni and Pando where it finished sixth with approximately three percent of the valid vote, but these thinly populated departments in the Bolivian Amazon represent a tiny fraction of the national electorate.

[30] The MAS even fared respectably in Beni and Pando in 2005, winning 16.5 percent and 20.9 percent of the vote, respectively.

departments of La Paz, Cochabamba, Oruro, Potosí, and Chuquisaca, where it won between fifty-four and sixty-three percent of the vote. In this election, however, it also finished first in Tarija, where it won 40.1 percent of the valid vote, and in Santa Cruz where it earned 26.4 percent.[31] As a result of this strong showing, the MAS gained more than half of the seats (137 of 255) in the constituent assembly, which enabled it to dominate the writing of a new constitution. As Chapter 6 discusses, the constituent assembly finally approved a proposed new constitution in late 2007 after a prolonged and highly contentious process.

The debate over the constitution exacerbated a highly polarized political environment and helped stimulate the autonomist movement in the eastern departments. In an effort to break the growing political impasse, in 2008 the government called a referendum on whether to recall President Morales and the departmental governors (prefects). Once again, the MAS triumphed. Approximately sixty-seven percent of voters nationwide cast their ballots in favor of retaining Morales in this referendum, and only two departments, Santa Cruz and Beni, voted to recall him. Support for Morales increased in comparison to 2005 in every department except for Chuquisaca. Moreover, none of the MAS prefects were recalled, while two of the opposition governors, Manfred Reyes Villa of Cochabamba and José Luis Paredes of La Paz, were. In the wake of this victory, the MAS negotiated an agreement with the opposition on the proposed new constitution that included more than one hundred modifications to the constitution. The new constitution was then submitted to a referendum in early 2009 where it was approved by sixty-two percent of the electorate. Nevertheless, four eastern departments, Santa Cruz, Beni, Pando, and Tarija, voted against the new constitution.

General elections were held in late 2009, as called for by the new constitution, and the MAS once again triumphed resoundingly. Morales was reelected with 64.2 percent of the vote, while his closest competitor, Manfred Reyes Villa, who ran as the candidate of the Plan Progreso para Bolivia – Concertación Nacional (PPB-CN), won only 26.5 percent. Morales won every department except for Santa Cruz, Beni, and Pando, but even in those departments he earned approximately forty percent of the vote. The MAS also won eighty-eight out of 130 seats (sixty-seven percent) in the Chamber of Deputies and twenty-six out of thirty-six seats (seventy-two percent) in the senate, providing it with the necessary votes to carry out the sweeping changes it envisions.

Thus, in the short time since its founding, the MAS has transformed itself into Bolivia's dominant party. The MAS now controls the country's major political institutions and it has consistently demonstrated its ability to win elections. The following sections explore the roots of the MAS's rapid and surprising success.

---

[31] The MAS finished second in Pando with 37.2 percent of the vote and third in Beni with 21.4 percent.

THE MAS'S ETHNIC APPEALS

The MAS has succeeded in part because it has appealed to Bolivia's indigenous population as indigenous people. It has used a variety of methods to woo indigenous voters. First, the MAS has established close ties with a vast number of indigenous organizations in the country. Second, the MAS has run numerous indigenous candidates, including for high-profile positions. Third, the MAS has made a variety of symbolic appeals to Bolivia's indigenous population. Fourth and finally, the MAS has aggressively promoted traditional indigenous demands. These ethnic appeals have helped the MAS consistently win an impressive share of the vote in indigenous areas.

The MAS had strong ties to the indigenous movement from the outset. The party originated in the Quechua-dominated coca growers unions based in the Chapare region of the department of Cochabamba. These unions date to the 1960s, but were strengthened and radicalized by the migration of large numbers of Quechua-speaking highlands Indians to the area in the 1980s. Many of these migrants were workers and peasants who had been hurt by the neoliberal economic reforms the Bolivian government undertook beginning in 1985. They included many former miners who had experience with labor activism. The residents of the Chapare depended heavily on coca growing for their livelihoods, and United States-supported efforts by the Bolivian government to eradicate coca growing in the region antagonized the coca growers and helped mobilize them (Healy 1991; Patzi Paco 1999, 48–50). The unions of coca growers, which exercised considerable authority within the Chapare, began to carry out numerous roadblocks, marches, rallies, sit-ins, and land seizures to protest the government's efforts to eradicate coca growing.[32]

By the early 1990s, the unified coca growers unions had become the most powerful and militant labor movement in the country. Moreover, they had largely gained control of the largest Bolivian peasant federation, the CSUTCB, traditionally dominated by Aymara activists from La Paz (Patzi Paco 1999, 89–90; Van Cott 2005). Under the leadership of the coca grower unions, the CSUTCB began to explore the idea of creating a vehicle to participate in elections, and in March 1995 a congress of peasant organizations voted to create a political instrument, the Asamblea por la Soberanía de los Pueblos, to compete in the municipal elections later that year. The leaders of the ASP did not manage to register the party in time for the elections, so they borrowed the inscription of the Izquierda Unida, a largely moribund left-wing party. Although the federation of coca growers spearheaded the creation of the IU/ASP, various other peasant organizations also supported the initiative, including the women's peasant federation, the Federación Nacional de Mujeres Campesinas

---

[32] The coca growers unions functioned as quasi-governments in the Chapare. They taxed peasants, regulated the coca leaf markets, set private land boundaries and carried out public works among other activities (Healy 1991, 89). Participation in union meetings and protest measures was typically obligatory (Stefanoni and Do Alto 2006, 37).

"Bartolina Sisa," and the Confederación Sindical de Colonizadores Bolivianos, a federation representing peasants from the highlands who had migrated to subtropical areas of Bolivia in search of land.

The IU/ASP did not initially enjoy strong organizational support outside of rural Cochabamba, and its leadership was dominated by the coca growers at the outset. Many Aymara organizations and leaders were resentful of the Quechua-speaking coca growers who had taken over the CSUTCB (Patzi Paco 1999, 117–18). As a result, the party initially fared poorly in Aymara areas of La Paz, the traditional stronghold of the Katarista parties. Indigenous leaders and organizations in the lowlands were also wary of the IU/ASP because it was dominated by the highlands Indians (Andolina 1999, 249–52). The main lowlands indigenous federation, the Confederación Indígena del Oriente Boliviano (CIDOB), initially considered forming its own party, but ultimately opted to let members of its regional organizations decide which parties to support in the elections (Andolina 1999, ch. 6; Van Cott 2005, 71–7). Most of the lowlands leaders and organizations supported small left-wing parties, such as the Movimiento Bolivia Libre (MBL), or the traditional parties, and thus the IU/ASP also fared quite poorly initially in lowlands indigenous areas.

Leadership conflicts led Evo Morales and his supporters to leave the IU/ASP in 1998 and found a new party, the Instrumento Político por la Soberanía de los Pueblos. The IPSP subsequently took over the registration of a largely defunct left-wing party, the MAS, in order to compete in elections. Under Morales's leadership, the MAS made efforts to build ties to indigenous organizations throughout Bolivia. The MAS, for example, reached out to the Quechua-speaking population outside of the department of Cochabamba, forging an alliance with Félix Vázquez, the powerful head of a peasant federation in northern Potosí. The MAS also built ties to organizations in the lowlands, striking a pact with the Coordinadora de Pueblos Étnicos de Santa Cruz, which it allowed to designate the party's candidates in the department of Santa Cruz. Perhaps most important, the MAS reached out to Aymara leaders and organizations, especially in the department of La Paz. These efforts were helped by the fact that Morales is of Aymara origin, although he had migrated to a predominantly Quechua-speaking area as a young man. The MAS was not able to obtain the support of all indigenous organizations, however. Some Aymara organizations, for example, supported Felipe Quispe and his party, the Movimiento Indígena Pachakuti, in the 2002 and 2005 elections, and CIDOB also has frequently maintained its distance from the MAS.[33] Nevertheless, the MAS gradually won the support of the majority of indigenous organizations in Bolivia.

The indigenous organizations provided a variety of benefits to the MAS. To begin with, the organizations provided the MAS with large numbers of experienced activists to staff the campaigns. As Van Cott (2005, 91) has argued, the MAS (and the MIP) "drew on resources of social movement organizations

---

[33] Quispe controlled one faction of the CSUTCB and used it to bolster his campaign.

with decades of experience and vast networks of free campaign labor...."
Although the organizations were poor, they supplied many material resources
to the campaigns, including posters and other campaign propaganda, venues
for meetings, and transportation to get candidates and supporters to rallies. In
a 2004 interview with the author, MAS deputy Gustavo Torrico stated, "The
federations do what they can. The coca growers give away coca leaf. The professional associations give away flags...." Perhaps most important, the indigenous organizations gave the MAS their seal of approval. By endorsing the
MAS, the organizations provided it with a degree of ethnic and organizational
legitimacy that the fledgling party would have otherwise lacked. In some rural
communities these organizations held a great deal of sway and residents often
voted en masse for the parties that they endorsed.

The MAS also attracted indigenous voters by running numerous indigenous
candidates. Although the proportion of indigenous candidates diminished over
time as more whites and mestizos entered the MAS, the party continued to
have many more indigenous candidates than did its principal competitors.
Moreover, in contrast to the traditional parties, it nominated indigenous people
for all types of positions, including the most important national-level offices.
Not only was the party's presidential candidate indigenous, but so too were
many, if not most, of the party's candidates for national deputy and senatorial
positions. Moreover, the MAS was careful to recruit candidates from the communities that they were supposed to represent. Thus, Aymara leaders would be
chosen as candidates in Aymara areas and Quechua leaders would be chosen
to represent Quechua districts. Local indigenous organizations and other social
movements typically played the lead role in nominating candidates, particularly in rural areas, which, according to some members of the MAS, gave the
party "a big advantage over the political parties that impose their candidates
from above" (Harnecker et al. 2008, 127). Evo Morales also handpicked many
candidates, however. Although it is difficult to measure how much of a role the
ethnicity of candidates played in vote choice in Bolivia, there is some evidence
to suggest that many indigenous voters preferred indigenous candidates. For
example, according to a 2006 LAPOP survey, twenty-nine percent of people
who self-identified as indigenous said that they felt better represented in the
government and legislature by leaders of their own ethnic background.

The MAS also sought to attract indigenous voters through symbolic appeals.
The party's candidates often dressed in indigenous clothing, participated in
indigenous rituals, invoked indigenous sayings, and made speeches in indigenous languages. The MAS, moreover, styled itself as the legitimate representative of the indigenous population and the leader of its historical struggle.
In its 2002 Program of Government, the MAS (2002, 30) declared: "In our
OWN POLITICAL INSTRUMENT, we will raise high the struggle of our ancestors,
struggles headed by Tupaj Katari and Bartolina Sisa, by Apiawayki Tumpa, by
Pedro Ignacio Muyba, by Pablo Zárate Willka, by Santos Marka T'ula and
thousands of heroes and martyrs" (emphasis in the original). Similarly, in his
2006 inaugural address, Morales extolled a long line of indigenous leaders

and denounced the discrimination they had struggled against. "Bolivia," he declared, "resembled South Africa, but threatened, condemned to extinction, we are [still] here. We are present.... We are here to say 'enough!' From 500 years of resistance we shift to taking control for another 500 years" (Stefanoni and Do Alto 2006, 132–3). The party's leaders also frequently idealized pre-colonial indigenous society. At the outset of its 2002 Program of Government, the MAS (2002, 3) referred to a precolonial era in which: "[M]isery and hunger were unknown. Everything was LIFE, everything was in its place. Nothing was lacking nor left over. We lived in communitarian societies of abundance, where life was complete harmony, brotherhood, and mutual respect with Mother Nature" (emphasis in the original).

In addition, the MAS appealed to indigenous voters by embracing a broad range of concrete ethnic demands. From the beginning, the MAS made the defense of coca growing a central part of its platform, and it sought to link coca leaf to indigenous culture. As Leonilda Zurita, one of the principal leaders of the MAS, argued, "To defend coca is to defend our culture, our wisdom, our natural medicine" (Harnecker et al. 2008, 42). The MAS's 2002 platform declared that "we will continue to defend with force the sacred coca leaf until the ultimate consequences, since it continues to be the symbol of our identity and expresses the millenary culture of our ancestors. It is life, medicine, and sustenance..." (Movimiento al Socialismo 2002, 15). The MAS also adopted other traditional indigenous demands. It advocated indigenous land and water rights in order to "reconstitute the historic territory of the original peoples and nations..." (Movimiento al Socialismo 2002, 13). It called for the recognition of indigenous forms of medicine and justice and the establishment of programs of intercultural and bilingual education that would incorporate indigenous traditions and knowledge. It also pledged to establish new labor laws to elimi-nate racial and ethnic discrimination (Movimiento al Socialismo 2002, 25). As Chapter 6 discusses, once the MAS took power, it moved to follow up on many of these pledges, incorporating indigenous rights into various laws as well as the new constitution.

The MAS's strong ties to indigenous organizations, its numerous indigenous candidates, its embrace of traditional indigenous demands, and its symbolic appeals to the indigenous population helped the party win the support of many indigenous voters. Initially, however, the MAS's support was largely confined to Quechua-speaking areas in the department of Cochabamba. As Figure 2.2 indicates, in the 1997 elections the IU/ASP won an average of 19.9 percent of the vote in municipalities where the majority of the population grew up speaking Quechua, but only 2.7 percent of the vote in municipalities where most people grew up speaking Aymara and 1.5 percent of the vote where the majority grew up speaking Spanish. The MAS's efforts to reach out in the early 2000s to the Aymara population as well as the Quechua population that lived outside of Cochabamba paid off, however. In the 2002 presidential elections, the MAS won 42.5 percent of the vote in municipalities where Quechua speak-ers represented a majority and 29.0 percent of the vote in municipalities where

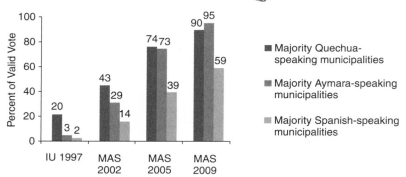

FIGURE 2.2. Mean municipal vote for the MAS in presidential elections, 1997–2009. *Source*: Corte Nacional Electoral

Aymara speakers represented a majority. By contrast, in municipalities where the majority of the population grew up speaking Spanish as their first language, the MAS won only 14.4 percent of the vote in the 2002 elections. The MAS's strong performance in Aymara municipalities in the 2002 elections came in spite of the fact that it faced strong competition in these areas from an Aymara ethnonationalist party, Felipe Quispe's Movimiento Indígena Pachakuti. Even in Aymara areas, however, the MIP's exclusionary rhetoric proved less appealing to voters than the MAS's inclusive ethnic appeals.[34]

The MAS built on this strong performance in the 2005 and 2009 presidential elections, sweeping both Quechua and Aymara areas with ease. In the 2005 elections, for example, it won seventy-four percent of the vote in municipalities where maternal Quechua speakers represented the majority and seventy-three percent of the vote in municipalities where maternal Aymara speakers represented the majority. By contrast, in those municipalities where a majority of the population learned Spanish as its first language, the MAS won only thirty-nine percent of the vote in the 2005 elections. In the 2009 elections, the MAS completely dominated indigenous areas, winning ninety percent of the vote in areas where a majority of the population learned to speak in Quechua and ninety-five percent of the vote in municipalities where a majority of the population learned to speak in Aymara. The MAS also fared quite well in Spanish-speaking areas in 2009, however, winning fifty-nine percent of the vote in municipalities where a majority of the population learned to speak in Spanish.

The MAS's strong performance in indigenous areas is not just a product of the fact that majority indigenous municipalities tend to be poorer than other municipalities. As Table 2.2 indicates, even controlling for the level of development of the municipality, the proportion of the population that grew up

[34] In the 2002 elections, the MIP won 19.5 percent of the vote in municipalities where the majority of the population grew up speaking Aymara, but the MAS won 29.0 percent of the vote in these areas.

TABLE 2.2. *The Correlates of the Municipal Vote Share of the MAS in Bolivian Presidential Elections, 1997–2009*

(Ordinary Least Squares Regression Analyses)

	1997 Elections	2002 Elections	2005 Elections	2009 Elections
Constant	−.034	.057	.289***	.743***
	(.076)	(.089)	(.085)	(.075)
Quechua speakers/total	.253***	.425***	.516***	.388***
population	(.030)	(.035)	(.034)	(.030)
Aymara speakers/total	.047	.283***	.580***	.554***
population	(.028)	(.033)	(.033)	(.029)
Index of Human	.038	.037	.017	−.354**
Development	(.122)	(.143)	(.129)	(.114)
N	309	313	313	314
R-squared	.314	.478	.615	.693

Note: Standard errors in parentheses
*p<.05, **p<.01; ***p<.001

speaking Quechua is a statistically significant determinant of the MAS's share of the municipal vote in all of the presidential elections between 1997 and 2009.[35] Other things being equal, each ten percentage point increase in the proportion of the population that grew up speaking Quechua leads to a 2.5 percentage point increase in the MAS's share of the municipal vote in 1997, a 4.3 percentage point increase in 2002, a 5.2 percentage point increase in 2005, and a 3.9 percentage point increase in 2009. As the table indicates, the proportion of the population that grew up speaking Aymara did not have a significant impact on the MAS's share of the vote in 1997, but it did have a strong and statistically significant effect in the 2002, 2005, and 2009 elections. *Ceteris paribus*, each ten percentage point increase in the proportion of the population that grew up speaking Aymara leads to a 2.8 percentage point increase in the MAS's vote share of the municipal vote in 2002, a 5.8 percentage point increase in 2005, and a 5.9 percentage point increase in 2009.[36]

THE MAS'S STRATEGY OF INCLUSION

The MAS was not content to rely on indigenous votes alone, however; in the early 2000s, the MAS also began to reach out to whites and mestizos. In a 2004

[35] The Index of Human Development used in this analysis is composed of indices of life expectancy, education, and income. This index is highly correlated with the urbanization rate (.679) and the literacy rate (.792), which is why these variables were excluded from the analysis. Data on these variables come from the Instituto Nacional de Estadística (INE).

[36] For ease of interpretation, these statistical analyses were performed using Ordinary Least Squares. Using a Tobit model does not appreciably change the results.

interview with the author, Dionisio Núñez, an Aymara legislator from the MAS, explained that initially the party was dominated by indigenous people, but:

[I]n the end we came to understand that we didn't want to go from being excluded to excluding others, that we had to include more people, business people, the middle classes.... Originally, there were three peasant organizations that founded the MAS. Two years ago, the reformulation of the MAS began.... The MAS ceased to be solely indigenous and peasant.

Similarly, Santos Ramírez, a former MAS senator, argued that:

[O]ne of the great qualities of Evo... has been the will to incorporate diverse sectors. This project was born in the indigenous movement and is going to continue being of the indigenous movement. But it has incorporated middle class sectors, progressive businessmen, intellectuals, union members, factory workers, artisans.... (Interview with author 2007)

The MAS used various strategies to woo white and mestizo voters. First, it was careful to avoid exclusionary rhetoric and to emphasize the inclusive nature of the party. MAS vice president Alvaro García Linera noted in a 2005 article that the party "has had to change its language to fit into the urban environment with a higher degree of cultural miscegenation; thus it can be said today that Morales heads a political proposition of a clear social mixed race content" (García Linera 2005, 17). According to Rafael Puente, a Jesuit priest who has served as vice minister of the interior in Morales's government, "the discourse of Evo is not characterized by radicalism; on the contrary he has taken great pains to always affirm that the project he leads is not exclusionary, that in it there will always be space for everyone..." (Harnecker et al. 2008, 104). In his 2006 inaugural address, for example, Evo emphasized that "We respect, we admire all sectors, professionals and non-professionals, intellectuals and non-intellectuals, businessmen and non-businessmen; we all have the right to live in this land.... There you can see that the indigenous movement is not exclusionary; it is inclusive" (Stefanoni and Do Alto 2006, 133).

In order to attract more white and mestizo voters, the MAS also broadened its platform. Initially, the MAS focused its platform and rhetoric largely on indigenous issues, especially coca growing. According to Leonilda Zurita, "people argued that [the party] was too focused on coca. Subsequently, [the party] changed. It had to address the entire nation" (interview with author 2007). Similarly, Senator Ricardo Díaz noted that the MAS "has moderated in the sense of greater inclusion. Before I saw it as very biased toward the indigenous. Now we are taking into account professionals, urbanites..." (interview with author 2007). The shift in the MAS's platform was particularly noticeable in its programs of government. Whereas the party's 2002 Program of Government focused heavily on indigenous issues and themes, the MAS's 2005 and 2009 Programs of Government addressed a much broader range of issues from infrastructure development to national security. Indeed, in many ways, the MAS's 2005 and 2009 platforms resembled those of traditional leftist and populist parties.

Beginning in the early 2000s, the MAS also tried to boost its support among whites and mestizos by establishing ties to urban mestizo-dominated organizations. These included associations of factory workers, artisans, small business-people, street vendors, the self-employed, truck drivers, adjudicators, teachers, and pensioners as well as many urban neighborhood associations. According to Santos Ramírez, "in the period from 2002 and 2004 the project of the MAS is assimilated by the urban population, by the intellectual middle class. This is the product, among other things, of the strategy deployed by Evo: he begins to set up meetings, events, seminars, and publicly invites those sectors to join" (Harnecker et al. 2008, 101). As a result of this strategy, the MAS managed to make alliances with more than fifty departmental and national organizations by 2005 in addition to countless municipal and neighborhood associations (Harnecker et al. 2008, 128). The MAS also forged ties to some smaller mestizo-dominated left-wing parties, although it eschewed alliances with the more powerful traditional parties for ideological reasons and also because it did not want the party to be controlled and co-opted in the way that some of the Katarista parties had been. The most important alliance the MAS struck was with the Movimiento Sin Miedo (MSM), a left-of-center party that was particularly strong in the city of La Paz where its founder, Juan del Granado, served as mayor.[37] The alliances with the MSM and other urban mestizo-dominated organizations helped the MAS by demonstrating its inclusiveness and providing it with an organizational base outside of the rural areas that were its traditional stronghold.

The MAS also sought to win the support of white and mestizo voters by recruiting white and mestizo candidates. During the 1990s, the vast majority of the party's candidates were indigenous, but this began to change in the early 2000s. It was not initially easy for the MAS to recruit white and mestizo leaders to the party since many of them were reluctant to affiliate themselves with a party that they viewed as having little electoral promise. Nevertheless, the MAS persisted in its efforts, and as its electoral performance improved, more and more prominent whites and mestizos joined the party. The MAS, for example, recruited the white/mestizo leftist intellectuals Antonio Peredo and Alvaro García Linera as its vice presidential candidates in 2002 and 2005, respectively. According to Ramírez, the nomination of García Linera, who was a well-known leftist academic and newscaster, proved particularly helpful in winning over white and mestizo supporters (Harnecker et al. 2008, 102). The MAS also recruited many well-known whites and mestizos, such as Filemón Escobar, a prominent union leader, and Ana María Romero, the former ombudswoman, as senatorial candidates. As a result of these efforts, the ethnic composition of the party's legislative contingent changed significantly over time.

---

[37] The MAS forged the alliance with the MSM in the run-up to the 2005 general elections and maintained it in the 2006 constituent assembly elections and the 2009 general elections.

Whereas in 1997 the MAS's legislative contingent was entirely indigenous, in 2002 more than one-third of the party's legislators were white or mestizo and by 2005 whites and mestizos represented at least half of the contingent.[38]

The MAS's inclusive approach has caused tensions within the party, however, particularly with respect to nominations for the legislature and bureaucratic and ministerial posts. Some indigenous leaders have complained that middle class whites and mestizos have seized many of the key positions within the government and the party. Indeed, most of the ministers in Morales's cabinets have been white or mestizo. In a 2007 interview with the author, Lino Villca, an indigenous senator and long-time MAS leader, complained that: "The indigenous movement is isolated. We have the president and the Ministry of Foreign Relations, but the middle class has the rest of the ministers.... Now the middle class defines the strategy of Evo Morales. The indigenous class is only for mobilizations." Nonetheless, as Villca acknowledged, the inclusive strategy of the MAS has yielded results, and the party is unlikely to abandon it any time soon in spite of any tensions it might cause.

The efforts to reach out to whites and mestizos helped the MAS boost its support steadily in predominantly Spanish-speaking areas, although it remained well below the overwhelming levels of support the party received in majority indigenous areas. As Figure 2.2 indicates, the MAS's share of the vote in municipalities where the majority of the population grew up speaking Spanish rose from 1.5 percent in 1997 to 14.4 percent in 2002 and 38.8 percent in 2005. In municipalities where more than ninety percent of the population grew up speaking Spanish, the share of the vote won by the MAS (or the IU) rose from 0.4 percent in 1997 to 4.2 percent in 2002 and 21.0 percent in 2005. National survey data also indicate the success of the MAS's efforts to reach out to whites and mestizos. According to the 2002 and 2006 LAPOP surveys, the MAS won only 5.8 percent of the vote of self-identified whites in the 2002 elections, but it won 31.6 percent of the self-identified white vote in 2005.[39] Similarly, the MAS's support among self-identified mestizos climbed from twenty percent in 2002 to fifty-one percent in 2005, according to the LAPOP surveys.

The large mestizo vote, especially the indigenous mestizo vote, proved crucial to the MAS's 2005 victory. According to the 2006 LAPOP survey, self-identified mestizos represented sixty-two percent of the party's total vote in 2005, whereas people who self-identify as indigenous represented twenty-eight percent of the MAS's total vote in 2005 and self-identified whites represented only seven percent.[40] Many of these self-identified mestizos were mostly or

---

[38] The author coded the ethnicity of legislators by studying their photos and biographies. Given the ambiguity and fluidity of ethnicity in Bolivia, these figures should be taken as rough estimates.

[39] According to the 2006 LAPOP survey, the MAS also substantially increased its share of the urban vote, winning the support of almost half of urban voters in 2005, as opposed to less than twenty percent in 2002.

[40] According to the 2006 LAPOP survey, sixty-five percent of the Bolivian population self-identified as mestizo that year, while nineteen percent self-identified as indigenous, and eleven percent self-identified as white (Seligson et al. 2006).

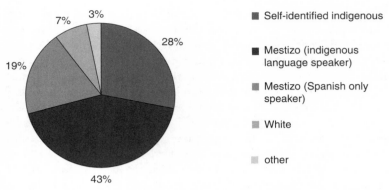

FIGURE 2.3. The ethnic composition of the vote for the MAS in 2005.
Source: LAPOP 2006 Bolivia survey

entirely of indigenous descent, came from indigenous communities, and had grown up speaking an indigenous language. As a result, they identified with many of the MAS's indigenous symbols and ethnic demands, felt more ethnically proximate to Morales and the MAS than to other parties and candidates, and voted for the MAS in large numbers. Indeed, more than two-thirds of the mestizos who reported voting for the MAS had grown up speaking an indigenous language, and as Figure 2.3 shows, these so-called indigenous mestizos accounted for forty-three percent of the MAS's total vote, more than any other group. Had the MAS adopted a more exclusionary platform, it likely would have alienated many of these indigenous mestizos, not to mention whites and non-indigenous mestizos. As we shall see, many of these whites and mestizos (as well as many of the MAS's indigenous supporters) were drawn to the party by its populist rhetoric and platform, but the MAS's inclusive approach helped make them feel comfortable with the party.

THE MAS'S POPULIST STRATEGIES

Equally crucial to the success of the MAS was its embrace of traditional populist electoral strategies. The MAS used four traditional populist approaches to attract supporters. First, it personalized its campaigns, relying heavily on the charismatic appeal of Evo Morales to win support. Second, it focused its campaigns on the lower classes in both urban and rural areas, employing a popular style and rhetoric. Third, the MAS adopted an anti-establishment message, taking advantage of widespread disenchantment with the traditional parties and elites. Fourth and finally, the MAS espoused redistributive, nationalist, and state interventionist policies, feeding on growing unrest with neoliberal policies and U.S. intervention. The MAS used each of these strategies from its inception, but it became increasingly reliant on them over time as it sought to reach out to whites and mestizos. As a result, a rough balance has emerged between the MAS's populist and ethnic appeals.

Over the last couple of decades, Evo Morales has become an increasingly popular figure who has attracted much support to the MAS. Morales's rise to prominence has been rapid. In the 1980s, Morales was a second-tier leader in the coca growers unions, but he rose steadily through the leadership ranks and in 1996 he was elected president of the six coca growers' federations of Cochabamba, which gave him an important base of power. Nevertheless, in the mid-1990s he was still largely unknown outside of Cochabamba. Moreover, within the IU/ASP, he was subordinate to Alejo Véliz, the party's presidential candidate in 1997. That year, Morales ran for congress from a single-member district in the Chapare and won seventy percent of the vote, more than any other congressional candidate in the country. Morales also received significantly more votes in this district than did the party's presidential candidate, which led Véliz to accuse Morales of promoting his own candidacy but not that of Véliz. This dispute led Morales and his supporters to leave the IU/ASP to form a new political instrument: the MAS.

Morales dominated the MAS from the outset. Like other populist leaders, Evo has mostly declined to build institutional structures that might constrain him or develop leaders who might challenge him, preferring instead to concentrate power in his person. According to one Bolivian scholar who has followed the indigenous movement closely for many decades, "Evo is very much of a *caudillo* [strongman], very personalistic. He does not allow any dissidence. He turns his back on or expels any legislator who competes with him" (interview with author 2004). The MAS is different from many populist parties, however, in that it does have a strong social movement base with which Morales consults regularly. When asked whether Morales was a *caudillo*, Álvaro García Linera replied: "He is a charismatic leader… a charismatic democratic leader. He is a man who permanently submits to popular assemblies and deliberation the big decisions…" (*"En la emancipación de los pueblos, Evo es sustituible"* 2006). According to García Linera and other MAS leaders, every single major decision that the party has taken has been discussed first with the party's social movement base (Carlsen 2007, 5). Nevertheless, consultation does not equate to real power sharing, and on issues he cares about Morales tends to have his way. In a 2004 interview with the author, García Linera acknowledged that Morales "concentrates the threads of the decision-making process. He is at the center of a network. He calls people and convinces them." Moreover, according to some leaders of the MAS, there are topics that Morales refuses to even discuss (*"Evo sacudió el sistema político y empoderó a los indígenas"* 2006).

Morales has proven to be a charismatic candidate and a tireless campaigner. By 2002, the first time Morales ran for president, he had already acquired some degree of fame. Antonio Peredo, the MAS's vice presidential candidate during the 2002 campaign, recounted that "everywhere we went people would meet us and ask us to come to their community. They weren't interested in hearing what our program was. They just wanted to meet Evo Morales" (interview with author 2004). Not surprising, the MAS's political campaigns have increasingly focused on him. According to Alex Contreras, Morales's spokesperson, the party has tried to project its leader as an "example of struggle, honesty, transparency and dignity. He is an example of an incorruptible, unyielding person and of change" (*"La imagen del Presidente no es elaborada, es espontánea"* 2006). Morales's personal popularity has grown so much in recent years that now some observers speak of *Evismo*, a phenomenon similar to the personality cults surrounding other populist leaders like Juan Perón (Benavente 2008, 61; *"El evismo ensalza a Evo en el poder"* 2006). According to García Linera, Evismo "implies an absolute respect for the leader and, fundamentally, his power. It implies acceptance that he is the creator of the phenomenon of the MAS" (*"En la emancipación de los pueblos, Evo es sustituible"* 2006). Morales's charisma and leadership have led some to question how well the party would do without him. Indeed, Morales has consistently fared much better than other candidates of the MAS in elections. In the 2005 elections, for example, he won a larger share of the vote than did the MAS's prefectural (gubernatorial) candidates in every single department.

The MAS has directed its appeals mostly, but not exclusively, at the poorer sectors of the population. Morales campaigned in rural areas of the country long neglected by national-level politicians, taking advantage of his party's strong ties to peasant and indigenous organizations. The party also aggressively sought out the support of the urban poor, forging alliances with many urban neighbor-hood groups and trade associations, such as associations of factory workers and self-employed people. Much of the party's discourse centered on redistributing income and addressing the needs of marginalized sectors of the population. Indeed, Morales has described inequality as one of the central reasons for the formation of the party, declaring that: "We have created our own political force because wealth and land are being concentrated in the hands of a few, and the majority of the people live in poverty" (Zimmerman 2002, 8).

Morales and many of the MAS's other candidates also adopted a popular and down-to-earth style in their campaigns. According to one Bolivian sociolo-gist, Morales "has generated a lot of empathy with the average citizen. That the President of the Republic calls you 'boss' almost with a feeling of humil-ity makes an impact. It's difficult to believe that someone of such importance could be such a regular guy" (Benavente 2008, 62). The MAS's efforts to reach out to the poor were helped by the fact that many of the party's candidates came from humble backgrounds and were not highly educated. According to a 2003 survey conducted by the University of Salamanca, less than half of the legislators from the MAS attended college, as opposed to one hundred percent of the legislators from the MNR and the NFR, and ninety-four percent of the legislators from the MIR (Instituto de Estudios de Iberoamérica y Portugal 2003, 114).[41] Morales himself came from a poor family and left high school before finishing his degree in order to help support his family.

---

[41] The percentage of legislators from the MAS who had attended university rose to sixty per-cent in 2006, but it remained well below that of other parties (Instituto Interuniversitario de Iberoamérica 2006, 70).

The humble background and popular style of Morales and the MAS's other candidates have helped them forge close ties to Bolivia's poor. Indeed, Samuel Doria Medina, one of Morales's opponents in the 2005 and 2009 elections, acknowledged that one factor in Evo's success is that he is "the candidate like you, like most people" (Benavente 2008, 61). Not surprising, the MAS has fared better among the poorer and less educated sectors of the population. The 2006 LAPOP survey, for example, found that in the 2005 elections Morales and the MAS won the support of sixty-one percent of voters who earned one thousand bolivianos or less (approximately $125 at current exchange rates) per month, but only forty-five percent of the vote of people who reported earning more than one thousand bolivianos per month. Similarly, the MAS won fifty-seven percent of the vote of people who had a high school education or less, and only forty-seven percent of the vote of people who had some postsecondary education.

Evo Morales and the MAS also have employed a great deal of anti-establishment and anti-elite rhetoric in an effort to win support among the poor and middle class voters. They have railed against the traditional parties and elites, accusing them of corruption, incompetence, and betrayal. "We all know that there are two Bolivias," Morales once proclaimed. "One Bolivia of 'charlatans' who always make promises and sign agreements that they never fulfill; and the other Bolivia which is always tricked, subjugated, humiliated, and exploited" (Barr 2006, 22; Postero 2004, 190). Similarly, in an interview with the author, Leonilda Zurita, the MAS's secretary for foreign relations, argued that the traditional parties "have looted our wealth. These parties have devoured Bolivia" (interview with author 2007). Interestingly, Morales and the MAS maintained this anti-establishment discourse even after they captured the presidency. Walter Chávez, an adviser to Evo, observed that: "Evo's discourse is always confrontational against the powers that be even when he is at the center of power... It is a populism like Perón" (Benavente 2008, 61).

The MAS's outsider status reinforced its anti-establishment rhetoric (Bohrt Irahola and Chávez Reyes 2002; Mayorga 2005; Romero Ballivián 2003; Van Cott 2003b). The MAS was not a typical Bolivian party in that it had no party bureaucracy to speak of and most of its candidates were social movement leaders rather than career politicians. Moreover, unlike the traditional parties, the MAS never participated in the various coalition governments that ruled Bolivia between 1985 and 2003. To the contrary, the MAS consistently criticized the ruling parties and their policies, and it participated in numerous social protests against them, ranging from marches and demonstrations to roadblocks. The ruling parties, for their part, treated the MAS and its leaders with disdain and sought to marginalize them. In early 2002, for example, the traditional parties voted to expel Morales from congress on unsubstantiated charges that he had played a role in the assassination of four policemen in the Chapare.[42]

---

[42] The charges were subsequently annulled by a ruling of the Constitutional Tribunal (Stefanoni and Do Alto 2006, 74).

This effort, however, only drew attention to Morales and strengthened his anti-establishment profile.

The MAS's anti-establishment rhetoric and outsider credentials helped it to capture the support of voters fed up with the traditional parties and political elites. As we have seen, support for the traditional parties declined precipitously during the late 1990s. By late 2001, almost half of the population said that parties were not necessary for democracy as opposed to only seventeen percent in 1993 (Calderón and Gamarra 2004, 17). In 2002, however, the MAS faced strong competition for politically disenchanted voters from a new party, the Nueva Fuerza Republicana (NFR), which also ran a populist, anti-establishment campaign. Nevertheless, Morales still managed to finish second in the 2002 elections behind Gonzalo Sánchez de Lozada of the MNR. The reputation of the traditional parties and elites deteriorated even further under Sánchez de Lozada. The Sánchez de Lozada administration failed to get the economy back on track or resolve the widening protests. Moreover, in October 2003, it violently repressed protests in the city of El Alto, leading to the deaths of more than fifty people. Abandoned by most of his former allies, Sánchez de Lozada resigned and fled the country, leaving the reputation of his party and the traditional parties that had supported him in shreds.[43]

In the 2005 elections, the MAS was the only one of the main contenders that had a clear anti-establishment profile. The NFR had largely fallen apart by then and was discredited by its participation in the Sánchez de Lozada administration. PODEMOS, the MAS's main rival in 2005, was little more than a collection of leading members of the traditional parties, particularly the ADN.[44] PODEMOS nominated Jorge Quiroga, a former leader of the ADN who had served as president of Bolivia from 2001 to 2002, as its presidential candidate.[45] Not surprisingly, Quiroga and PODEMOS held little appeal for anti-establishment voters. According to the 2006 LAPOP survey, in the 2005 elections the MAS won 54.7 percent of the votes of people who expressed no trust in parties, whereas PODEMOS won only 19.5 percent. The MAS's appeal to politically disenchanted voters was even more apparent from the high levels of support it won from voters who participated in protests against previous governments. The MAS won seventy-seven percent of the vote of people who participated in protests against the previous administration, whereas PODEMOS earned the support of less than ten percent of these voters.

The MAS also has attracted voters with its nationalist and state interventionist rhetoric and policy positions. As we have seen, disenchantment with market-oriented policies grew considerably in the late 1990s and early 2000s.

---

[43] A survey carried out in 2004 found that parties were the least trusted institution in Bolivia that year (Seligson et al. 2004, 102).

[44] The only traditional party that ran a candidate in the 2005 presidential elections was the MNR, and its candidate won a mere 6.5 percent of the vote.

[45] Unidad Nacional (UN), which finished third in the 2005 elections, was also composed principally of former members of the traditional parties, especially the MIR.

The market-oriented policies Bolivia implemented beginning in the mid-1980s had successfully stabilized the economy and generated some initial growth, but in the late 1990s and early 2000s, the Bolivian economy stagnated. In 2005, Bolivia's gross domestic product per capita was actually lower than it was in 1998, leading to widespread disenchantment with the market-oriented economic model. The MAS capitalized on this disenchantment by denouncing neoliberal policies and proposing state interventionist measures, including the nationalization of privatized companies, in order to redistribute income and generate an economic recovery. According to Evo, the MAS's program was "about stopping and reversing privatization. We want to get our companies and natural resources back, because we can't allow them to be concentrated in the hands of a few transnational corporations.... In concrete terms, we'll promote national production and block free trade in that way. We'll reverse the economic reforms that have brought more inequality and poverty over us" (Zimmerman 2002, 8).

In opposing neoliberal policies, the MAS often appealed to nationalist sentiments. For example, in its 2002 governing program, the MAS (2002, 9) declared:

The neoliberal parties such as the MNR, ADN, MIR, MBL, UCS, NFR, CONDEPA and other small groupings of their corrupt circle, are characterized by the submission and betrayal of the country, by the handing over of the national patrimony almost without charge to the voraciousness of international capital and its directors, who impose conditions of poverty on the legitimate owners of natural resources.

The MAS made control over Bolivia's considerable natural gas deposits a centerpiece of its platform, particularly in the 2005 campaign. It helped block Sánchez de Lozada's plan to export gas through Chile, and then pressed the ensuing government of Carlos Mesa to renegotiate its contracts with the foreign firms that exported the gas. After winning election as president, Morales went so far as to seize control of the natural gas fields and demand that the foreign firms pay a higher share of their profits to the state. These moves proved quite popular. Indeed, President Morales's public approval rating soared by thirteen points to eighty-one percent in the wake of his takeover of the gas fields ("Bolivians Love Evo: Want Closer Ties with the U.S." 2006, 16).

The MAS also successfully appealed to nationalist sentiments in opposing the coca eradication program that the Bolivian government expanded in the late 1990s under pressure from the U.S. government. The party's 2002 governing plan, for example, declared that "We will defend the national territory against all forms of North American penetration, [and we will defend] the coca leaf growers against the criminal repression of mercenary forces paid by U.S. organisms" (Movimiento al Socialismo 2002, 16). The MAS's opposition to coca eradication provoked the intervention of the U.S. ambassador to Bolivia, Manuel Rocha, who warned Bolivians not to vote for Morales in a speech shortly before the 2002 election. In the wake of this speech, which many Bolivians viewed as inappropriate interference in their internal affairs,

Morales's support went up by five points in surveys taken in the principal cities of the country (Romero Ballivián 2003, 251).

Left-of-center voters have been particularly attracted by the MAS's statist and nationalist agenda (Romero Ballivián 2002, 191; Seligson et al. 2006, 89–90). According to the 2006 LAPOP survey, the MAS won 75.3 percent of the vote of people who identified with the left in the 2005 election, whereas PODEMOS won only 12.0 percent of these voters.[46] Nearly half of the people who reported voting for the MAS in 2005, as in 2002, identified with the left, with most of the remainder self-identifying as centrists. Many of these left-wing voters felt abandoned by the traditional parties' embrace of the United States and neoliberal policies. The MAS, moreover, aggressively courted this left-of-center constituency by recruiting well-known leftists to serve as candidates for the vice presidency and the legislature and by developing a traditional left-wing platform in many areas (Patzi Paco 2004; Van Cott 2005; Zegada Claure 2002, 51).

The MAS's nationalist and state interventionist agenda appealed to some centrist and right-wing voters as well, however. Bolivians who self-identified as being on the right or the center were almost as likely to support the nationalization of the gas industry as people on the left, and many of these nationalistic centrists and rightists voted for the MAS.[47] According to the 2006 LAPOP survey, 53.8 percent of centrists who strongly supported the nationalization of the gas industry reported voting for the MAS, as opposed to only forty-one percent of those who mildly supported it, and 29.6 percent of those who disapproved of it. Overall, the MAS won 48.2 percent of the vote of people who self-identified as centrists and 32.3 percent of the vote of people who self-identified as being on the right – an impressive performance for a left-wing party.[48]

AN ANALYSIS OF THE MAS VOTE

Table 2.3 presents the results of a multinomial logit analysis of the characteristics of voters for the MAS in the 2005 elections.[49] For simplicity, I report

---

[46] The survey asked people to place themselves on a left–right scale from one to ten. Here, I classify people who place themselves from one to four as leftists, five to six as centrists, and seven to ten as rightists. In the 2006 LAPOP survey, thirty-one percent of the people who answered this question identified themselves as being on the left, 46.5 percent on the center, and 22.5 percent on the right. However, a significant percentage of the interviewees (24.5 percent) failed to respond.

[47] According to the 2006 LAPOP survey, sixty-two percent of people who self-identified as being on the left strongly approved (eight to ten on a ten point scale) of the nationalization of the gas industry, as did sixty percent of centrists and/or rightists.

[48] Ethnic ties also help explain why many people on the center and the right supported the MAS. According to the 2006 LAPOP survey, 61.4 percent of centrists and 56.8 percent of rightists who grew up speaking an indigenous language supported the MAS in 2005, as opposed to only 30.0 percent of those centrists and 14.3 percent of those rightists who did not grow up speaking an indigenous language.

[49] Dow and Endersby (2004, 108) argue that multinomial logit is superior in some aspects to multinomial probit, particularly for applications such as this, where "a voter casts a ballot for a candidate or party selected from a fixed, stable pool of alternatives...." For a contrasting view, see Alvarez and Nagler (1998).

TABLE 2.3. *Predictors of Voting for the MAS (over PODEMOS) in the 2005 Bolivian Elections (Multinomial logit model using 2006 LAPOP survey)*

	Coefficient	Standard Error	P > |z|
Constant	3.722	.949	.000
Self-identifies as indigenous	.561	.273	.040
Self-identifies as white	−.676	.247	.006
Aymara maternal language	1.434	.285	.000
Quechua maternal language	.637	.199	.001
Other indigenous maternal language	.413	.548	.452
Prefers ethnic representation	.299	.207	.149
Supports indigenous language education (1–7 scale)	.129	.056	.023
Trust in political parties (1–7 scale)	−.042	.055	.448
Protested against Mesa administration	.835	.283	.003
Left–right ideological self-placement (left–right 1–10 scale)	−.298	.041	.000
Support for nationalization of gas industry (1–10 scale)	.106	.037	.004
Participation in trade associations (1–4 scale)	.268	.100	.007
Resides in *media luna* (southern and eastern departments)	−1.030	.193	.000
Urbanization level (1–4 scale)	−.013	.078	.864
Monthly income (0–8 scale)	−.142	.069	.038
Female	−.016	.166	.921
Age (in years)	.015	.006	.013
Pseudo R^2	.184		
N	1162		

only the results of a comparison of the likelihood of voting for one of the two main parties, the MAS and PODEMOS, which together won eighty-two percent of the valid vote.[50] Each parameter estimate in the first column represents the predicted marginal effect of the variable on the log-odds ratio of voting for the MAS over PODEMOS. The data for this analysis come from the 2006 LAPOP survey.[51] As with most postelection polls, this survey slightly overestimated the percentage of the population that reported voting for the winner of the election, the MAS in this case, and slightly underestimated the percentage of the population that reported voting for the other parties.[52] In addition, the

---

[50] None of the six other parties that competed in this election earned more than seven percent of the vote.

[51] For more information on the survey and the wording of the questions, see Seligson et al. (2006).

[52] In the 2006 LAPOP survey, fifty-three percent of voters reported casting their ballots for the MAS and twenty-five percent reported voting for PODEMOS. According to the official returns, the MAS received fifty percent of the total vote and PODEMOS earned twenty-six percent.

survey overestimated voter turnout in the election: 90.9 percent of registered voters reported voting in the survey, whereas only 84.5 percent of registered voters actually voted in the election, according to the Corte Nacional Electoral (2006).[53]

The analysis generated a number of noteworthy findings. First, as Table 2.3 indicates, the MAS's populist appeals – that is, its focus on the subaltern sectors, and its anti-establishment, nationalist, and state interventionist message – were clearly successful in winning support among certain categories of voters. Low-income voters, self-identified leftists, people who participated in trade associations such as organizations of merchants or peasant unions, people who favored the nationalization of the gas industry, and people who had participated in protests against the administration of Carlos Mesa (2003–5) were all significantly more likely to report having voted for the MAS, according to the analysis. In order to estimate precisely what effect these variables had on the probability of voting for the MAS, I carried out a series of simulations using Clarify (King et al. 2000).[54] These simulations indicated that someone who strongly favored the nationalization of the gas industry had a sixty-three percent likelihood of voting for the MAS when other variables are held at their means, whereas someone who strongly opposed it had only a thirty-six percent probability of doing so. The effects of ideological self-placement were even stronger. Someone who identified strongly with the left had a seventy-eight percent likelihood of voting for the MAS, whereas someone who identified strongly with the right had only a twenty-seven percent probability of doing so. Meanwhile, voters who participated in protests against the administration of Carlos Mesa (2003–5) had a seventy percent probability of voting for the MAS when all other variables are held at their means, as opposed to only a fifty-three percent probability for those voters who did not participate in any protests against the Mesa administration. Surprisingly, voters who had little trust in political parties were not more likely to vote for the MAS when other variables are controlled. This may be because by 2005 the MAS had established itself as the most important political party in the country, causing the level of trust in political parties among supporters of the MAS to increase.[55]

Self-identifying as indigenous also increases the likelihood of voting for the MAS even after controlling for language, ideology, dissatisfaction with parties, participation in protests, support for nationalization of the gas industry, and

---

[53] There is little evidence to suggest that the increase in votes for the MAS in 2005 is due to increased voter turnout. Voter turnout as a percent of the estimated voting age population actually declined between 2002 and 2005, both nationwide and in majority indigenous provinces.

[54] I present graphs illustrating these simulations in Madrid (2008).

[55] According to the 2002 LAPOP survey, MAS supporters in 2002 were more likely to express low levels of confidence in parties, presumably because in 2002 the MAS had not yet established itself as one of the country's main parties. In 2002, 38.8 percent of MAS supporters reported having no trust in parties, as opposed to 29.2 percent of all voters.

a host of other variables.[56] This suggests that people did not vote for the MAS just because of the party's populist platform, but also because the party's ethnic demands and profile presumably appealed to them as indigenous people. The dual ethnic and populist appeal of the MAS also helps explain why the MAS fared significantly better in the 2005 elections than traditional populist parties have fared in recent elections. While populist parties, such as the NFR and UCS, managed to win approximately twenty percent of the vote in some elections during the 1990s and early 2000s, none of them approached the fifty-three percent of the vote the MAS captured in 2005.

The analysis also found that people who self-identify as white were less likely to vote for the MAS, even controlling for other variables. However, the probability that a self-identified white person would vote for the MAS was still relatively high, other things being equal. A simulation found that when all other variables are held at their means people who self-identify as white had a forty-two percent probability of voting for the MAS, people who self-identify as mestizo had a fifty-seven percent probability of doing so, and people who self-identify as indigenous had a sixty-three percent probability of voting for the MAS.[57] This suggests that the MAS's ethnopopulist appeals resonated particularly strongly among self-identified indigenous people, but that they were inclusive enough to attract many mestizos and whites.

Speaking an indigenous language also increased the likelihood of voting for the MAS, even controlling for indigenous self-identification and other variables. The variables measuring whether the respondent grew up speaking Aymara or Quechua were both positive and highly statistically significant, although the variable for speaking a lowlands indigenous language was not.[58] When all other variables are held at their means, people who grew up speaking Aymara had a sixty-nine percent probability of voting for the MAS, whereas native Quechua speakers had a sixty percent probability of doing so, and people who did not grow up speaking an indigenous language had only a forty-five percent probability of supporting the MAS. Why does speaking an indigenous language have such a strong effect on the likelihood of voting for the MAS even after controlling for indigenous self-identification?[59] The main reason is that

---

[56] The modest level of statistical significance of the indigenous identification variable is presumably the result of the fact that indigenous self-identification is correlated with other variables in the analysis, such as the Aymara and Quechua linguistic variables. The vast majority (eighty-four percent) of people who self-identify as indigenous grew up speaking an indigenous language.

[57] The ninety-five percent confidence intervals of the estimates for self-identified indigenous people overlap with those of mestizos, so we do not have a high level of certainty that someone who self-identifies as indigenous is more likely to vote for the MAS than someone who self-identifies as mestizo.

[58] Speakers of lowlands indigenous languages may not have been significantly more likely to vote for the MAS because the MAS may have been perceived as a party that principally represented highlands indigenous populations, reflecting ongoing lowlands–highlands indigenous divides.

[59] I view growing up speaking an indigenous language as a reasonable proxy for having indigenous roots and the cultural attachments and life experiences that go with them. It is these cultural attachments and life experiences, I assume, that draw indigenous language speakers to the MAS.

the MAS's inclusive ethnic appeals attracted not only people who self-identified as indigenous, but also many people who grew up speaking an indigenous language, but do not self-identify as indigenous. These indigenous mestizos may not self-identify as indigenous, but their indigenous roots, their cultural attachments, and their experiences with socioeconomic disadvantage and discrimination made them receptive to the inclusive ethnic profile and agenda of the MAS.

The analysis also found that views on ethnic issues had only a modest effect on the likelihood of voting for the MAS, presumably because the MAS's inclusive appeals attracted many people who did not have a strong position on these issues. The ethnic representation variable had the expected sign but it was not statistically significant, suggesting that people who felt better represented by members of their own ethnic group were not significantly more likely to vote for the MAS. The support for teaching indigenous languages variable, meanwhile, was positive and statistically significant, but a simulation revealed that we cannot be sure (at the ninety-five percent confidence level) that someone who strongly advocated that schools teach indigenous languages was more likely to support the MAS than someone who did not support education in indigenous languages at all.

These findings thus provide support for the argument that the MAS's inclusive ethnopopulist appeal played a crucial role in its resounding electoral victory, attracting the support of a broad variety of people with indigenous backgrounds as well as low-income and politically disenchanted voters and people with leftist and nationalist views. The statistical analysis, however, also showed that a number of other variables, not directly related to the MAS's ethnopopulist appeal, influenced the likelihood that a voter would support the MAS. Other things being equal, voters from the eastern and southern departments known as the *media luna* were much less likely to support the MAS. By contrast, older voters were significantly more likely to support the MAS. Surprisingly, however, neither urbanization level nor gender had a statistically significant relationship with voting for the MAS once other variables were controlled for.

CONCLUSION

This chapter has shown that the ascent of the MAS was due in large part to its inclusive ethnopopulist appeals. These appeals resonated widely because of growing levels of indigenous consciousness and organization in Bolivia as well as the high levels of disenchantment with the traditional parties. Equally important, the low levels of ethnic polarization and fluid ethnic boundaries made it possible for the MAS to win the support not only of self-identified indigenous people, but also of many voters who typically identify as white or mestizo.

The MAS started out as a party that appealed primarily to Quechua-speaking coca growers in the department of Cochabamba, but it gradually reached out to other people as well. It recruited white and mestizo candidates, forged alliances with a variety of indigenous and non-indigenous organizations, and avoided exclusionary rhetoric and demands. The MAS also used traditional populist strategies to build a broad, multi-ethnic coalition. It emphasized Morales's leadership, focused its campaigns on the poor, employed anti-establishment rhetoric, and made numerous nationalist and state interventionist appeals.

The MAS has demonstrated remarkable electoral stability to date, consistently winning more than fifty percent of the vote in the numerous elections held since it took power in 2005. This level of success is particularly astonishing given that, from the return to democracy until the MAS's resounding 2005 victory, no Bolivian party had captured more than forty percent of the vote. It is unclear, however, how long the MAS will be able to hold its diverse multi-ethnic coalition together. The MAS should be able to maintain the support of much of its rural indigenous base in large part because this population has benefited the most from the party's policies and identifies most strongly with its ethnic project and appeals. It will have a more difficult time maintaining the support of the ethnically diverse urban poor and middle class, however, particularly if the economy begins to falter. Indeed, in late 2010 and 2011, support for Morales declined considerably in polls carried out in the major cities of the country.

Nevertheless, the MAS already has carried out important changes unlikely to be reversed, regardless of the length of the party's hold on power. The expansion of the role of the Bolivian state in the natural gas industry, the recognition of many indigenous rights, and the transformation of Bolivia's political institutions, including the creation of a new constitution, are just a few of the many legacies that the MAS will bequeath to its successors.

3

The Rise and Decline of Pachakutik in Ecuador

> We are no longer Indians that you go to see in a museum. We are not only present;
> we are also here with proposals.
>> Luis Macas, in the wake of Pachakutik's impressive performance in the
>> 1996 elections (Cited in Escobar 1996, A12)

In Ecuador, like in Bolivia, the indigenous movement gave birth to a political party in the mid-1990s.[1] This party, the Movimiento Unidad Plurinacional Pachakutik – Nuevo País (MUPP-NP), performed surprisingly well from the start. In the 1996 elections, for example, its presidential candidate, Freddy Ehlers, finished third with 20.6 percent of the valid vote and it won eight seats in the legislature. Its most important breakthrough, however, came in the 2002 elections when the candidate it supported, Lucio Gutiérrez, was elected president, and Pachakutik took control of four cabinet ministries in the new government.[2] Thus, in less than a decade, Pachakutik emerged as a major player in Ecuadorian politics.

The success of the MUPP-NP, like the MAS, was due in part to its ethnic appeals. Pachakutik used a variety of symbolic and substantive appeals to win the support of Ecuador's indigenous population. It ran numerous indigenous candidates, it campaigned extensively in indigenous areas, and it embraced traditional ethnic demands. Pachakutik also benefited significantly from its close ties to Ecuador's powerful indigenous movement, which provided it with organizational legitimacy as well as human and material resources. These appeals and resources helped Pachakutik capture much of the indigenous vote beginning in 1996.

From the outset Pachakutik sought to win the support not just of indigenous people, but of Ecuadorians of all ethnicities. As a result, the party

---

[1] For simplicity, I will refer at times to Pachakutik as a party, even though it is technically an independent electoral movement rather than a party.

[2] Neither Ehlers nor Gutiérrez were actually members of Pachakutik, but they ran as the candidates of alliances between their movements and Pachakutik.

employed inclusive rhetoric, recruited numerous white and mestizo candidates, and formed alliances with mestizo-led parties and movements. Pachakutik, like the MAS in Bolivia, also used traditional populist strategies to reach out to whites and mestizos. It nominated famous, politically independent personalities as its presidential candidates and severely criticized the traditional parties and existing political elites. It focused its appeals mainly on the lower classes and emphasized its own humble grassroots origins. And it adopted a strongly nationalist and state interventionist platform, denouncing neoliberal policies and foreign intervention in Ecuador.

These appeals proved successful in part because many Ecuadorians had grown disenchanted with the traditional parties and their economic and social policies. Moreover, the fluidity of ethnic identity and the low level of ethnic polarization in Ecuador meant that an indigenous party could win support not only from self-identified indigenous people, but also from many whites and mestizos. This was crucial given that people who self-identify as indigenous only represent a small proportion of the population in Ecuador. Nevertheless, Pachakutik still won less support than did the MAS in Bolivia, in part because the indigenous electorate was much smaller in Ecuador, but also because Pachakutik faced difficult competition from other populist candidates and movements.

Moreover, the success of Pachakutik proved relatively short-lived. In the 2006 presidential elections, the party won only 2.2 percent of the national vote, and it has struggled to maintain its relevance since that time. Pachakutik encountered difficulties beginning in 2006 for several reasons. First, in the run-up to the 2006 elections, the party abandoned its inclusive approach in favor of a more ethnonationalist posture. Whereas in previous elections it had forged alliances with non-indigenous organizations and supported white or mestizo candidates for president, in the 2006 elections it eschewed alliances and concentrated most of the key candidacies, including its presidential nomination, in the hands of indigenous leaders. Partly as a result, many prominent white and mestizo leaders and organizations abandoned the party, as did non-indigenous voters.

Second and relatedly, Pachakutik's decision to nominate an internal candidate rather than to support a better known outsider, such as Rafael Correa, in the 2006 election weakened its appeal in traditional populist constituencies. Moreover, Pachakutik's decision to go it alone in 2006 meant that it faced extensive competition for these traditional populist constituencies from other candidates, including Correa and Gilmar Gutiérrez, the brother of former president Lucio Gutiérrez. Correa ran on a populist platform that resembled Pachakutik's in many ways, except that it was less focused on indigenous issues. Moreover, Correa was better known and financed than Pachakutik's candidate, and he managed to win over many of the politically disenchanted and anti-neoliberal voters who had supported Pachakutik in previous elections. Similarly, Gilmar Gutiérrez's populist campaign strategies proved effective in many of the indigenous and mestizo communities that had previously supported his brother and Pachakutik.

This chapter is organized as follows. The first section discusses institutional explanations for the emergence of Pachakutik. The second section discusses the ethnic landscape in Ecuador and explains why it was conducive to inclusive ethnic appeals. The third section details how the traditional parties in Ecuador largely failed to make ethnic appeals. In the fourth section, I show how Pachakutik's inclusive ethnic appeals enabled it to capture the support of many indigenous voters in the 1996, 1998, and 2002 elections, without antagonizing white and mestizo voters. The fifth section discusses how Pachakutik also used traditional populist strategies to win the support of voters of all ethnic backgrounds. The sixth section analyzes the poor performance of Pachakutik in the 2006 elections, detailing how the party's abandonment of its successful ethnopopulist approach undermined its support, particularly among whites and mestizos. The conclusion discusses the impact and future of ethnopopulism in Ecuador.

INSTITUTIONAL EXPLANATIONS

Some scholars have argued that the emergence of Pachakutik in Ecuador is the result of institutional reforms (Birnir 2004; Macdonald Jr. 2002, 184–5; Van Cott 2005). Birnir (2004, 14), for example, maintains that "until 1995, restrictive ballot-access requirements prevented the indigenous communities from registering a political party, let alone competing in elections." Similarly, Van Cott (2005, 113) argues that "as in Bolivia, restrictive party registration requirements were the main impediment to the formation of ethnic parties." Both Birnir and Van Cott suggest that the principal barrier was the requirement that political parties have "a national organization, which should extend to at least ten provinces of the country, among which there should be at least two of three most populous" (*Leyes de elecciones, partidos políticos y reglamentos* 1991, 99). Birnir and Van Cott argue that this requirement made it difficult or impossible for the indigenous movement to form a party because there were few indigenous people on the coast where two of the three most populous provinces were located. In 1995, however, the electoral law was changed to permit independent movements, which did not need to demonstrate that they had a national organization, to compete in elections. This reform, they argue, paved the way for the creation of Pachakutik.

These scholars, however, overestimate the legal impediments to party formation in Ecuador. Parties did not have to demonstrate they had a certain number of provincial members as Van Cott (2005, 113) claims. In order to demonstrate that they were a national organization, parties only needed to show that they had a directorship in at least ten provinces, which required nothing more than the naming of some provincial party leaders.[3] Carlos

---

[3] Moreover, the Supreme Electoral Tribunal (TSE) was not required to verify the accuracy of the provincial directorships (interview with Aguinaga 2007).

Aguinaga, the former president of the Supreme Electoral Tribunal, argued that Pachakutik could have formed a party without difficulty, asserting that "to form a party in Ecuador is easy" (interview with author 2007). Similarly, Gandhi Burbano, a former member of the Supreme Electoral Tribunal, maintained that Pachakutik "would not have had difficulty in satisfying the requirements of the laws. It would have registered candidates and created a directorship in those provinces" (interview with author 2007). Pachakutik also could have formed a party the way the MAS in Bolivia did, by borrowing an existing party's registration.

As Andolina (1999, 212) points out, the change in the law that permitted independent movements to compete "was more 'ideologically enabling' than anything else" since it enabled Pachakutik to distinguish itself from the traditional parties.[4] (See also Collins 2001, 9). Although this change may have encouraged the indigenous movement to participate in the elections, it is quite possible that they would have done so in any event.[5] Indeed, both Nina Pacari and José María Cabascango, long-time Pachakutik leaders, told the author that if the law had not been changed to permit movements to run in elections, they would have created a party or found another way to participate (interviews with author 2005).

This is not to suggest that institutional factors played no role in the emergence of Pachakutik. The change in registration requirements clearly made it easier for Pachakutik to register as a party even though Pachakutik might have overcome or circumvented these requirements in any event. Institutional factors, however, cannot explain Pachakutik's strong performance in presidential elections between 1996 and 2002, including in some white and mestizo-dominated areas.[6] Nor can institutional factors explain why the party suddenly declined beginning in 2006. To account for these developments, we must examine the campaign strategies and appeals of Pachakutik and how they resonated in Ecuador's complex political and ethnic landscape.

---

[4] It is not clear, however, whether voters distinguish between parties and independent movements such as Pachakutik that compete in elections.

[5] The decision to create an independent movement rather than a party also had some negative implications for Pachakutik by depriving it of access to state financing for parties. On a number of occasions, Pachakutik has debated whether to reconstitute itself as a political party (interview with Talahua 2007).

[6] Another institutional change, the 1996 reform that permitted parties or movements to make alliances in legislative (pluripersonal) elections, may have boosted Pachakutik's performance in legislative elections somewhat. As we shall see, Pachakutik's alliances have helped the party expand its base of support beyond the rural indigenous population and have enabled it to reduce the number of competitors it faces. Nevertheless, even this reform has had a relatively modest impact on Pachakutik's fortunes since it only affected legislative elections. Ecuadorian parties have always been permitted to make alliances in presidential elections and these presidential alliances have arguably had a greater impact on Pachakutik's electoral performance than the legislative alliances. Indeed, in some provinces Pachakutik has eschewed alliances in legislative elections altogether.

ETHNICITY AND ETHNOPOPULISM IN ECUADOR

This chapter argues that Pachakutik succeeded in large part because it made inclusive ethnopopulist appeals. Pachakutik won the support of much of the indigenous population because it appealed to them as indigenous people. Pachakutik was the first major party in Ecuador to originate in the indigenous movement, to nominate numerous indigenous candidates, to extensively invoke indigenous symbols, and to embrace the full array of traditional indigenous demands. Nevertheless, during the first decade of its existence, Pachakutik also reached out to whites and mestizos. It avoided exclusionary language, recruited numerous white and mestizo candidates and leaders, formed alliances with non-indigenous organizations, and developed a broad and classically populist platform. This inclusive approach helped the party win the support of voters of all ethnic backgrounds, although it fared best among the indigenous population.

The inclusive approach was successful because of the long history of *mestizaje* in Ecuador, which was even more far-reaching than in Bolivia. *Mestizaje* in Ecuador, like elsewhere in Latin America, was a cultural as well as a biological process facilitated by the rapid urbanization of the country that took place during the twentieth century. As Indian peasants migrated to the cities, they and their children abandoned indigenous customs and embraced mestizo identities (Belote and Belote 1984; Whitten 1981). Widespread discrimination against the indigenous in both the cities and the countryside did much to hasten the assimilation process. Many people abandoned indigenous customs and identities in order to avoid the discrimination to which they were often subjected. The Ecuadorian state also played an active role in promoting *mestizaje*, particularly through educational programs that penetrated rural areas. Indeed, General Guillermo Rodríguez Lara, who ruled Ecuador from 1972–6, reportedly said that, "There is no more Indian problem [in Ecuador]. We all become white men when we accept the goals of the national culture" (Cited in Yashar 2005, 95; Burbano de Lara 2005, 240).

By any measure, *mestizaje* significantly reduced the proportion of the population in Ecuador that is indigenous. The first colonial census of 1780 classified sixty-four percent of the population as indigenous, but by 1850 this figure had declined to forty-six percent, and it continued to decline in the decades that followed (Sánchez-Parga 1996, 17–21).[7] The 1950 census, which was the first modern census carried out in Ecuador, did not specifically seek to measure the number of indigenous people, but it did include questions about language use (Clark 1998). It found that by that time only fourteen percent of the population spoke Quichua, the dominant indigenous language of Ecuador (Knapp 1987, 11–14; Sánchez-Parga 1996). The percentage of indigenous language speakers continued to fall in the decades that followed, dropping to only

---

[7] These censuses used somewhat different methods to identify indigenous people and they are therefore not strictly comparable.

4.6 percent in the 2001 census (León Guzmán 2003).[8] The 2001 census also included a question about ethnic self-identification for the first time. It found that only 6.1 percent of Ecuadorians above the age of fifteen self-identified as indigenous (León Guzmán 2003, 2).[9] By contrast, 77.7 percent of the population surveyed in the census self-identified as mestizo, 10.8 percent as white, and 5.0 percent as black or mulatto (León Guzmán 2003, 2). Other recent surveys have reached relatively similar findings.[10]

Because people who self-identify as indigenous represent a small proportion of the population, Pachakutik has had to reach out to people who self-identify with other ethnic categories in order to fare well in elections. As Pachakutik legislator Raúl Ilaquiche acknowledged, "With just indigenous votes you can't win. You need white, mestizo, and urban votes" (interview with author 2007). Similarly, Valerio Grefa (1996, 56), an indigenous leader of Pachakutik, notes that from the beginning, "there was a consensus on the necessity that the indigenous people alone could not transform the country."

Winning votes from people who self-identify as white or mestizo was feasible for Pachakutik because ethnic boundaries in Ecuador are fluid and ambiguous as a result of widespread *mestizaje*. Many people who self-identify as white or mestizo, for example, have indigenous roots and identify to some degree with indigenous culture. In a 2000 survey carried out by the census bureau, more than twice as many people (12.5 percent of the respondents) reported that their parents spoke an indigenous language than self-identified as indigenous or spoke an indigenous language themselves (León Guzmán 2003). In all, 14.3 percent of the respondents in this survey either self-identified as indigenous, spoke an indigenous language, or had parents that spoke an indigenous language (León Guzmán 2003). Moreover, an even larger percentage of Ecuadorians identify to some degree with indigenous culture. A 2006 Latin American Public Opinion Project survey asked interviewees to what extent they identified with Quichua culture on a scale of one to seven. Only 10.4 percent of the national sample reported that they strongly identified with Quichua culture

[8] A 2000 survey by the census bureau found that 4.4 percent of the population spoke an indigenous language (León Guzmán 2003, 3). In the 2006 LAPOP survey, only 1.4 percent of the respondents reported speaking Quichua, but another 4.6 percent reported understanding it.

[9] Critics have objected to the wording of this question and argued that many indigenous people are reluctant to self-identify as indigenous because of discrimination against them. The wording of the ethnic self-identification question on the 2001 census was as follows: "Do you consider yourself indigenous, black (Afro-Ecuadorian), mestizo, mulatto, white or other?"

[10] The indigenous movement and some scholars have claimed that indigenous people represent as much as forty percent of the Ecuadorian population, but data on ethnic self-identification (and language) do not support these claims. A 2000 survey by the census bureau, like the 2001 census, found that only about six percent of the population self-identified as indigenous (León Guzmán 2003, 3). A subsequent survey by the census bureau reported that 8.5 percent of the population self-identified as indigenous (Sistema Integrado de Indicadores Sociales del Ecuador 2007b, 6, 2007a, 8). Surveys by the Latin American Public Opinion Project, which have used similar questions as the census, have found that an even lower percentage of the population – less than three percent – has self-identified as indigenous.

(six to seven on the seven point scale), but another 29.4 percent of the population reported a moderate degree of identification with Quichua culture (three to five on the seven point scale).

As we have seen, people who have indigenous roots or identify with indigenous culture may be receptive to ethnic appeals, even if they do not self-identify as indigenous. Many of these indigenous mestizos feel more ethnically proximate to indigenous candidates and parties than to the largely light-skinned candidates and elite parties that have traditionally dominated Ecuadorian politics. To attract these voters, however, Pachakutik has had to be inclusive, avoiding exclusionary anti-white or anti-mestizo rhetoric. Indeed, even many self-identified indigenous people in Ecuador object to exclusionary ethnonationalist rhetoric.

Pachakutik's efforts to win the support of white and mestizo voters have also been facilitated by the fact that ethnic polarization is quite low in Ecuador. Although discrimination against indigenous people is commonplace in Ecuador and indigenous people are disproportionately poor and disadvantaged, this has not translated into widespread ethnic hostility or major outbreaks of ethnic violence.[11] The absence of ethnic polarization is, no doubt, at least partly a byproduct of *mestizaje,* which has blurred and softened the lines between different ethnic groups in the country (Zamosc 1994). The low level of ethnic polarization in Ecuador has meant that even people who do not identify with indigenous culture have sometimes been willing to vote for a party that was established by the indigenous movement and is led principally by indigenous people. Indeed, Pachakutik has also drawn a significant share of its votes from whites and non-indigenous mestizos. These voters have supported Pachakutik, however, largely because it has adopted highly inclusive rhetoric and demands.

Nevertheless, we should not exaggerate either the extent of ethnic harmony in Ecuador or the level of support for Pachakutik among whites and mestizos. Although Pachakutik has made inroads in mestizo and white areas, in no legislative election has it ever won more than twelve percent of the vote in cantons that are less than one-half indigenous. Pachakutik has fared better in presidential elections, but it has done so only by allying with other parties and supporting white or mestizo candidates. It is difficult to know to what extent ethnic prejudice has limited support for Pachakutik, but many indigenous leaders are skeptical that Ecuador is ready to elect an indigenous president (interviews with Atamaint 2007; Miranda 2007; and Sucuzhañay 2007). Indeed, in the 2006 LAPOP survey, 21.2 percent of the respondents reported that they were concerned that an indigenous person could be elected president in that year's election, and this figure may underestimate the actual level of concern since people are typically reluctant to admit prejudice in surveys. In a 2004 survey

---

[11] According to the census bureau's 2006 Survey on Living Conditions, seventy percent of indigenous people in Ecuador live below the poverty line, as compared to 34.9 percent of mestizos and 33.2 percent of whites (Sistema Integrado de Indicadores Sociales del Ecuador 2007a, 8).

carried out by the census bureau, sixty-five percent of the respondents said that they believed Ecuadorians are racist, although only ten percent admitted to being racist themselves (Sistema Integrado de Indicadores Sociales del Ecuador 2007a, 8; Secretaría Técnica del Frente Social 2006, 40–5).

Given its ethnic demographics, Ecuador is a much less favorable environment for the success of an indigenous party than is Bolivia. That Pachakutik was able to succeed for a time is a testament to the effectiveness of its inclusive ethnopopulist appeals and the party's determination to reach out across ethnic lines.

THE EMERGENCE OF THE INDIGENOUS VOTE

Before the 1990s, there was little reason to believe that an indigenous party might be successful in Ecuador since the indigenous population traditionally played little role in the country's electoral politics. Until 1978 the Ecuadorian constitution restricted suffrage to literate citizens, which effectively disenfranchised much of the indigenous population. According to the 1950 census, ninety-two percent of Quichua speakers in Ecuador were illiterate, compared to only thirty-six percent of Spanish speakers (Collins 2001, 6). Although illiteracy rates declined considerably in the latter half of the twentieth century, they remained relatively high in indigenous areas.[12] As a result, much of the indigenous population did not participate in the intermittent elections held in Ecuador during the first three-quarters of the twentieth century. The 1978 constitution eliminated these restrictions on the franchise, however, which led to a sharp increase in voter registration, particularly in indigenous areas. Between 1978 and 1980, the number of people registered to vote increased by thirty-five percent (Darlic Mardesic 1987, 37). In the most heavily indigenous provinces (Bolivar, Cañar, Cotopaxi, Chimborazo, Imbabura, Morona Santiago, Napo, and Pastaza), voter registration went up by an average of forty-eight percent (Darlic Mardesic 1987, 37). The number of votes cast, meanwhile, increased by ninety-one percent in the indigenous provinces between the 1978 and 1984 presidential elections, as opposed to seventy-four percent in the other provinces.[13]

In spite of the increase in the size of the indigenous electorate, the traditional parties largely shied away from making ethnic appeals to indigenous voters. During the 1980s and early 1990s, the traditional parties recruited relatively few indigenous candidates for important positions. Indeed, only one indigenous person, Manuel Naula, served in the Ecuadorian legislature during the 1980s, and he was an alternate. Nor did the traditional parties embrace many of the demands of the indigenous movement, establish close links to indigenous

---

[12] Quintero López (1978, 281) estimates that approximately 23.3 percent of the adult population was illiterate in 1978, but the illiteracy rate was much higher in the countryside, particularly in indigenous areas. (See also Larrea and Sommaruga 1984).

[13] The 1984 elections were the first presidential elections in which illiterates participated.

organizations, or nominate indigenous people for important leadership positions within their parties. The traditional parties did oppose racial discrimination and they called for the preservation of indigenous cultures and the economic and social advancement of indigenous communities, but they offered little in the way of programs designed to achieve these goals (Grijalva 1992; Tribunal Supremo Electoral 1981). In fact, many parties explicitly opposed ethnically oriented policies such as quotas, territorial autonomy for indigenous people, and the recognition of Ecuador as a plurinational state (Andolina 1999, 195–7; Frank et al. 1992; Patiño 1996). The declaration of principles of the Partido Social Cristiano (PSC), for example, stated that policies toward the indigenous should not "foment racial differences" but should instead provide equal opportunities to all "so that progress could be the result of creative competition within equality of possibilities" (Tribunal Supremo Electoral 1981, 156–7). The PSC also condemned "all demagogical exaltation that takes the indigenous population as a banner of political propaganda" (Tribunal Supremo Electoral 1981, 157).

Leftist parties reached out somewhat more to the indigenous population.[14] Some smaller leftist parties, such as the Partido Comunista de Ecuador, the Partido Socialista de Ecuador, the Frente Amplio de la Izquierda, and the Movimiento Popular Democrático had long had ties to the indigenous movement and embraced many indigenous causes (Andolina 1999, 195–7; Becker 2008, 104–5; Van Cott 2005). The larger center-left parties such as Izquierda Democrática (ID) and Democracia Popular (DP) also made direct appeals to the indigenous population. DP's governing plan, for example, decried the "shameful and inhumane living conditions" of indigenous people and called for the creation of an "indigenous institute that would focus exclusively on the promotion of the indigenous population and coordinate all the public sector programs that have to do with it" (Tribunal Supremo Electoral 1981, 144). ID, meanwhile, recruited a number of indigenous leaders to its side, including Manuel Naula, the only indigenous person to serve in the Ecuadoran legislature during the 1980s.

Rodrigo Borja, the leader of Izquierda Democrática, also adopted some indigenous movement demands during his presidency (1988–92). As president, he initiated a dialogue with the main indigenous federation, Confederación de Nacionalidades Indígenas del Ecuador (CONAIE), legitimizing it as the representative of the indigenous population. He also allowed CONAIE to appoint the directors of the state's bilingual education program, and he accelerated land

---

[14] Some populist parties, notably the Concentración de Fuerzas Populares (CFP), also reached out to indigenous voters. According to Valerio Grefa (1996, 55), Jaime Roldós, the CFP leader who was elected president in 1979, "stuck very much in the sentiments of indigenous people in the country, not because he brought the indigenous people to his side, but rather because his message got through to indigenous people, because he began to speak of adult education, of the need to support indigenous peoples, to recognize that we existed. He was one of the first presidents to speak in Quichua and that impacted a great deal in the conscience of indigenous people."

reform, recognizing the communal land rights of some Amazonian indigenous groups (Andolina 1999, 192–3; Selverston 1994, 145–6). Borja even declared his support for the recognition of Ecuador as a pluricultural state (Selverston 1994, 146). Not surprisingly, ID and other left and center-left parties fared disproportionately well in indigenous areas. Indeed, in the eight most indigenous provinces, Borja won an average of 38.0 percent of the valid vote in the first round and 60.3 percent of the valid vote in the second round of the 1984 presidential elections. By contrast, in Ecuador as a whole he won 28.7 percent of the valid vote in the first round and 48.5 percent in the second round.[15]

Nevertheless, whites and mestizos dominated the leadership of the leftist parties as well as the centrist and rightist parties and their concerns, not the interests of the indigenous population, drove the parties' agendas. Indigenous people often expressed frustration and disenchantment even with all of the traditional parties, including leftist parties. In a 1988 election day survey of eleven indigenous parishes, forty-six percent of the respondents declared that none of the parties represented the indigenous population, even though seventy percent of the total respondents reported voting for left or center-left candidates (Chiriboga and Rivera 1989, 195, 213–15). CONAIE considered supporting the left in the 1988 presidential elections, but in the end it voted to maintain its independence from parties. Many indigenous leaders favored maintaining their autonomy because they felt that parties, including the leftist parties, used them to win the support of indigenous voters but did not allow them to play a role in decision making (Andolina 1999, 218–20; Becker 2008, 182–4). As a leader of CONAIE, Blanca Chancosa, put it: "They would speak for us, but it was out of the question for an Indian to be in the leadership" (Becker 2008, 184).

Frustration with the existing parties, including the leftist parties, led to high levels of electoral volatility in indigenous areas. Izquierda Democrática won the most support in indigenous areas during the 1980s, but many indigenous people grew disillusioned with ID during Borja's presidency in spite of his concessions to the indigenous movement. In the first round of the 1992 presidential elections, ID's support in the most indigenous provinces dropped to 16.1 percent, down from 33.2 percent in 1988. Thus, by the mid-1990s, no party could claim to have locked up a significant share of the indigenous vote.

THE INDIGENOUS MOVEMENT AND THE RISE OF PACHAKUTIK

It was not until the emergence of Pachakutik in 1996 that a major party made ethnic appeals a central part of its campaigns. Pachakutik not only made symbolic appeals to the indigenous population, it also took up a whole range of traditional demands of the indigenous movement. Moreover, Pachakutik, in stark contrast to the traditional parties, had close ties to a variety of

---

[15] Similarly, in 1988, Borja won an average of 33.2 percent of the first round vote and 65.6 percent of the second round vote in the eight most indigenous provinces. In Ecuador as a whole, he won only 24.5 percent of the first round vote and 54.0 percent of the second round vote in 1988.

indigenous organizations, ran numerous indigenous candidates for important political offices, and possessed a mostly indigenous leadership. Not surprising, Pachakutik won a large share of the vote in indigenous areas in the first three elections in which it participated.

The indigenous movement in Ecuador was the main actor behind the creation of Pachakutik, and it helped the party win support in indigenous areas by providing it with various organizational resources (Andolina 1999; Beck and Mijeski 2001; Collins 2001; Van Cott 2005).[16] Nevertheless, the indigenous movement only played a modest role in the overall electoral success of Pachakutik. The large vote share earned by the party in the 1996, 1998, and 2002 elections was mostly due to its ability to go beyond its indigenous base. Pachakutik fared well because it was able to win votes not only in rural areas where the indigenous movement is strong, but also in cities and medium-sized towns where the indigenous movement is weak.

The Ecuadorian indigenous movement was traditionally the strongest in the region. The modern indigenous movement in Ecuador dates to the mid-1940s when the Federación Ecuatoriana de los Indios was created by the Communist Party. In the decades that followed, left-wing parties and church groups helped organize other important indigenous organizations, such as the Federación Nacional de Organizaciones Campesinas (FENOC), Ecuador Runacunapac Riccharimui (ECUARUNARI), and the Confederación de Nacionalidades Indígenas de la Amazonía Ecuatoriana (CONFENAIE). As a result, Ecuador's indigenous population gradually became the most densely organized in the region. A unified nationwide indigenous movement in Ecuador did not emerge until 1986, however, when the main highlands indigenous federation, ECUARUNARI, came together with the largest Amazonian organization, CONFENAIE, and some smaller indigenous groups to form CONAIE.[17] Some indigenous organizations, such as the Federación Ecuatoriana de Iglesias Evangélicas (FEINE), an evangelical indigenous organization, and the Federación Nacional de Organizaciones Campesinas, Indígenas y Negras (FENOCIN), a leftist organization that has a significant presence on the coast, did not join the new confederation. Nevertheless, these groups represent a much smaller percentage of the indigenous population than CONAIE.

CONAIE very quickly made its presence felt on the national political scene. In 1990, the organization led an uprising in which its members withheld farm produce, occupied buildings, and blocked the main highways in the highlands for over a week (Zamosc 1994). In response, the administration of President Rodrigo Borja agreed to open negotiations with CONAIE on a list of grievances. CONAIE and its member organizations carried out further protests in

---

[16] There is an extensive English and Spanish language literature on the Ecuadorian indigenous movement. See, for example, Barrera Guarderas 2001; Ramón Valarezo 1993; Becker 2008; Clark and Becker 2007; Guerrero Cazar and Ospina Peralta 2003; Ibarra 1992; Lucero 2008; Pallares 2002; Sánchez-Parga 2007; Santana 1995; Selverston-Scher 2001; Yashar 2005.

[17] ECUARUNARI and CONFENAIE had set up a precursor of CONAIE, the Consejo de Coordinación de las Nacionalidades Indígenas in 1980 (Yashar 2005, 131).

the years that followed. The most important of these demonstrations came in 1994 when CONAIE mobilized to block the government's agrarian development law. That same year, CONAIE also helped defeat some proposals that the government of President Sixto Durán Ballén had submitted to a popular referendum, including a proposal that would have opened the way for the privatization of the country's social security system.

The leadership of CONAIE was initially reluctant to participate in elections because of its distrust of the political system. Since its founding, CONAIE had largely eschewed participating or even taking sides in elections, and in 1992, it called on its membership to cast null ballots in the elections, proclaiming that "We want actions and not elections" (Becker 2008, 182–4; Sánchez López and Freidenberg 1998, 70). Participation in elections was resisted in particular by the leaders of highlands organizations who feared that indigenous leaders would be co-opted by political parties. As the national political influence of the indigenous movement grew, however, many indigenous leaders, especially those representing Amazonian organizations, began to advocate forming a party in part because they believed that it would be highly successful. This topic was the subject of repeated debates in CONAIE assemblies.[18] In 1995, some Amazonian leaders and a few highlands leaders demonstrated their resolve to participate in the 1996 elections by forming an electoral vehicle that they called the Pachakutik Movement. In order not to divide the movement, the leadership of CONAIE acquiesced, voting at the organization's thirteenth assembly to create an independent electoral movement named the Movimiento de Unidad Plurinacional Pachakutik (MUPP), which would participate in both local and national elections (Andolina 1999; Collins 2001; Sánchez López and Freidenberg 1998).[19]

Pachakutik's ties to the indigenous movement helped it win support among the indigenous population. CONAIE has been estimated to represent approximately eighty percent of the indigenous population and it has influence in most indigenous communities. Thus, its backing of Pachakutik carried a great deal of weight. The indigenous movement also provided Pachakutik with candidates and leaders. Indeed, many of the party's best known leaders have come from CONAIE, including Luis Macas, the former congressman and the party's 2006 presidential candidate; Nina Pacari, the former minister of foreign relations and vice president of congress; and Gilberto Talahua, the former congressman and national coordinator of the party. According to Freidenberg and Alcántara (2001), CONAIE provided more than half of the members of Pachakutik's executive committee in 1998. In addition, CONAIE provided Pachakutik with a network of organizations and activists that it could mobilize in its campaigns.

---

[18] CONAIE made the decision to participate in the 1996 elections in its fourth congress in December 1993, but it initially planned to participate only in local and provincial elections (Andolina 1999, 221). Moreover, this initial decision was not entirely clear and was not immediately acted upon (interview with Cabascango 2005).

[19] See Andolina (1999, ch. 6), Barrera Guarderas (2001, ch. 6), Massal (2005, ch. 5), and Mijeski and Beck (2011, ch. 3) for details on the founding of the movement.

A 2000 World Bank study reported that Ecuador had approximately twenty-three hundred grassroots indigenous organizations organized into 180 second-tier organizations (Beck and Mijeski 2001; Van Cott 2005, 110). Many of these organizations have participated in Pachakutik's campaigns. The organizations, for example, have sought to motivate and educate the rural population through workshops and popular theater programs that have acquainted the participants with the ballot, explained to them how to register to vote, and told them for whom to vote (Freidenberg and Alcántara 2001, 249–50). This organizational support was particularly crucial considering that neither Pachakutik nor CONAIE had much in the way of financial resources.[20]

Thus, the indigenous movement played the central role in the establishment of Pachakutik and helped the party make inroads among indigenous voters. The support of the indigenous movement could only take the party so far, however. As we shall see, Pachakutik's ability to win the support of the vast majority of voters who had few, if any, ties to the indigenous movement stemmed in large part from the party's inclusive ethnic and populist appeals.

PACHAKUTIK'S ETHNIC APPEALS

Pachakutik has used a variety of ethnic appeals to attract indigenous voters. To begin with, the party has often used rhetoric and symbols designed specifically to appeal to indigenous people. Indeed, the party's name, Pachakutik; its banner, the *wiphala*; and its logo, the multicolored rainbow, are all indigenous symbols. *Pachakutik* refers to a cosmic cataclysm that is supposed to herald the arrival of a new country or era, the *wiphala* is a traditional highlands Indian banner, and the rainbow colors symbolize the unity of the indigenous peoples. Party leaders also have often made direct rhetorical appeals to the indigenous population. The party has styled itself at times and been characterized by others as the political arm of the indigenous movement and the legitimate representative of the indigenous population, a claim that has been given some credibility by its close relations and leadership overlap with CONAIE.

In addition, Pachakutik has recruited numerous indigenous leaders as candidates for important positions in the national legislature as well as in local government. At the outset approximately two-thirds of the top leadership of the party, including its legislative contingent, was indigenous. Recruiting indigenous candidates turned out to be an effective strategy because many indigenous voters preferred to support people from similar ethnic backgrounds. In a survey carried out in heavily indigenous parishes on the day of the 1996 elections, the most common reason given for voting for a particular candidate was the fact that the candidate was indigenous – forty-eight percent of

---

[20] Efrén Calapucho, a leader of CONAIE, lamented that "the indigenous don't have money to make campaigns.... In the typical case, the social organizations don't contribute money but rather yucca, chicha, etc." (Interview with author 2005). Interviews with legislators from Pachakutik also confirmed that CONAIE did not contribute financially to their campaigns.

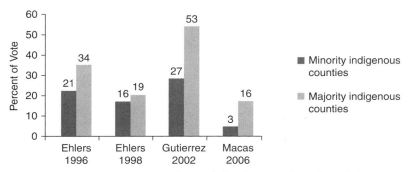

FIGURE 3.1. Mean county vote for Pachakutik's presidential candidates, 1996–2006.
Source: Tribunal Supremo Electoral

the respondents mentioned this as the motive for their vote (Wray 1996, 25). Interestingly, more educated indigenous people were particularly likely to cite the candidate's indigenous ethnicity as a motivating factor (Wray 1996, 25).

Pachakutik's platform and legislative initiatives also have aimed at attracting indigenous voters. The party has embraced many of the traditional ethnic demands of the indigenous movement, including indigenous autonomy, land reform, water rights, multicultural and multilingual education, and the inclusion of members of indigenous organizations in government agencies. At the constituent assembly of 1997, Pachakutik helped get a sweeping chapter on indigenous collective rights included in the constitution, although it failed to gain approval for declaring Ecuador a plurinational state (Andolina 2003, 747). Article 84 of the 1997 constitution recognizes and guarantees the right of indigenous people to maintain their customs, their community lands, their natural resources, their agricultural practices, their organizational forms, their intellectual property, and their traditional medicine. It also grants them the right to bilingual education, to formulate development policies with adequate state financing, and to participate in state organisms. In the national legislature, Pachakutik has also presented a wide range of bills aimed at benefiting the indigenous population. These bills included legislation seeking to create an indigenous development fund, to expand the power of rural parish councils, and to forgive debts owed to the National Institute of Agrarian Development.[21]

Pachakutik's ties to the indigenous movement and its various ethnic appeals have helped the party win support in indigenous areas. As Figure 3.1 indicates, in counties where self-identified indigenous people constitute a majority of the population, Pachakutik's presidential candidates won an average of 33.9 percent of the vote in the 1996 elections, 18.8 percent of the vote in the 1998 elections, 53.1 percent of the vote in the first round of the 2002 elections, and

---

[21] See Collins (2006, appendix 1) for a list of bills presented by Pachakutik in the legislature between 1996 and 2002.

83.3 percent of the vote in the second round of the 2002 elections.[22] By contrast, in each of these elections the MUPP-NP's presidential candidates won a much smaller share of the vote in those counties where self-identified indigenous people represent a minority of the population.

Moreover, as Table 3.1 shows, in each of these elections, the proportion of the population that self-identifies as indigenous is a highly statistically significant determinant of the likelihood of voting for Pachakutik's presidential candidates even controlling for the proportion of poor people in these counties.[23] Other things being equal, a ten percentage point increase in the proportion of the county population that is indigenous would result in a 3.9 percentage point increase in the vote for Pachakutik's presidential candidate in the 1996 election, a 1.6 percentage point increase in the 1998 election, a 6.0 percentage point increase in the first round of the 2002 election, and a 5.1 percentage point increase in the second round of the 2002 election.[24]

Pachakutik's indigenous profile and appeals also helped it fare well in indigenous areas in the legislative elections that took place during this period. As Figure 3.2 indicates, Pachakutik and its allies won an average of 23.5 percent of the vote in majority indigenous counties in the 1996 legislative elections, 36.8 percent in these counties in the 1998 legislative elections, and 37.3 percent in the 2002 legislative elections.[25] By contrast, as the figure indicates, it won a much smaller share of the vote in counties where the indigenous population was in the minority. Table 3.1 shows that the proportion of the population that is indigenous is also a highly statistically significant determinant of the legislative vote for Pachakutik, even controlling for the proportion of poor people in each county. According to these models, each ten percent increase in the proportion of the population that self-identifies as indigenous in a county would lead to a 3.5 percent increase in the county-level vote for Pachakutik's legislative candidates in 1996, a 4.9 percent increase in their vote in 1998, and a 4.5 percent increase in their vote in 2002.

---

[22] The proportion of the population that is indigenous is calculated here using data on ethnic self-identification from the 2001 census.

[23] The proportion of the population that self-identifies as indigenous is only modestly correlated with the proportion of the population that is poor ($r = .193$). The proportion of the population that is poor is highly correlated with the urbanization ($r = -.654$) and literacy rates ($r = -.583$), however, which is why these variables were excluded from the analysis. Data on all of these variables come from the 2001 census.

[24] For ease of interpretation, these statistical analyses were performed using Ordinary Least Squares. Using a Tobit model does not appreciably change the results.

[25] These data refer to the legislative elections for provincial deputies (i.e., deputies elected from provincial districts to the national legislature). In many provinces, Pachakutik ran in alliance with other parties and the data include the votes won by those alliances. In 1996 and 1998, Ecuador also held separate elections to select a smaller number of national deputies (i.e., deputies elected in a single national district). In counties where the majority of the population self-identifies as indigenous, Pachakutik and its allies won 27.3 percent of the vote in these elections in 1996 and 32.0 percent in 1998.

TABLE 3.1. *The Correlates of the County Vote Share for Pachakutik's Legislative and Presidential Candidates, 1996–2006*

(Ordinary Least Squares regression models)

	Constant	Indigenous / Total Population	Poor people / Total Population	Summary Statistics
Vote for Ehlers in 1996 presidential elections	.390*** (.060)	.390*** (.061)	−.281*** (.079)	N = 199 R² = .191
Vote for Ehlers in 1998 presidential elections	.274*** (.041)	.158*** (.038)	−.172** (.054)	N = 209 R² = .101
Vote for Gutiérrez in 2002 presidential elections (1st round)	.363*** (.055)	.600*** (.050)	−.193** (.072)	N = 215 R² = .408
Vote for Gutiérrez in 2002 presidential elections (2nd round)	.785*** (.066)	.505*** (.059)	−.277** (.086)	N = 215 R² = .262
Vote for Macas in 2006 presidential elections	−.013 (.017)	.209*** (.015)	.034 (.022)	N = 215 R² = .502
Vote for MUPP-NP in 1996 legislative elections (provincial deputies)	.084* (.035)	.347*** (.036)	−.063 (.047)	N = 199 R² = .318
Vote for MUPP-NP in 1998 legislative elections (provincial deputies)	.092** (.032)	.485*** (.029)	−.069 (.042)	N = 209 R² = .572
Vote for MUPP-NP in 2002 legislative elections (provincial deputies)	.106** (.035)	.447*** (.032)	−.026 (.046)	N = 215 R² = .490
Vote for MUPP-NP in 2006 legislative elections	.033 (.025)	.370*** (.023)	.003 (.033)	N = 219 R² = .561

Note: Standard errors in parentheses
* p<.05; ** p<.01; *** p<.001

PACHAKUTIK'S INCLUSIVE APPROACH

Pachakutik not only aimed to win the support of indigenous voters; at the outset, it also actively sought out support from Ecuadorians of other ethnic backgrounds. Thus, it avoided exclusionary rhetoric, developed a broad and inclusive political platform, recruited white and mestizo candidates and leaders, and forged alliances with many urban mestizo-dominated organizations and parties.[26] This inclusive strategy largely paid dividends. Between 1996 and 2002, Pachakutik won a significant share of the vote not only in indigenous areas, but also in many places where the self-identified indigenous population represented only a small portion of the electorate.

---

[26] Some whites and mestizos had also helped found Pachakutik.

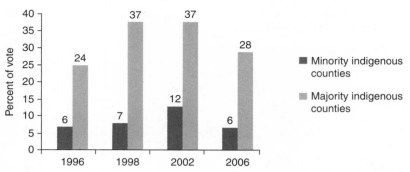

FIGURE 3.2. Mean county vote for Pachakutik in legislative elections, 1996–2006.
Source: Tribunal Supremo Electoral

In its founding Declaration of Ideological Principles, Pachakutik pronounced that it was "a space open for all Ecuadorians," it called for tolerance and respect for diversity, and it pledged "to construct a broad national, social, and political alliance with the participation of all of the social sectors" (Movimiento Unidad Plurinacional Pachakutik – Nuevo País 1998, 1–6). In the years that followed, leaders of Pachakutik made good on these promises, constructing a diverse coalition of supporters. Patricio Miranda, a Pachakutik legislator from the province of Chimborazo, told me: "Pachakutik is the combination of all that is the country. We bring together diversity. We can't do it with just one sector. Our base is the indigenous movement, but there are also other sectors, environmentalists, young people, etc." (interview with author 2007). Similarly, Luis Macas has stressed that: "Within Pachakutik there are not only Indians, there are workers, unions, professional associations of lawyers, doctors, etc., there are the non-governmental organizations that work in concrete ways within the communities, there are environmentalists, a women's caucus made up of indigenous and non-indigenous women. We all participate" (Cited in Collins 2006, 211).

Pachakutik aggressively recruited whites and mestizos as candidates and nominated them for important positions in the party's leadership and on its electoral lists. As a result, Pachakutik's executive committee and national legislative delegation typically had a significant proportion of white and mestizo members. Pachakutik's first executive committee, for example, was approximately one-third white or mestizo as were its first two legislative delegations (Collins 2006, ch. 5). Moreover, the legislative delegation elected in 2002 was one-half white or mestizo.[27] Pachakutik also recruited numerous white and mestizo candidates for local elections, especially in mestizo-dominated areas. Indeed, in the 2000 municipal elections, the majority of Pachakutik's winning mayors and prefects were whites or mestizos (Collins 2006, 212).

Candidates from Pachakutik, at times, had to face accusations that they were trying to gain control of the government to serve indigenous interests

[27] Data supplied to author by Pachakutik's national headquarters, Quito, July 5, 2007.

alone. Auki Tituaña (1996, 102), a leader of Pachakutik elected mayor of Cotacachi, recounted that "the parties even began to direct a dirty campaign against my candidacy, alleging that if I won, the Municipal Government would be full of indigenous people, something that was very absurd because legally I couldn't do it, fire all the mestizos and put in indigenous people." Similarly, Klever Guevara (1996, 98), the mayor of Guaranda, reported that "the people say now that there is a Pachakutik mayor, soon the Indians are going to want to be in the Municipal Government. But the Indians want absolutely nothing, not a single position." In most instances, Pachakutik was able to refute these charges by pointing to the multi-ethnic nature of their movement. According to Tituaña (1996, 104): "We have said that our commitment is with the people of Cotacachi, be they black, mestizos, or Indians, be they women, young people or the elderly. We have said [we will not have any] sectarianism or ... problems of race, religion, or ideology."

Pachakutik also reached out to whites and mestizos by developing a broad platform that addresses issues relevant to people of all races and ethnicities. Macas has asserted that: "Strategically, there are two main directions in which we work: to fight for our rights as indigenous peoples and to help work for proposals for political change, together with other sectors of society. Therefore, we have made concrete political proposals not only for indigenous peoples, but for all of Ecuadorian society" ("Interview with Luis Macas" 2003, 197). These concrete proposals included constitutional reforms, the expansion of state intervention in the economy, and a host of social policy initiatives. Some indigenous leaders used the slogan "nothing just for the indigenous" to emphasize that their demands would benefit all people and not just indigenous people (Guerrero Cazar and Ospina Peralta 2003, 143). In an interview with Collins (2006, 372), Mesías Mora, a mestizo former Pachakutik legislator, argued that "the indigenous movement is gaining leadership stature through the various mobilizations, uprisings, and, above all, because the indigenous movement's demands have not been *indigenista*, they have not been of a particularistic nature, like union demands.... Our demands are a little more generous, more open to other sectors, and this has meant that the indigenous movement at the national and provincial levels, in particular, has been gaining authority among these social sectors...."

Perhaps the most effective way in which Pachakutik reached out to whites and mestizos was by forming alliances.[28] In the first three presidential elections in which it competed, Pachakutik made pacts with important non-indigenous parties and movements. In the 1996 elections, for example, it forged an alliance with Freddy Ehlers, a white television personality, and his Movimiento Ciudadano Nuevo País (MCNP). Under this alliance, Ehlers ran as the coalition's presidential candidate, and Luis Macas, the former president of CONAIE, headed the coalition's list of candidates for the legislature.

---

[28] Pachakutik itself had many mestizo-dominated organizations among its members, although CONAIE was the most powerful organization within it.

Ehlers and Pachakutik also obtained the support of the Coordinadora de Movimientos Sociales (CMS), a broad grouping of energy sector unions, women's groups, human rights groups, environmental organizations, and neighborhood associations. In addition, some left-of-center parties, including Izquierda Democrática and the Partido Socialista – Frente Amplio (PS-FA), agreed to support Ehlers's presidential candidacy, although they ran their own candidates for the legislature. The alliance with ID was particularly crucial because it brought aboard a party that would have been one of Ehlers's most significant competitors in the highlands.

Pachakutik's relationship with Ehlers deteriorated after the 1996 elections, and in 1998 Ehlers decided to run as the candidate of his own movement, the MCNP, rather than as the candidate of the MUPP-NP. After first considering several other candidates, including Rodrigo Borja, the former president and head of ID, and Paco Moncayo, the former head of the armed forces, Pachakutik opted to support Ehlers again in 1998, as did the CMS and the PS-FA. The indigenous movement's relationship with Ehlers was considerably frostier in 1998 than in 1996, however, and Ehlers's campaign complained that many indigenous organizations and leaders did not actively support him. Moreover, ID ran its own presidential candidate, Rodrigo Borja, in 1998, which further undermined Ehlers's support.[29]

For the 2002 elections, the indigenous movement was divided initially over whom to choose as its presidential candidate. Antonio Vargas, an Amazonian indigenous leader who was the former head of CONAIE, was determined to run and he established his own political movement to advance his candidacy with the support of CONFENAIE, the Amazonian indigenous federation. Many indigenous leaders, particularly in the highlands, distrusted Vargas, however, and they coalesced behind another indigenous candidate, Auki Tituaña, the mayor of Cotacachi. Efforts to unite behind a single candidate failed, and in July 2002, CONAIE asked both candidates to withdraw in order to preserve the unity of the movement. Tituaña dropped out of the race shortly thereafter, but Vargas continued his campaign, ultimately winning the endorsement of the Movimiento Independiente Amauta Jatari (MIAJ), a new indigenous electoral movement sponsored by FEINE, the evangelical indigenous organization.[30]

Pachakutik, CONAIE, and most other indigenous organizations declined to support Vargas, however. Instead, they threw their support behind Lucio Gutiérrez, a former military colonel who had joined with CONAIE in a 2000 uprising that brought down the government of Jamil Mahuad. Gutiérrez ran as the joint presidential candidate of Pachakutik and his own fledgling party, the Partido Sociedad Patriótica 21 de Enero (PSP). Some left-wing parties, namely the Movimiento Popular Democrático and a sector of the PS-FA, also endorsed Gutiérrez, although they were not official members of the

---

[29] ID did run in alliance with Pachakutik in the legislative elections in some provinces, as did the MCNP and DP.
[30] MIAJ subsequently changed its name to the Movimiento Independiente Amauta Yuyay.

alliance.[31] In addition, the Gutiérrez campaign won the support of the country's most important unions, associations of teachers and professionals, the organization of rural social security affiliates, the CMS, and various other social movements (Quintero López 2005, 115–16). Thus, in 2002, as in previous elections, the presidential candidate supported by Pachakutik had a diverse coalition behind him.

The efforts by Pachakutik to appeal to whites and mestizos largely paid off. As Figure 3.1 indicates, both Ehlers and Gutiérrez fared relatively well in mestizo-dominated areas, although they fared even better in indigenous areas. Indeed, in counties where the indigenous population represented a minority of the population, Pachakutik's presidential candidates won an average of 21.1 percent of the vote in 1996, 15.9 percent in 1998, and 26.7 percent in the first round of the 2002 presidential elections. More significant, both Ehlers and Gutiérrez won most of their votes in mestizo-dominated counties, which were more numerous and more populous than the indigenous majority counties. In the 1996, 1998, and 2002 elections, Ehlers and Gutiérrez won approximately three-quarters of their total vote in counties where the self-identified indigenous population represented less than ten percent of the total population. Survey data also indicate that Pachakutik's presidential candidates fared well among whites and mestizos. According to the 2004 LAPOP survey, Gutiérrez won approximately thirty-two percent of the vote of people who self-identified as mestizo and a similar percentage of the vote of people who self-identified as white in the first round of the 2002 elections.[32] He fared even better among self-identified indigenous voters, winning approximately fifty-eight percent of their votes, but indigenous people represented only a small portion of his total voters. Nearly ninety percent of the people who reported voting for Gutiérrez self-identified as white or mestizo, roughly equivalent to their share of the population in this survey.

Pachakutik did not fare quite as well in mestizo areas in the legislative elections. In counties where indigenous people represent a minority of the population, Pachakutik and its allies won 6.3 percent of the vote for provincial deputies in 1996, 7.4 percent in 1998, and 12.1 percent in 2002, as Figure 3.2 shows. Nevertheless, most of Pachakutik's votes in the legislative elections came from these areas. Indeed, in the 1996 and 1998 legislative elections for national deputies, Pachakutik and its allies won almost three-quarters of its votes in counties where the indigenous population represents less than ten percent of

---

[31] The leadership of the PS-FA had originally agreed to support Gutiérrez, but most leaders threw their support to León Roldós once he announced his candidacy.

[32] These figures should be regarded with some caution because the 2004 LAPOP survey was taken almost two years after the 2002 elections. In this survey, 40.2 percent of those people who remembered which candidate they voted for reported casting their votes for Gutiérrez in the first round of the 2002 elections. In fact, Gutiérrez actually won 20.6 percent of the valid vote in the first round: It is common in postelection surveys for more respondents to report having voted for the winner than actually did.

the total population. According to the 2001 LAPOP survey, eighty-three per-cent of the people who reported voting for Pachakutik's legislative candidates in 1998 self-identified as white or mestizo and only fifteen percent self-iden-tified as indigenous. Similarly, the 2004 LAPOP survey found that eighty-six percent of the people who reported voting for Pachakutik in the 2002 legisla-tive elections self-identified as white or mestizo, whereas only fourteen percent self-identified as indigenous.[33]

By contrast, Antonio Vargas and the MIAJ, which pursued a more ethnona-tionalist approach, fared relatively poorly in non-indigenous areas.[34] Vargas won 6.6 percent of the vote in majority indigenous counties in the 2002 presi-dential elections, but less than one percent in those counties where the indigen-ous people represented a minority of the population. As a result, he finished dead last out of eleven candidates. The MIAJ fared even worse in the 2002 legislative elections when it won less than 0.5 percent of the total vote and failed to capture a single seat. The party did not even field candidates in the legislative elections in most of the mestizo-dominated provinces. In contrast to Pachakutik, the MIAJ largely eschewed alliances, although it did ally with the populist Partido Roldosista Ecuatoriano (PRE) in one province. One leader of the MIAJ said: "We don't want alliances with non-Indian parties. They aren't going to give us the same treatment, the place that belongs to us. They are going to signal with the finger what we have to do. We can't go back" (Andrade 2003, 124). Instead, the MIAJ nominated indigenous candidates and relied mostly on its base within the indigenous movement, and this strategy generated meager results outside a few of the FEINE's strongholds.

PACHAKUTIK'S POPULIST APPEALS

Another key to Pachakutik's success in winning votes among whites and mes-tizos as well as indigenous people was its traditional populist rhetoric and platform. Populism has been a recurrent phenomenon in Ecuador, and many leaders, from José María Velasco Ibarra to Abdalá Bucaram, have employed populist appeals to win votes (de la Torre 2000, 2004; Freidenberg 2003). Pachakutik's presidential candidates, like earlier populist leaders in Ecuador, used a combination of personalistic, anti-establishment, nationalist, and state interventionist appeals to woo voters. They directed these appeals primarily at the popular sectors, which they made the focus of their electoral campaigns.

---

[33] In both 1998 and 2002, a much larger percentage of the indigenous population than the white or mestizo population voted for Pachakutik's legislative candidates. According to the 2001 LAPOP survey, Pachakutik won twenty-eight percent of the vote of the self-identified indig-enous population in the 1998 elections, but only four percent of the self-identified white and mestizo population. Data from the 2001 LAPOP survey on voter behavior, like data from the 2004 LAPOP survey, should be regarded with caution, however, because the 2001 poll was taken three years after the 1998 elections.

[34] One of the mestizo leaders of Pachakutik went so far as to accuse Vargas of being anti-mestizo (interview with Barrera 2005).

These appeals succeeded in attracting many voters who were discontent with the traditional parties and their record of governance.

For its 1996, 1998, and 2002 electoral campaigns, Pachakutik deliberately chose independent and well-known presidential candidates who had no ties to the traditional parties.[35] These candidates used personalistic appeals extensively in their election campaigns. Ehlers, for example, was well-known for his television show and his journalistic exposés, and his campaign revolved to a large extent around his telegenic personality (Sánchez-Parga 1999, 396–7). Rather than campaign on his governing plan, Ehlers "promoted his persona, his characteristic as a non-politician, of being an 'ordinary person ...'" (Sánchez-Parga 1999, 397). Ehlers did not belong to a political party, nor did he seek to create one. Instead, he built a largely personalistic movement, the MCNP, to back his campaigns.

Gutiérrez similarly lacked a well-defined governing plan or platform on which to campaign (Quintero López 2005, 116–17). Rather, his campaign centered on his achievements in the military and his role in the overthrow of former president Jamil Mahuad. Like many populists, Gutiérrez presented himself as the savior of the nation. When asked why he wanted to be president, he replied:

First, because I love profoundly my country. What I did on the 21st of January in uniting myself to a popular rebellion in which I risked my military career, the tranquility of my family and even my life, speaks of the profound love I feel for my country. Second, because I feel completely trained [for the position]. In military life you acquire a lot of experience in administering human resources, economics.... I am a civil engineer, with degrees in administration and physical education. I have always been first [in my class]. Third, I believe that Ecuador needs a president with a new conception of administering the state.... We need a man with a new global way of thinking, someone who doesn't commit the errors of the past and thinks only in the positive. It's not time to curse the darkness, but rather to turn on the light, mark the path, and illuminate the destination. ("Lucio y las elecciones" 2002, 41)

Gutiérrez, like Ehlers, did not belong to an established party, but instead created his own movement, the Partido Sociedad Patriótica 21 de Enero, which he named after the date of his uprising. The PSP was a very weakly institutionalized party controlled by Gutiérrez along with a small circle of his closest friends and family members.

Both Ehlers and Gutiérrez focused their appeals to a large extent on the poor. During his 1996 and 1998 campaigns, Ehlers constantly toured marginal areas. He employed traditional populist techniques to try to win the support of these poorer voters, riding on mules and promising computers to everyone to bring them into the new information age (Sánchez-Parga 1999, 397). Gutiérrez similarly centered his campaign on the poor. "I have no ideology,"

---

[35] Ehlers had once been affiliated with Izquierda Democrática and was friendly with its leader, Rodrigo Borja, but he had no official role in the party.

he proclaimed. "My ideology is the desire to change the situation of the country, to struggle for the poorest" (Ibarra 2002, 28). He argued that "politicians should imitate Jesus Christ, because he came to serve the neediest" ("Lucio y las elecciones" 2002, 41).

Pachakutik's candidates for other positions also directed their appeals at the poor. They campaigned mainly in poorer regions of the country, developed numerous proposals to combat poverty, and recruited their leaders and candidates mainly from the poor sectors of the population. According to a study of the 1996 legislature, sixty-two percent of Pachakutik's legislative delegation came from the lower classes as opposed to only four percent of the legislators from the three other main parties, the PSC, the PRE, and the DP (Mateos Díaz and Alcántara Sáez 1998, 23).

Not surprisingly, Pachakutik's legislative candidates drew their votes principally from the poorer sectors of the population. According to the 2001 LAPOP survey, 80.4 percent of Pachakutik's votes in the 1998 legislative elections came from people who earned less than $200 per month, as opposed to only 57.9 percent of people who reported voting for other parties. Similarly, the 2004 LAPOP survey found that 58.6 percent of the people who reported voting for the PSP's and the MUPP-NP's legislative candidates in the 2002 legislative elections earned less than $200 per month, as opposed to 44.3 percent of people who reported voting for other parties. Gutiérrez also drew his support disproportionately from the poorer sectors of the population during his presidential campaign. According to the 2004 LAPOP survey, 53.7 percent of Gutiérrez's supporters reported that they had a monthly family income of less than $200, as opposed to 45.8 percent of people who reported voting for other candidates. Ehlers, however, actually fared worse among poorer voters. According to the 2001 LAPOP survey, only 55.0 percent of people who reported voting for Ehlers in 1998 had monthly earnings of less than $200, as opposed to 64.5 percent of people who reported voting for other candidates. This may be explained in part by Ehlers's roots in the middle- and upper-income sectors of Cuenca, which was his strongest bastion of support, as well as by the tepid support that Ehlers received in 1998 from the indigenous movement and population.

Another key facet of the campaigns of Ehlers and Gutiérrez was their anti-establishment appeals. Ehlers had broadcast exposés of political corruption as a journalist, and as a candidate he launched steady criticisms of the political elite. He regularly contrasted himself to the other main candidates by referring to himself as a nonpolitician and an ordinary citizen. Ehlers sought to overhaul Ecuador's existing political institutions, which he blamed in part for the country's problems. He called for a constituent assembly and he even went so far as to broadcast a television advertisement in which he declared that he was ready to dissolve congress "democratically" with the support of the people (Sánchez-Parga 1999, 398).

Gutiérrez had even stronger anti-establishment credentials than Ehlers, given his leadership of the uprising that overthrew Mahuad. On the campaign trail, he regularly denounced the traditional parties and other candidates in harsh terms. In one interview, he stated:

Those are the parties of the last century that have not elaborated anything new and have not been positive for democracy. I believe that, just as vaccines are obtained from the venom of vipers, our party emerges from the putrefaction of the [traditional] parties to give the Ecuadorian people an antidote. ("Lucio y las elecciones" 2002, 42) (*Sente* 2002, 42)

Like Ehlers, Gutiérrez supported overhauling the constitution, and he proposed a series of institutional reforms calling for the downsizing of congress and the de-politicization of the Constitutional Tribunal, the Supreme Court, the Supreme Electoral Tribunal, and other state organisms. He threatened to call a plebiscite in the event that congress blocked these measures "because 100 deputies cannot impose themselves on 12 million Ecuadorians" ("Gutiérrez dice sí al capital foráneo para el petróleo" 2002).

The leadership of Pachakutik also attacked the existing political elite in harsh terms. Macas, for example, declared that "since the beginnings of the life of the republic there has been a group that wants to end our country, fill their pockets and take advantage of our resources because they are demagogues and liars; because they are not sensitive to the problems of poverty of the people: because they are corrupt and have submerged the country in the most terrible crisis" ("Dr. Luis Macas: Barreré a los corruptos del Congreso" 1996). Pachakutik presented itself as an honest grassroots alternative to these parties, and it developed a strong anticorruption platform that stressed transparency, accountability, and permanent monitoring. Pachakutik presented this anticorruption platform as grounded in the indigenous principles of *ama shua*, *ama quilla*, and *ama llulla* (Do not lie, do not steal, and do not be lazy).

These personalistic and anti-establishment appeals were successful in large part because of the high levels of disenchantment with the traditional parties in Ecuador (Mejía Acosta 2002; Pachano 2007). Even before the emergence of Pachakutik, the traditional parties in Ecuador had been losing ground in elections, particularly in indigenous areas, and this support declined even more rapidly after Pachakutik's arrival. According to Latinobarometer surveys, only eighteen percent of the Ecuadorian population expressed trust in parties in 1996, and by 2001 this figure had declined to eight percent, the lowest of any Andean country (Verdesoto Custode 2005, 123). Surveys carried out by an Ecuadorian survey firm between December 1995 and August 1999 indicated even lower levels of support for the country's parties, with only six to nine percent of respondents expressing trust in them (Córdova C. 1999, 79).[36] The high levels of dissatisfaction with the traditional parties meant that it was more important to have an appealing candidate than a strong party and that political independence was prized. Indeed, according to one 2002 survey, seventy-six

---

[36] By contrast, trust in indigenous leaders fluctuated between thirty and forty-nine percent during this period (Córdova C. 1999, 79).

percent of voters said that they cared about the personal characteristics of the candidate, while only twenty-four percent said they cared what party the candidate belonged to ("El presidente ideal" 2002, 16–17).

Ehlers and Gutiérrez were able to capitalize on this disenchantment with their anti-establishment discourse. They won the support of many of the voters fed up with the political establishment. According to the 2001 LAPOP survey, 86.3 percent of people who reported voting for Ehlers in the 1998 presidential elections had low levels of trust (one to three on a seven point scale) in parties, as opposed to 77.2 percent of people who reported voting for other candidates. Similarly, 53.9 percent of people who reported voting for Ehlers in 1998 had little respect for Ecuadorian political institutions (one to three on a seven point scale), as opposed to 43.7 percent of Ecuadorians who said they voted for other candidates. Gutiérrez supporters, by contrast, showed only marginally lower levels of respect for political institutions and trust in parties than supporters of other candidates in the 2002 elections.[37] According to the 2004 LAPOP survey, 42.1 percent of people who reported voting for Gutiérrez had little respect for Ecuadorian political institutions, as opposed to 37.0 percent of people who reported voting for other candidates. And 80.1 percent of Gutiérrez's supporters had little trust in parties, compared with 79.5 percent of people who reported voting for other candidates. Nevertheless, it is clear from surveys taken at the time of the election that Gutiérrez was widely perceived as being independent from parties, which presumably helped in the elections ("Perfil de los candidatos" 2002, 7).

Pachakutik and its presidential candidates also took a strong stance against neoliberal policies and foreign intervention in Ecuador. The indigenous movement played an important role in the struggle against neoliberal policies during the early 1990s when it carried out various demonstrations against market-oriented reforms. CONAIE, for example, helped defeat a series of constitutional reforms proposed by President Sixto Durán Ballén, which would have cleared the way for privatization of the social security system, among other things. As a result of their vigorous opposition to these policies, the indigenous movement came to be seen as "the principal condensing force of resistance to structural adjustment" (Ibarra 2002, 28). When Pachakutik was formed, it took up this banner. In its declaration of principles, the party announced its "opposition to the neoliberal model and those who sustain it" and called for income redistribution, the strengthening of state enterprises, and a halt to privatization (Movimiento Unidad Plurinacional Pachakutik – Nuevo País 1998, 1). Pachakutik also adopted a highly nationalistic stance on many issues, opposing foreign debt payments, a free trade agreement with the United States, and the presence of a U.S. military base in Manta, Ecuador.

---

[37] These minor differences may stem from the fact that by the time the 2004 LAPOP survey was taken Gutiérrez had been in power for more than a year, which may have increased the respect his supporters had for Ecuadorian parties and political institutions.

Ehlers and Gutiérrez took up many of these same themes in their campaigns. Ehlers, for example, criticized the privatization policies of the Durán Ballén administration and promised to defend the rights of state employees. Gutiérrez, meanwhile, declared that he was going to form "a government of the people against neoliberalism" (Quintero López 2005, 142). As Zamosc (2004, 147) recounts, "since the coup, Gutiérrez had presented himself as a radical populist. He talked 'with rage' about the utter poverty of the masses, denouncing the foreign debt as a looting mechanism, and arguing that the dominant classes had surrendered national sovereignty. To counter these evils, he promised to reject the neoliberal model and wage war on corruption." After the first round of the 2002 election, however, Gutiérrez began to shift to the right. He traveled to the United States to meet with members of the Bush administration and the financial community, and subsequently announced that he would preserve the dollar as Ecuador's currency, sign an agreement with the IMF, and allow the United States to maintain its base in Manta. Once in office, he alienated Pachakutik and other left-leaning allies by naming market-oriented technocrats to key positions, maintaining close ties to the United States and international financial institutions, and implementing strict market-oriented policies.

Unfortunately, the LAPOP Ecuadorian surveys do not have any questions that allow us to directly assess the degree of nationalist or state interventionist views among Pachakutik supporters, but the surveys did ask participants whether they identified more with the left, the right, or the center. As we might expect, given the left's traditional association with nationalism and state interventionism in Latin America, people who supported Pachakutik's legislative candidates were significantly more likely to be on the left. According to the 2001 LAPOP survey, 50.1 percent of the people who reported voting for Pachakutik's legislative candidates in the 1998 elections identified themselves as being on the left (one to four on a ten point scale), as opposed to 26.5 percent of people who supported other parties. Voters who supported Ehlers and Gutiérrez were more likely to be centrists, however. According to the 2001 LAPOP survey, 53.9 percent of Ecuadorians who reported voting for Ehlers in the 1998 elections identified themselves as being in the political center (five to six on a ten point scale), as opposed to 46.5 percent of people who supported other candidates. Similarly, in the 2004 LAPOP survey, 53.5 percent of Gutiérrez's supporters identified themselves as centrists, as opposed to 44.9 percent of the people who reported voting for other candidates. This is not especially surprising, given that neither candidate explicitly identified with the left, although they allied themselves with various leftist parties and movements.

THE RISE AND DECLINE OF PACHAKUTIK

The combination of ethnic and populist appeals helped Pachakutik and the presidential candidates it supported fare surprisingly well in the initial elections in which they competed. In 1996, the party's presidential candidate,

Freddy Ehlers, finished third with 20.6 percent of the vote in the 1996 elections, a remarkable performance for an inexperienced candidate from a new and underfinanced party. In 1998, Ehlers lost ground, finishing fourth, but he still won 14.8 percent of the vote. Moreover, Pachakutik rebounded in 2002 when Lucio Gutiérrez finished first with 20.6 percent of the first round vote. This was the same share of the vote that Ehlers had won in 1996, but in 2002 it was enough to qualify Gutiérrez for the runoff election, which he won easily with 54.8 percent of the vote.

Pachakutik's legislative candidates also fared relatively well between 1996 and 2002. In 1996, they won 10.8 percent of the vote in the elections for national deputies and 7.1 percent of the vote for provincial deputies, giving them a total of eight deputies in the national legislature. In 1998, their share of the vote declined slightly: They won 9.2 percent of the vote in the elections for national deputies and 5.3 percent of the vote for provincial deputies. They again won eight deputies in an expanded national legislature, however. Moreover, Pachakutik bounced back in the 2002 elections, capturing 7.9 percent of the vote and ten seats in the elections of provincial deputies that year.[38] (In 2002, there were no elections for national deputies.) Pachakutik also fared quite well in the municipal and provincial elections in which it competed during this period, winning dozens of mayoralties and municipal councilmember positions as well as some provincial prefect and councilor positions.

Thus, in a relatively short period of time, Pachakutik established itself as a major political actor in Ecuador. It also demonstrated a considerable degree of electoral stability between 1996 and 2002, unusual for any party in Ecuador but particularly surprising for a new party. In recent decades, Ecuador has had one of the highest levels of electoral volatility in Latin America and numerous parties have come and gone (Madrid 2005a, 6; Mustillo 2007; Payne et al. 2002, 132).

At least a couple of factors, however, prevented Pachakutik from becoming a dominant party like Bolivia's MAS. First, as we have seen, ethnic demographics are not nearly as favorable for indigenous parties in Ecuador as in Bolivia. Indigenous parties have consistently fared best among self-identified indigenous people and ethnically proximate groups. Pachakutik, like the MAS, was able to draw some support from mestizos and, even, whites, but its relatively small indigenous base inhibited its growth.

Second, Pachakutik faced tougher competition from leftist and populist parties than did the MAS in Bolivia. In each election between 1996 and 2002, Pachakutik had to contend with important populist or leftist candidates and parties. In the 1996 election, for example, long-time populist leader Abdalá Bucaram won the support of many poor and anti-establishment voters who might have otherwise supported Ehlers. In the 1998 election, Ehlers faced competition not only from Alvaro Noboa, a wealthy businessman who ran as the

---

[38] In all of these legislative elections, Pachakutik ran in alliance with other parties in some of the districts in which it competed.

candidate of Bucaram's populist party, the Partido Roldosista Ecuatoriano, but also from two center-left candidates, Jamil Mahuad of Democracia Popular and Rodrigo Borja of Izquierda Democrática, with strong parties and long political biographies. Each of these candidates made inroads among traditional populist constituencies, winning the support of many anti-establishment and poorer voters who might have otherwise supported Ehlers. Finally, in the 2002 election, Gutiérrez faced stiff competition from two populist candidates: Alvaro Noboa, who this time ran as the candidate of his own party, Partido Renovador Institucional Acción Nacional (PRIAN); and Jacobo Bucaram, the brother of Abdalá Bucaram, who ran as the candidate of the PRE. In addition, two center-left candidates, Borja of ID, and León Roldós, who ran as an independent, also won the support of many poor and anti-establishment voters. Thus Pachakutik's presidential candidates were not the only ones that successfully used populist appeals during this period.

Nevertheless, before 2006, Pachakutik and its presidential candidates fared relatively well in spite of the difficult competition that they faced. In the 2006 elections, however, the party suffered a stunning setback. Its presidential candidate, Luis Macas, won a mere 2.2 percent of the valid vote and he finished a distant sixth. Pachakutik fared somewhat better in the legislative elections in which it won 4.1 percent of the vote and six seats, but this, too, represented a sharp decline from 2002. Moreover, Pachakutik has performed even worse in elections held since that time.

The decline of Pachakutik in recent years has stemmed in large part from the party's shift away from ethnopopulism. In the run-up to the 2006 elections, Pachakutik abandoned the inclusive alliance-oriented strategy that it had pursued previously and shifted in a more ethnonationalist direction. Whereas in previous elections it had nominated well-known white/mestizo personalities from outside of the indigenous movement as its presidential candidates, in the 2006 elections, it nominated one of its own indigenous leaders. Pachakutik also put forth fewer white and mestizo candidates for other positions, and, partly as a result, many of the party's mestizo leaders and organizations abandoned it. At the same time, the effectiveness of the party's nationalist, state interventionist, and anti-establishment appeals was undermined by its initial participation in the Gutiérrez administration and strong competition from other populist candidates.

In the wake of the 2002 electoral victory of Lucio Gutiérrez, Pachakutik assumed an important role in the new government, causing some of its leaders to even speak of a "co-government." Gutiérrez gave four cabinet posts to leaders of Pachakutik, including the ministry of foreign relations (Nina Pacari) and the ministry of agriculture (Luis Macas). In all approximately fourteen percent of all government appointments went to members of Pachakutik, according to a study by Ecuadorian newspaper *El Comercio* (Beck and Mijeski 2006, 12).[39] Nevertheless, tensions between Gutiérrez and Pachakutik emerged

---

[39] Miguel Lluco (2005, 130) claimed that according to the agreement Pachakutik had made with Gutiérrez, thirty percent of government appointments were supposed to go to Pachakutik.

quickly in large part because of the new president's shift to the right. In the wake of the elections, Gutiérrez appointed a conservative economist as minister of the economy, signed an austerity agreement with the International Monetary Fund, and pursued close relations with the United States. Leaders of Pachakutik, meanwhile, voiced frequent criticisms of Gutiérrez's policies and complained of being marginalized from decision making. In August 2003 when Pachakutik's congressional delegation refused to support one of his bills, Gutiérrez called an end to the alliance and asked all of Pachakutik's political appointees to resign.[40]

The alliance with Gutiérrez, even though it was short-lived, had several negative effects on Pachakutik and the indigenous movement. First, it undermined Pachakutik's populist credentials. Pachakutik's willingness to tolerate and, in some cases, even support the Gutiérrez administration's policies tarnished its reputation as the country's most important opponent of neoliberalism and U.S. intervention. Partly as a result, other parties were able to capture much of the anti-establishment and anti-neoliberal vote in subsequent elections. Second, the alliance worsened regional and religious fissures within the indigenous movement, which Gutiérrez sought to exploit. From the outset of his tenure, Gutiérrez had sought to build his own base of indigenous support. He created a new indigenous organization, established a new indigenous advisory group, and developed his own clientelist networks in some indigenous areas in spite of the objections of CONAIE (Beck and Mijeski 2006, 13–14). After the rupture with Pachakutik, Gutiérrez redoubled these efforts. He pursued closer ties with the Amazonian and evangelical indigenous organizations; he appointed Antonio Vargas, the estranged former head of CONAIE, as the minister of social welfare; and he issued a decree that allowed the president to name the head of the Consejo de Desarrollo de las Nacionalidades y Pueblos del Ecuador, the agency that coordinated state programs for the indigenous population, without consulting with CONAIE (Beck and Mijeski 2006, 18–20; Zamosc 2004, 149–50). All of these measures helped divide the indigenous movement between those who supported Gutiérrez (many of the Amazonian and evangelical organizations) and those who opposed him (most of the highlands organizations).

Perhaps the most important impact of the alliance with Gutiérrez was that it soured many indigenous leaders on alliances and helped lead to Pachakutik's disastrous decision to nominate an internal candidate for the 2006 elections. Pachakutik had initially leaned toward running in alliance with Rafael Correa, the populist former minister of the economy who was the presidential candidate of a new movement called Alianza País.[41] At Pachakutik's Extraordinary

---

[40] For a discussion of Pachakutik's alliance with Gutiérrez, see Barrera (2004); Zamosc (2004); León (2005); and Beck and Mijeski (2006).

[41] Correa actively sought the support of Pachakutik. In one interview, he argued that the alliance made sense because "we have much affinity. I have even advised the indigenous movement. I am an *indigenista* in the good sense of the term." See Zeas (2006, 225).

Congress of April 2006, the majority of Pachakutik's delegates voted to form an alliance with Correa, including representatives of fourteen of the twenty-two provincial organizations and the Confederation of Rural Social Security Affiliates ("Pachakutik va en alianza: Rafael Correa es su primera opción" 2006). Nevertheless, a significant sector of the indigenous movement, including the leadership of CONAIE and ECUARUNARI, was opposed to such an alliance in part because of the problems that had occurred with previous alliances (interviews with Miranda 2007 and Talahua 2007).

In addition, some indigenous leaders believed that it was time for the movement to put forward an indigenous presidential candidate. From the outset, Pachakutik's inclusive strategy had generated debate within the party. Some indigenous leaders opposed the inclusion of whites and mestizos in the party, particularly in top leadership positions. As Carlos Sucuzhañay, a national deputy from Pachakutik, put it, "there are indigenous comrades who do not understand the need to have a plurinational party. They want to exclude mestizos" (interview with author 2007). Similarly, Shiram Diana Atamaint, another member of Pachakutik's legislative delegation, acknowledged: "There are different groups, different ways of thinking. Some are radical. Some believe that we [indigenous people] should be first in everything, although [Pachakutik] is a plurinational organization. Others say no, that we must be open" (interview with author 2007).

In the run-up to the 2006 elections, the more ethnonationalist faction of the party seized the upper hand. At a May 2006 meeting of Pachakutik's political council, the leadership chose to ignore the previous vote in Pachakutik's congress and named Luis Macas as the party's presidential candidate.[42] According to Ramsés Torres, the head of Pachakutik's legislative delegation, "The ethnocentric cradle [of Pachakutik] wanted to find out how many we were in truth – how many votes we could win with our candidates" (interview with author 2007). Macas and other Pachakutik leaders continued to discuss the possibility of allying with Correa and other leftist parties, but the negotiations failed to prosper largely because of disagreements over who should be the presidential candidate. In June 2006, Macas and Pachakutik proposed the holding of primaries to choose the candidate, but Correa rejected this proposal on the grounds that there was insufficient time. Correa, in turn, proposed carrying out a survey to evaluate who was the more popular candidate, but Pachakutik rejected this idea. As a result, in 2006 Pachakutik ran its own presidential candidate for the first time.

Not only did Pachakutik's effort to ally with Correa run aground in 2006, but it also failed to establish an alliance with any of the other leftist and populist parties. Moreover, many of the mestizo-dominated unions and organizations that had supported Pachakutik in past elections abandoned the party in the run-up to the 2006 elections in part because of concerns about the

---

[42] Macas easily prevailed over Auki Tituaña, the mayor of Cotacachi, who sought the nomination for a second time ("Luis Macas es el candidato de Pachakutik a la Presidencia" 2006).

growing dominance of the ethnonationalist faction within Pachakutik (Beck and Mijeski 2006, 17). The unions of teachers, oil workers, and electrical workers, for example, all linked up with other parties and movements in 2006, as did some urban organizations, such as the Urban Forum, and peasant and indigenous organizations like FENOCIN. Fernando Buendía, a former member of Pachakutik, explained the decision of some peasant organizations to leave Pachakutik by arguing that "the agenda of the movement only responds to the interest of the indigenous communities ... in Pachakutik they only speak of indigenous education, indigenous health and there is no space for peasant proposals" ("La desintegración de Pachakutik continua" 2005).

In 2006, the party also nominated fewer mestizo candidates and leaders than it had in the past (interviews with Atamaint 2007; Talahua 2007; and Torres 2007). Whereas Pachakutik's legislative delegation had traditionally included various mestizos, after the 2006 elections, all but one of its national deputies were indigenous. Ramsés Torres, the only mestizo in Pachakutik's 2007–2011 legislative delegation, attributed the absence of mestizo candidates to leadership errors, noting that: "There are indigenous leaders who have a perspective that is very ethnic and not pluralistic" (interview with author 2007). Similarly, Miguel Lluco, a long-time Pachakutik leader, observed that "the comrades believe that Pachakutik has to be a reference only for Indians or at least led by Indians" ("Pachakutik se requesbraja por el indigenismo" 2005). Some prominent mestizo leaders, such as Augusto Barrera and Virgilio Hernández, left the party specifically because of concerns about its growing ethnocentrism. In announcing his departure, Barrera said that "there is a clearer tendency to see Pachakutik as a space for the political representation of the indigenous movement, which is a legitimate aspiration, but in our judgment, a broader and more diverse project is necessary" ("Pachakutik pierde su fuerza urbana" 2005). Thus, Pachakutik increasingly resembled an exclusionary ethnic party, rather than the ethnopopulist party it had traditionally been.

Pachakutik's failure to establish an alliance with Correa meant that it faced significant competition from him for the anti-establishment and anti-neoliberal vote.[43] The Pachakutik deputy, Raúl Ilaquiche, argued that the party had problems in 2006 because "the discourse of Correa was similar to Pachakutik: the nationalization of natural resources, the struggle against the TLC, to not increase prices etc.... all the themes were gathered from Pachakutik" (interview with author 2007).[44] Similarly, another Pachakutik deputy maintained that: "What Correa is leading is not his invention. It comes from the social and indigenous movements. The proposal of a Constitutional Assembly et cetera, comes

---

[43] The early frontrunner in the campaign was León Roldós, the former Socialist Party leader who ran as the candidate of Izquierda Democrática and a new movement called Red Ética y Democrática, but Roldós gradually lost ground to Correa, who employed much more radical populist rhetoric.

[44] For a discussion of Correa's 2006 campaign, see Conaghan (2011) and de la Torre and Conaghan (2009).

from us.... He has our image and discourse" (interview with Miranda 2007).[45] Correa attracted the support of some politicians, like Barrera and Hernández, who had previously been members of Pachakutik as well as many of the labor unions and civil society organizations that had previously backed Pachakutik. Moreover, Correa forged an alliance with the PS-FA, which enhanced his credibility on the left. Correa even made some ethnic appeals, describing himself as an *indigenista* and speaking Quichua on the campaign trail.[46]

Pachakutik also faced a surprising degree of competition from Lucio Gutiérrez's Partido Sociedad Patriótica. Gutiérrez, who had been ousted from the presidency in a largely middle class uprising in 2005, originally sought to run as the PSP's presidential candidate in 2006. The Supreme Electoral Tribunal barred him from running, however, so he proposed his brother, Gilmar Gutiérrez, instead. During the campaign, the PSP capitalized on the strong ties that it established to numerous indigenous leaders and organizations during Gutiérrez's administration. It also benefited from Gutiérrez's neopopulist discourse and policies. Although Gutiérrez had embraced some neoliberal policies, such as free trade and dollarization, during his tenure in government, he accompanied these measures with traditional populist rhetoric and policies. He denounced the political establishment and boosted government spending in poorer areas, especially rural zones, in an effort to win support. The Gutiérrez administration, for example, established a poverty subvention payment that Gilmar promised to double during his campaign. One leader of the indigenous community explained Gutiérrez's strong performance in indigenous areas by noting that, "Gutiérrez gave away food, picks and shovels for two years to the communities. The people became accustomed to the giveaway" (Vaca and Muñoz 2006).

Pachakutik thus lost votes to both Correa's Alianza País and Gutiérrez's PSP in the 2006 presidential elections. The party fared particularly poorly in non-indigenous areas where its ethnonationalist profile and lack of ties to mestizo organizations and leaders undermined its performance. Macas won only 2.8 percent of the vote in cantons where self-identified indigenous people were in the minority. Even in indigenous areas, however, Macas's electoral results were a disappointment. He won only 15.9 percent of the vote in counties where the self-identified indigenous population represented a majority.[47] By contrast, Gutiérrez won an astonishing 42.1 percent of the vote in these counties, while

---

[45] The similarity between Correa's proposed policies and Pachakutik's policies led one leader of Pachakutik to say that the voters "didn't reject Pachakutik's proposals. Pachakutik's proposals won" (interview with Quishpe 2007). Similarly, a leading pollster argued that "Correa stole [from Pachakutik] the rhetoric of the struggle against the traditional parties" (interview with Babar 2007).

[46] Correa studied Quichua and practiced it during a year-long stint at a Catholic mission in a rural highlands community.

[47] Pachakutik's legislative candidates fared somewhat better than its presidential candidate, winning twenty-eight percent of the votes in areas where the self-identified indigenous population represented a majority.

Correa won 14.6 percent. According to a parish-level analysis by Báez Rivera and Bretón Solo de Zaldívar (2006, 22–3), Macas finished first in twenty-one highlands parishes where the indigenous people represented at least twenty percent of the population, whereas Gutiérrez won fifty-seven of these parishes and Correa won twenty-seven of them.[48] Outside of the highlands, Macas fared even worse, winning only eleven parishes in the Amazon and only two on the coast (Báez Rivera and Bretón Solo de Zaldívar 2006, 22–3).

Nevertheless, the winner of the first round of the 2006 elections was neither Correa, nor Gutiérrez, but rather Alvaro Noboa of PRIAN, who picked up 26.8 percent of the vote largely on the strength of his performance on the coast. Correa, who fared well on the coast as well as in the highlands and the Amazon, finished second with 22.8 percent of the vote, while Gutiérrez, whose support was confined mostly to highlands and the Amazon, came in third with 17.4 percent of the vote. In the second round of the elections, Pachakutik and most of the left-wing parties threw their support behind Correa. The PSP did not endorse either candidate, but Correa worked hard to win over the voters who had backed Gutiérrez in the first round, promising various populist measures including increases in poverty bonds, housing programs, and electrical and telephone subsidies for the poor (de la Torre 2006, 74; Recalde 2007, 21). Correa also tried to assuage those sectors of the population that feared his radical policies by promising that he would maintain the dollar as Ecuador's currency in spite of his misgivings about it (Recalde 2007, 21). Correa's efforts paid off, as he easily won the second round with fifty-seven percent of the vote. He fared particularly well in indigenous areas, winning 73.6 percent of the vote in counties where the indigenous represent the majority of the population.

Since the 2006 elections, Correa has consolidated his control of the country. In 2007, he convoked elections for a constituent assembly in which his party triumphed, winning almost seventy percent of the votes for parties. He then used his majority in the constituent assembly to rewrite the constitution, which was approved by a large majority in a referendum in September 2008. The new charter expands the powers of the presidency and allows Correa to serve for two more terms, enabling him potentially to stay in power until 2017. As called for in the constitution, new presidential and legislative elections were held in 2009. Correa triumphed in these elections, winning fifty-two percent of the presidential vote: the first time any candidate had won a majority of votes in the first round since the return to democracy in 1979. Correa's party also won fifty-nine of the 124 seats in the legislature. Lucio Gutiérrez and the PSP finished in second place with twenty-eight percent of the presidential vote and nineteen seats in the legislature.

Pachakutik, meanwhile, has continued its decline. It is now more dominated than ever by indigenous leaders and demands, and it has been unable to regain

---

[48] Macas won an average of 18.3 percent of the vote in parishes where indigenous people represented at least twenty percent of the vote, as opposed to 49.6 percent for Gutiérrez and 23.5 percent for Correa (Báez Rivera and Bretón Solo de Zaldívar 2006, 22–3).

the support of the mestizo voters, leaders, and organizations that formerly backed the party. Correa, with whom Pachakutik has had an often contentious relationship, has won over most of the party's former mestizo supporters with his populist appeals, but other parties, including the PSP, have also made inroads. In the 2007 elections for the constituent assembly, Pachakutik won less than one percent of the vote for parties, which earned it only four seats. Pachakutik did not even nominate a candidate for the 2009 presidential elections, and it captured only 1.4 percent of the vote and four seats in the 2009 legislative elections. The party's support is now confined mostly to certain indigenous areas in the highlands and even there it faces tough competition from Correa and Alianza País and Gutiérrez and the PSP, both of which have maintained close ties to some indigenous organizations and leaders outside of CONAIE. Latin America's first major indigenous party is now only a shell of its former self.

CONCLUSION

Pachakutik's shift away from ethnopopulism toward a more ethnocentric approach has thus been an unmitigated disaster for the party. As we have seen, Pachakutik's inclusive ethnic and populist appeals played a crucial role in the surprising success of the party in the late 1990s and early 2000s, and the abandonment of this inclusive strategy, along with intense competition from other populist leaders and movements, hurt Pachakutik considerably beginning in 2006. The party now has little support in white and mestizo areas, and even in indigenous areas it has lost a lot of ground.

Ethnopopulism has not disappeared from Ecuadorian electoral politics, however. Other Ecuadorian politicians and parties, including Correa and Gutiérrez, have adopted many of Pachakutik's ethnopopulist strategies, although they have emphasized populist more than ethnic appeals.

Moreover, as Chapter 6 discusses, Pachakutik has helped transform Ecuadorian politics in other important ways. The most impressive changes have come in the area of political representation. Pachakutik was the first Ecuadorian party to nominate indigenous people for important political positions, but many other parties have followed its example. As a result, indigenous people now regularly serve as mayors, prefects, national legislators, and government ministers in Ecuador, whereas prior to the 1990s, they rarely did. Pachakutik's advocacy of indigenous issues has also paid off. Many of the traditional demands of the indigenous movement, from multicultural education to the recognition of Ecuador as a plurinational state, have been achieved. Progress has even been made in addressing ethnic discrimination and inequality in the last decade, although much remains to be done. A variety of actors have helped realize these achievements, but Pachakutik has played a crucial role in placing these issues on the policy agenda. Thus, Pachakutik has left an enduring mark on Ecuadorian politics that far outshines its electoral achievements.

4

Ethnopopulism without Indigenous Parties in Peru

> I am a symbol of every one of you ... we are not going to lose this opportunity for
> the cholos. Our turn has arrived, that is not anti-anybody, but rather pro-us.
>
> Alejandro Toledo in a 1994 campaign speech

Peru, like Bolivia and Ecuador, has some of the key ingredients necessary for
the success of indigenous parties. Specifically, it has a large politically and economically marginalized indigenous population with only weak attachments to
the existing political parties. This population, along with some other sectors of
the electorate, has expressed considerable dissatisfaction with the traditional
political parties and their economic policies in the last decade or so, and thus
we might expect it to be attracted to a party that combines ethnic and populist
appeals. Peru also has a long tradition of *mestizaje*, which has blurred ethnic
boundaries and reduced ethnic polarization, thus making it feasible for an indigenous party to win support across ethnic lines.

Surprisingly, however, no major indigenous party has emerged in Peru. As
we shall see, a large number of regional parties based in local indigenous or
peasant organizations have competed successfully in local elections. None of
these parties has been able to translate their local successes to the national
level, however.

Nevertheless, some politicians have effectively used a combination of ethnic and populist appeals to woo indigenous as well as non-indigenous voters,
and they have thus demonstrated the viability of ethnopopulism in Peru. These
politicians, namely Alberto Fujimori, Alejandro Toledo, and Ollanta Humala,
have used these appeals to capture the support of the majority of indigenous
voters in their presidential campaigns. Indeed, voters of indigenous descent
helped catapult all three of these politicians to the presidency.

Ethnic appeals, however, have been less central to the campaigns of these
Peruvian politicians than they have been to the campaigns of their counterparts
in Bolivia and Ecuador. None of these Peruvian leaders originated in the indigenous movement, nor did they recruit nearly as many indigenous candidates and
leaders as the MAS or Pachakutik. Instead, Fujimori, Toledo, and Humala all

relied more on populist than ethnic linkages to voters. These populist appeals enabled them to win support among diverse sectors of the electorate, but they have not (yet) been enough to establish enduring ties to indigenous voters.

This chapter proceeds as follows. The first section discusses local indigenous parties in Peru and why they have failed to scale up to the national level. It argues that the absence of major indigenous parties in Peru stems mainly from the weakness and fragmentation of the country's indigenous movement, rather than from institutional factors, as some scholars have argued. The second section shows how Fujimori, Toledo, and Humala used ethnic appeals in their presidential campaigns to attract disproportionate support from indigenous voters. The third section demonstrates how populist appeals played an even more important role in their electoral campaigns, helping them win the support of voters of all ethnicities. The conclusion briefly discusses the implications of the Peruvian case and the future prospects for ethnopopulism in Peru.

REGIONAL INDIGENOUS PARTIES

Over the last several decades, a large number of indigenous-based electoral movements have been formed at the local level in Peru. According to Paredes (2008, 18), the number of political groups with indigenous or peasant names competing in provincial elections rose from three in 1995 to seven in 1998 and fifteen in 2002, the vast majority of which were located in the southern highlands.[1] By my calculations, fourteen distinct movements with indigenous or peasant names competed in the 2006 provincial elections. These movements won an average of 14.8 percent of the vote in the eighty-three provincial elections in which they competed in 2002, and an average of 19.7 percent of the valid vote in the fifty-nine provinces in which they competed in 2006.[2] These figures, moreover, count only those movements competing in municipal elections in the provincial capitals: An even larger number of movements with indigenous or peasant names competed in elections in smaller, district municipalities in all of these years. As I discuss later in this chapter, some of the indigenous parties have been particularly successful, winning control of provincial or district municipalities. Nevertheless, none of these parties has yet managed to move up to the national level.

One of the first attempts at forming an indigenous-based party in Peru was undertaken in the mid-1990s when the most important Amazonian indigenous organization, the Asociación Interétnica de Desarrollo de la Selva Peruana (AIDESEP), created the Movimiento Indígena Amazónico del Perú (MIAP). In the 1998 municipal elections, the MIAP, supposed to be the electoral arm of the movement, won ten mayoralties on its own and a number of others in alliance

---

[1] By provincial elections, I mean municipal elections in the provincial capitals.

[2] Political movements with indigenous or peasant names won approximately three hundred and seventy-six thousand votes in provincial elections in 2002 and approximately three hundred and fifty-eight thousand votes in 2006.

with other parties (Aroca Medina 1999). The MIAP's success was short-lived, however. It was only able to register in one province on its own for the 2002 municipal elections, and it won no mayoralties there, although it did manage to win some offices elsewhere in alliance with other parties (Van Cott 2005, 174–5). Nor did MIAP fare any better in the general elections. MIAP participated in national congressional elections in the Amazon region in alliance with other parties in 2000 and 2001, but it did not manage to win any seats in those elections (Van Cott 2005, 175). The party subsequently changed its name to the Movimiento Intercultural Amazónico del Perú to try to appeal more broadly across ethnic groups, but this failed to reverse the party's decline (Huber 2008, 23; Quispe Lázaro 2007) (interviews with Lajo 2008 and Huber 2008).

Other indigenous-based parties have emerged in the Amazon in recent years. In 2002, for example, twelve indigenous mayors, who represented a variety of regional and national parties, won office in the Peruvian Amazon, and in 2006, fourteen representatives of indigenous communities were elected as provincial councilors (Huber 2008, 19–20). None of these parties competed in national elections, however. In the 2011 elections the head of AIDESEP, Alberto Pizango, sought to run for president as the candidate of a new indigenous party called the Alianza para la Alternative de la Humanidad (APHU). The movement's organizers, however, did not manage to register APHU as a party in time for the elections, and efforts by Pizango to forge alliances with other parties such as the Partido Fonavista del Perú and the Partido Nacionalista Peruano (PNP) foundered because of disagreements over the allocation of key candidacies. As a result, the Amazonian indigenous movement remained largely on the sidelines in the 2011 elections.

Another early effort to establish an indigenous-based party took place in the province of Angaraes in the department of Huancavelica in the southern highlands. In the early 1990s, the indigenous leaders of a number of peasant communities banded together with a group of unaffiliated professionals to form the Movimiento Independiente de Campesinos y Profesionales (MINCAP). The new party developed a strong *indigenista* discourse partly out of genuine conviction, but also because some of the professionals in the party were convinced that such a discourse would win votes (Durand Guevara 2006, 559). MINCAP finished third in the 1993 elections in Lircay, the provincial capital of Angaraes, and it might have won if many of the peasants of one district had not voted mistakenly for a party whose symbol resembled that of MINCAP but which did not even have a candidate in the race (Durand Guevara 2006, 553). After this defeat, the party regrouped and managed to win the 1998 municipal elections in the province, thanks in part to the inclusion of some indigenous authorities on its party list (Durand Guevara 2006, 555). Once in office, however, MINCAP split up in large part because of differences over the extent to which the party should emphasize an *indigenista* agenda. Some of the more *indigenista* leaders went on to found a new party, the Movimiento Rikcharisun Ayllu, which competed in the 2002 elections. The Movimiento Rikcharisun Ayllu finished third in the 2002 municipal elections in Angaraes, but it took away enough votes from MINCAP to prevent it from winning. MINCAP recovered from this defeat, however, and recaptured the mayoralty of Angaraes in the 2006 elections. Thus, it has established itself as an important regional indigenous-based party, albeit one whose strength is limited to just one province.

Other indigenous parties have sprung up elsewhere in the southern highlands in recent years. In the early 2000s, a party with a marked ethnic discourse, the Alianza Electoral Frente Popular Llapanchik, emerged in the province of Andahuaylas, located in the department of Apurimac. Seven provincial organizations founded Llapanchik, but the key role was played by the Frente de Defensa Regional Agrario de Apurímac which had spearheaded some regional protests against a drop in the price of potatoes in 2000 (Huber 2008; Pajuelo Teves 2006). The new party embraced an *indigenista* discourse from the outset, although this discourse co-existed with more traditional agrarian demands. Llapanchik fared quite well in the 2002 regional elections in Andahuaylas, winning the provincial capital as well as five of the eighteen districts (Huber 2008, 15). In the 2006 regional elections, the party again won the provincial capital and five districts in Andahuaylas, but it also managed to win enough support in other provinces in the department of Apurimac to get its candidate, David Salazar, elected regional president (Huber 2008, 109–12; Pajuelo Teves 2006). In spite of these successes, however, Llapanchik remains a predominantly Andahuaylas-based movement with some influence in neighboring provinces (Pajuelo Teves 2006, 109–10). Although leaders of Llapanchik have undertaken discussions about creating a broader indigenous party in Peru, those discussions have yet to bear fruit ("Regional Parties Make Gains at García's Expense" 2006, 13).

The coca growers' movement in Peru also has attempted to create its own party. In June 2006, a leader of the coca growers, Nelson Palomino, formed Kuska as the political arm of the coca growers' movement in the department of Ayacucho. Kuska did not manage to register in time for the November 2006 regional elections, so it formed an alliance with the Movimiento Independiente Tarpuy, a regional party that had fared relatively well in the 2002 elections (Huber 2008, 42–50). This new alliance participated in the 2006 regional elections under the name of the Movimiento Independiente Qatun Tarpuy and finished second in the department of Ayacucho, winning a couple of provincial mayoralties and fifteen district mayoralties (Huber 2008, 43, 49). Not surprisingly, the new alliance, which emphasized the defense of the coca leaf and, to a lesser extent, indigenous rights, fared particularly well in the coca growing districts, where all of the mayors it elected were coca grower leaders (Huber 2008, 47–9). The leaders of Kuska hoped to participate in the 2011 presidential elections, but they ultimately failed to register the party ("Is this the New Evo Morales?" 2007). The Movimiento Independiente Qatun Tarpuy, meanwhile, lost ground in the 2010 regional elections.

The region of Puno, located in the southern highlands on the border with Bolivia, is another area that has seen an increase in ethnic discourse by politicians in recent years. None of the local parties that have been founded specifically to promote indigenous rights and culture have had much success, however. One prominent local *indigenista* leader, Hugo Llano, tried to create an indigenous party, Sentimiento y Unidad por el Mundo Andino, but could not gather enough signatures to register for the 2006 regional elections (Huber 2008, 33). Another indigenous-based party, the Movimiento Andino Socialista, did manage to register for the 2006 regional elections and finished fourth in the region of Puno, but it did not win enough votes to maintain its registration (interview with Vilca 2008). In addition, a wide variety of local politicians, such as the current and past regional presidents David Jiménez and Hernán Fuentes, along with some mayors, such as Eugenio "Papalindo" Barbaito of Juli and Fortunato Calli of Ilave, have employed ethnic discourse at times (Huber 2008) (interview with Vilca 2008). These leaders have not sought to create an indigenous party per se, however, preferring to create personalist vehicles or affiliate with national or regional parties as it has suited their interests. In 2007, a few of the Aymara-speaking mayors did form an umbrella organization, the Unión de Municipalidades Aymaras, but this organization has done little in the face of personal and political differences among the mayors (Huber 2008, 40–1).

Thus, regional indigenous-based parties have sprung up throughout Peru in the last decade or so. These parties have enjoyed significant success in municipal and regional elections, but they have not managed to translate their local-level achievements to the national level. Indeed, most of them have not even sought to compete in national elections. The following pages discuss the causes of this surprising omission. As we shall see, some scholars have argued that the failure of these regional parties to compete in national elections in Peru is due mostly to institutional factors. This study, however, suggests that a more fundamental factor has been the absence of a powerful nationwide indigenous movement in Peru. Given the weakness and fragmentation of the Peruvian indigenous movement, it is no surprise that indigenous parties in Peru are weak and fragmented as well.

INSTITUTIONAL EXPLANATIONS

Some scholars have attributed the absence of national-level indigenous parties in Peru to institutional barriers to party formation at the national level (Rice 2006; Van Cott 2005). Van Cott (2005, 163) argues that obstacles to gaining access to the ballot have limited the possibilities for indigenous parties, noting that a "1979 law required parties to present a list of 100,000 *members* (less than 1 percent of the national electorate) to register, which must include voters in at least half of the country's districts" (emphasis added). She also notes that "obstacles to ballot access increased in Peru in 1995 when signature requirements increased for registering national parties from 100,000 to 480,000" (Van Cott 2005, 163).

The signature requirements have impeded some weak regional indigenous movements from forming parties, but the significance of these laws should not be exaggerated. First, the 1979 law refers not to members, but rather to adherents, and adherents are much easier to find than members.[3] As Blancas Bustamante (2005, 108) notes, in order to express his or her adhesion to a party, a citizen needed only to sign a form, which does not imply any commitment or legal relationship to a party. By contrast, membership implies a commitment or legal relationship, and thus laws that require parties to have a certain number of members are considerably more onerous. Second, the 1995 law was never rigorously enforced – parties frequently submitted fraudulent signatures and the Fujimori regime only challenged these signatures when it suited its own interests (Blancas Bustamante 2005) (interview with Tuesta 2008).[4] Moreover, the signature requirement was reduced from four percent to a much more manageable one percent in 2001 with the passage of Law No. 27505.

The most significant obstacle to gaining access to the ballot in Peru is not the signature requirement but rather the stipulation that parties demonstrate they have provincial committees composed of at least fifty members in one-third of the provinces and two-thirds of the departments of the country (Blancas Bustamante 2005) (interview with Tuesta 2008). Nevertheless, even this requirement, which has only been in force since the Law of Political Parties (Law No. 28094) was enacted in 2003, has not prevented numerous parties from being formed. In 2006 alone, twenty parties, many of which were formed only recently, participated in the presidential elections, and twenty-four parties participated in the congressional elections. In 2011, ten parties ran candidates for president and thirteen parties ran candidates for congress, including a number of new parties. Thus, registration requirements in Peru are hardly an insurmountable obstacle to party formation, although they are a significant impediment to local movements without a national base of supporters.

Another institutional explanation for the absence of a significant indigenous party in Peru focuses on the Fujimori regime's centralization policies. Van Cott (2005, 163), for example, argues that Fujimori "restrict[ed] the powers and resources of municipal governments and dismantled regional governments," thereby limiting the ability of indigenous parties to use local offices as a stepping stone to higher offices. This explanation is also problematic, however. Although the Fujimori administration eliminated regional governments, the regional governments were less likely than municipal governments to serve as an initial stepping stone for indigenous parties. Moreover, as Van Cott acknowledges (2005, 166), the regional governments were reinstated by the Toledo

---

[3] In recent presidential and legislative elections, a large number of parties have earned less than one percent of the vote, suggesting that many listed as adherents of these parties were not members or even firm supporters of the parties.

[4] The 1995 law was superseded by the 1997 Organic Law of Elections (Law No. 26589), which also called on parties to present a list of adherents that represented four percent of the national electorate.

administration in 2002. In addition, the Fujimori regime's policies toward municipal governments were more complicated than she suggests. Fujimori weakened the powers of the provincial municipalities, but he strengthened the authority of the district municipalities, which are predominantly rural and often largely indigenous (Barr 2002) (interview with Tuesta 2008). Thus, the Fujimori administration actually increased the importance of local offices likely to elect indigenous people.

Some scholars argue that the enactment of a quota law in 2002 has also served as an impediment to indigenous-based parties (Davila Puño 2005, 36–40; Htun 2004, 449; Rice 2006, 142; Van Cott 2005, 167). The 2002 Law of Regional Elections and a 2002 amendment to the 1997 Law of Municipal Elections required that a minimum of fifteen percent of the members of each political party's list of candidates in elections for regional and municipal councils come from "native communities." Van Cott (2005, 167) argues that these quotas "hurt fledgling indigenous parties because the major parties have a better chance of winning and, thus, of recruiting the most qualified indigenous candidates."[5] Similarly, Rice (2006, 142) argues that the quota law "has served to fracture and divide the Amazonian indigenous movement according to partisan interests, as potential indigenous candidates are aggressively wooed and co-opted by parties from across the ideological spectrum." The quota law, however, has been deemed applicable only to "native communities," which are located almost exclusively in the Amazon. The much more numerous Quechua- and Aymara-speaking highlands Indians were defined as belonging to peasant communities, rather than native communities, and they were therefore excluded from the quota. Thus, although the quota law may well have undermined indigenous parties in the Amazonian region, it has had no impact on the fortunes of indigenous parties in the highlands, where more than ninety percent of the indigenous population is concentrated.

Institutional factors thus can offer only a partial explanation for the absence of indigenous parties in Peru. The indigenous movement has faced some institutional obstacles to forming parties, but Peru's institutional environment is not clearly more inimical to the formation of indigenous parties than those of its neighbors. As we shall see, what distinguishes Peru from its neighbors is the weakness and fragmentation of the country's indigenous movement.

PERU'S WEAK INDIGENOUS MOVEMENT

Some scholars, most notably Van Cott (2005), have also attributed the absence of indigenous parties in Peru to the weakness and fragmentation of the country's indigenous movement. The Peruvian indigenous movement is fragmented into numerous organizations, none of which has a strong presence throughout

---

[5] Indigenous organizations had therefore pushed unsuccessfully for a law that would have set aside reserved seats for indigenous people, and not just positions on the party lists (Htun 2004; Rice 2006; Van Cott 2005).

the country. A plethora of organizations are active in the highlands and on the coast, but none of these commands the allegiance of more than a tiny fraction of the indigenous language-speaking population. Most of these organizations, moreover, have only recently begun to adopt an ethnic discourse and make ethnic demands. The situation in the Peruvian Amazon is somewhat different. There, a strong and relatively representative indigenous movement has emerged, which has consistently made ethnic claims over the last several decades (García and Lucero 2004; Greene 2006; Yashar 2005). Nevertheless, the Amazonian indigenous movement does not have any appreciable influence outside of the Amazon where the vast majority of the indigenous population is located. As a result, it has been unable to serve as the basis for a national indigenous party.

The oldest peasant confederation operating in Peru is the Confederación Campesina del Perú (CCP), which was founded in 1947. Although many of the CCP's members are Quechua- or Aymara-speaking, it has traditionally styled itself as a peasant, rather than an indigenous, organization, and only in recent years has it begun to employ ethnic discourse. The CCP, which had close ties to a variety of leftist parties, participated actively in the numerous peasant mobilizations that occurred in the 1950s, 1960s, and 1970s, but it lost impetus beginning in the 1980s in part because its leaders were targeted by the Shining Path and repressed by the military (Fernández Fontenoy 2000). The CCP currently claims to have nineteen departmental federations along with a number of sectoral federations, but it has an important presence only in the southern highlands and its membership base is quite limited (interview with Palacín 2008). Only 10,215 people claimed to be affiliated with the CCP in the 1994 agricultural census, out of the more than 1.75 million agricultural producers surveyed (Instituto Nacional de Estadística e Informática 1994).[6] The CCP also has few sources of income. Its member confederations no longer contribute regularly to the organization, which relies on occasional assistance from foreign aid agencies and other donors for support (interview with Gallo Carhuachinchay 2008).

A second peasant federation, the Confederación Nacional Agraria (CNA), was created by the military regime of General Juan Velasco Alvarado in 1974. With the sponsorship of the government, the CNA rapidly became the most important peasant confederation in the country, displacing the CCP (Fernández Fontenoy 2000, 204–5; Yashar 2005, 233).[7] Beginning in the 1980s, the CNA entered into a crisis in part because of the guerrilla violence, but also because it lost the support of the government after the overthrow of Velasco. Currently, the CNA has fifteen departmental federations, but it has even fewer members than the CCP. In the 1994 agricultural census, only 1,615 people identified themselves as belonging to the CNA (Instituto Nacional de Estadística

---

[6] The survey included both landed and landless peasant farmers.

[7] According to the CNA, at the outset, it had eighteen agrarian federations, 149 provincial agrarian leagues, and three thousand base organizations. See Confederación Nacional Agraria 2008.

e Informática 1994). The CNA has also suffered from considerable financial difficulties in recent years, which has curtailed its activities (interview with Huascar 2006).

A third indigenous-based organization, the Confederación Nacional de Comunidades del Perú Afectados por la Minería (CONACAMI), arose in the highlands in the late 1990s, and quickly surpassed both the CCP and the CNA in terms of its dynamism (García and Lucero 2004, 177–9; Van Cott 2005, 153). CONACAMI was formed to bring together under a single umbrella organization the different community organizations protesting environmental and health problems caused by mining activities, which had expanded under Fujimori. CONACAMI did not initially present itself as an indigenous organization, but it has done so increasingly over time, in part because most of the communities affected by the mining operations are Quechua-speaking (García and Lucero 2004, 178–9; Paredes 2006).[8] CONACAMI has grown steadily since its creation and, by 2008, it was active in eighteen regions and incorporated more than 1,650 base organizations (Palacín Quispe 2008, 86). Moreover, in recent years it has had a better track record than either the CCP or the CNA in soliciting assistance from a variety of foreign development organizations, including Oxfam (García and Lucero 2004, 179; Palacín Quispe 2008, 94). It has won a number of important victories in communities throughout the highlands, forcing private companies and the government to alter and, in some cases, eliminate their mining activities (Palacín Quispe 2008; Paredes 2006). Nevertheless, CONACAMI has yet to demonstrate that it can mobilize large numbers of people or that it has influence outside of the area of mining policy.

Another highlands peasant movement that has grown in power in recent decades is the movement of the coca growers. Cabieses (2004) estimated that there were fifty thousand coca growers in Peru during 2004, of which thirty-five thousand belonged to the most important federation of coca growers, the Confederación Nacional de Productores Agropecuarios de las Cuencas Cocaleras del Perú. Coca growers have aggressively fought efforts to eradicate their crops, and some of the leaders of the coca growers have recently embraced ethnic demands and discourse as well. The coca growers have demonstrated an ability to bring people into the streets, notably in a 2003 march on Lima and 2005 strikes across Peru, but they have been plagued by internal divisions that have reduced their clout (Durand Guevara 2005; Felbab-Brown 2006; "Cocaleros intentan volver a unirse" 2006, A24). Moreover, the grassroots influence of the coca growers is limited to a few isolated coca growing regions located far from the country's center of power (Durand Guevara 2005; Felbab-Brown 2006).

The strongest indigenous movement in Peru is located in the Amazon, where a number of organizations have emerged to represent the lowlands

---

[8] Paredes (2006), however, questions whether CONACAMI can form the basis for a powerful indigenous movement, noting that the communities involved in CONACAMI have diverse identities and they do not focus on ethnic demands.

indigenous population. The most important of these organizations, the Asociación Interétnica de Desarrollo de la Selva Peruana (AIDESEP), was founded in 1980 by several local federations. The Amazonian federations, unlike the CCP and the CNA, presented themselves as indigenous organizations from the outset and they have advocated a variety of ethnic causes (García and Lucero 2004; Greene 2006; Yashar 2005). During the late 1980s, conflicts within AIDESEP led some federations to break away and found a rival organization, the Confederación de Nacionalidades Amazónicas del Perú (CONAP). Nevertheless, AIDESEP continues to be the much larger of the two organizations and claims to represent fifty-seven federations and territorial organizations, covering thirteen hundred and fifty communities in which three hundred and fifty thousand people live (Asociación Interétnica de Desarrollo de la Selva Peruana 2009). CONAP, by contrast, claims thirty-five affiliated federations that represent a population of one hundred and fifty thousand (Van Cott 2005, 159). Like CONACAMI, AIDESEP has been relatively successful at raising funds from external donors for its projects and it has established a high international profile. It also has registered some success in resisting the government's efforts to open up the natural resources of the Amazon to commercial exploitation. The administration of Alan García, for example, was forced to backtrack on its Amazonian development plans in both 2008 and 2009 in the face of sometimes violent resistance by the followers of AIDESEP.

AIDESEP and other organizations have made efforts to unify the indigenous movement and create a national-level indigenous organization, but these efforts have so far been unsuccessful. Perhaps the most important attempt was the creation of the Conferencia Permanente de Pueblos Indígenas del Perú (COPPIP) in 1997. The CCP, CNA, AIDESEP, CONAP, and other organizations all participated in the founding of COPPIP, but tensions gradually emerged over who should lead the organization and how much it should cooperate with the government (Pajuelo Teves 2006, 74). These tensions ultimately led COPPIP to split up in 2002 (interview with Palacín 2008; interview with Lajo 2008). Another attempt to unify the indigenous movement was initiated in 2006 with the establishment of the Coordinadora Andina de Organizaciones Indígenas (CAOI). CAOI, which groups together not only the Peruvian indigenous groups but also organizations from Bolivia, Ecuador, Chile, Argentina, and Colombia, is led by Miguel Palacín, the founder of CONACAMI (Coordinadora Andina de Organizaciones Indígenas n.d.). CAOI only recently began to operate, however, so it is too soon to know whether it will be able to bring together the fragmented Peruvian movements.

Thus the indigenous movement in Peru continues to be relatively weak and divided. As a result, it lacks the organizational resources that enabled its counterparts in Bolivia and Ecuador to create parties that could compete on the national level. It has no national network of activists, not much access to the national media, and only minimal material resources. Nor does it have much in the way of organizational legitimacy or even name recognition to lend to a party. This has made it difficult for it to create and sustain a nationally competitive indigenous party.

ETHNICITY AND ETHNIC APPEALS IN PERU

Although no party based in the indigenous movement has emerged at the national level, several important politicians in Peru have used ethnic appeals to win support from indigenous voters. Alberto Fujimori was the first major presidential candidate in Peru to make significant ethnic appeals, but these appeals were used even more widely by Alejandro Toledo and, most recently, by Ollanta Humala.[9] None of these candidates were indigenous leaders per se, nor were their parties based in the indigenous movement. Consequently, they did not focus on ethnic appeals nearly as much as the leaders of the MAS in Bolivia or Pachakutik in Ecuador, both of which originated in the indigenous movement and have indigenous leaders. Nevertheless, ethnic appeals were an important part of the efforts of these Peruvian politicians to attract voters of indigenous descent.

Fujimori, Toledo, and Humala employed a variety of ethnic appeals. Some of these appeals were symbolic. For example, all three leaders recruited numerous indigenous and cholo candidates to their campaigns, and they contrasted their own ethnic backgrounds with those of their competitors. They also donned indigenous clothing, used indigenous sayings and languages, and invoked indigenous cultural symbols. Other appeals were more substantive. Toledo, Humala, and, to a lesser extent, Fujimori embraced many of the traditional demands of the indigenous movement, calling for education in indigenous languages, indigenous territorial rights, and the elimination of discrimination. In all of their appeals, however, Fujimori, Toledo, and Humala were careful to be inclusive. They avoided exclusionary language and policy proposals, they maintained an ethnically diverse leadership, and they developed broad and inclusive platforms.

The ethnic landscape in Peru and, in particular, the country's high level of *mestizaje*, has made this inclusive strategy feasible. From the outset of the colonial period in Peru, there were frequent, often coercive, sexual relationships between Spanish colonists and the native indigenous population.[10] This intermixing led to the emergence of a mestizo population, which gradually

---

[9] Some other national politicians and parties also have made ethnic appeals in recent years, but they have not been nearly as successful as Fujimori, Toledo, and Humala. For example, Ciro Gálvez Herrera, a Quechua-speaking intellectual and lawyer from Huancavelica who has developed an eclectic *indigenista* philosophy, founded his own party, Renacimiento Andino, in 1996. Renacimiento Andino is little more than a personalist electoral vehicle for Gálvez. It does not have much of an organization, nor does it have close ties to any indigenous or peasant movement, and it has fared poorly in the various elections in which it has competed (interviews with Torres 2008, Huber 2008, and Lajo 2008).

[10] This intermixing grew to include immigrants from other regions (e.g., Africa and Asia) as well as their descendants.

became dominant in Peru. As elsewhere in the region, social and economic pressures helped drive the process of *mestizaje* in Peru. Over the course of the twentieth century, numerous indigenous immigrants migrated from the countryside to the cities in search of jobs. In the face of widespread social and economic discrimination, many of these indigenous immigrants and their children abandoned indigenous practices and customs. Government policies also encouraged *mestizaje*. The government of Juan Velasco Alvarado, for example, reclassified indigenous people in the highlands as peasants and created new local authorities that undermined traditional ones (Remy 1995, 115–16).[11] The penetration of Spanish-language education into the countryside, meanwhile, led to the decline of indigenous languages in many areas. The percentage of Peruvians who identified an indigenous tongue as their maternal language in the census declined from fifty-one percent in 1940 to thirty-six percent in 1961, twenty-eight percent in 1972, twenty-four percent in 1981, and eighteen percent in 2006 (Instituto Nacional de Estadística e Informática 2007, 94–7; Pajuelo Teves 2006, 43).

Mestizaje had several important consequences for Peru. To begin with, it significantly reduced the relative size of the indigenous population in Peru. Most Peruvians came to identify themselves as mestizo. Indeed, the 2006 census found that fifty-eight percent of the population self-identified as mestizo, while only twenty-seven percent identified with some indigenous category (Instituto Nacional de Estadística e Informática 2007, 94–7).[12] The decline in the proportion of indigenous people in Peru meant that no party could win in national elections with indigenous votes alone. This was especially true prior to the 1980 elections when many indigenous people could not vote because of literacy requirements. As a result, parties and politicians have had strong incentives to reach out beyond ethnic lines.

Mestizaje also has made it easier for parties to reach across ethnic lines by reducing ethnic polarization. Although ethnic discrimination is widespread in Peru, ethnic relations are generally harmonious and ethnic conflict is rare. Peru did experience an intense internal conflict during the 1980s and early 1990s that devastated indigenous areas in the highlands and, to a lesser degree, the Amazon. Approximately three-quarters of the victims of this conflict were indigenous. Nevertheless, the conflict was driven by ideology rather than ethnicity. Indeed, both the military and the Shining Path guerrillas were multi-ethnic and neither side presented its struggle in ethnic terms. The country has experienced

---

[11] Velasco also carried out important agrarian reforms and made Quechua a second official language in Peru.

[12] According to the 2006 census, 57.6 percent of the population above twelve years of age self-identified as mestizo, 22.5 percent as Quechua, 2.7 percent as Aymara, 1.7 percent as Amazonian indigenous, 4.8 percent as white, 1.5 percent as black or mulatto, and 9.1 percent as other (Instituto Nacional de Estadística e Informática 2007, 110). The precise wording of the 2006 census question was: "According to your ancestry and your customs, do you consider yourself: 1) Amazonian indigenous; 2) Of Quechua origin; 3) Of Aymara origin; 4) Of black, mulatto or zambo origin; 5) Of mestizo origin; 6) Of white or Caucasian origin; 7) Other."

a few incidents of ethnically related violence since then, such as the 2009 conflict at Bagua in which thirty-four police officers and indigenous protestors were killed, but these incidents have been relatively uncommon, and they have not led to widely generalized ethnic tensions. The low level of ethnic polarization in Peru has meant that ethnic demands and appeals do not typically alienate those Peruvians who do not have indigenous roots. Indeed, many whites and mestizos have supported ethnopopulist leaders in Peru.

Mestizaje has also made it easier for parties and politicians to reach across ethnic lines by blurring the boundaries between members of different ethnic groups. As de la Cadena (2000) has shown, many Peruvians who self-identify as white or mestizo have not abandoned their indigenous identities altogether. These so-called indigenous mestizos, who are often popularly referred to as cholos, typically speak indigenous languages or practice some indigenous customs. They also usually have some degree of ethnic consciousness and may even identify with their ethnolinguistic group, although they are reluctant to identify as Indian or indigenous because of the social stigma attached to these terms. Many of these so-called indigenous mestizos have thus been receptive to the ethnic appeals of Peruvian politicians, as long as those appeals are made in an inclusive manner.

Both self-identified indigenous people and indigenous mestizos are disadvantaged socioeconomically and are frequently the subject of discrimination. A clear social hierarchy prevails in Peru in which people of European descent and appearance are located at the top and people of indigenous background and appearance are located at the bottom. Various surveys have found that Peruvians who speak indigenous languages are more likely to report having personally experienced discrimination and to believe that ethnic discrimination is widespread (Paredes 2007; Sulmont Haak 2005). People who speak indigenous languages also tend to be poorer than non-indigenous language speakers and have less access to education and healthcare. In 2000, for example, sixty-three percent of indigenous households fell under the poverty line, as opposed to only forty-three percent of non-indigenous households (Trivelli 2005, 17). Thus people of indigenous descent in Peru have numerous grievances, which they may act upon in the ballot booth.

Although indigenous people have not had the option of voting for indigenous parties or candidates in presidential elections in Peru, they have had the possibility of voting for candidates from ethnically proximate groups and against candidates from ethnically distant groups. Neither Fujimori, nor Toledo, nor Humala self-identified as indigenous, nor did they run as the candidates of indigenous parties. Nevertheless, they were all relatively dark-skinned, ethnic outsiders who were seen as more ethnically proximate to the indigenous population than their principal competitors. Toledo and Humala, for example, were both clearly of indigenous descent and were of highlands origins, while their main competitors in 2001 and 2006 represented the white Lima elite. Fujimori is a more complicated case because he is of Japanese origin and is therefore not in an ethnic group that one would normally think of as ethnically proximate to the indigenous population. Nevertheless, in the 1990 elections Fujimori effectively played on resentment of the white Lima elite, which his main competitor, Mario Vargas Llosa, embodied. Moreover, as we shall see, Fujimori, Toledo, and Humala all sought to enhance their attractiveness to indigenous and cholo voters by recruiting many candidates of indigenous descent and making direct ethnic appeals.

THE EMERGENCE OF THE INDIGENOUS VOTE

The use of ethnic appeals in national electoral campaigns in Peru is a relatively recent phenomenon. Until the 1980s, most of the indigenous population could not vote because of the literacy requirements imposed in 1896 after the War of the Pacific (Paredes 2008, 5). As a result, presidential candidates initially had little reason to make ethnic appeals. It was only after the 1978 constitution granted suffrage to illiterates that the indigenous population became an important part of the electorate.[13] In the wake of this reform, which also lowered the voting age from twenty-one to eighteen years of age, voter turnout in indigenous areas soared. The number of votes cast in majority indigenous provinces rose by an average of 145 percent between the 1978 constituent assembly elections – the last elections to have literacy restrictions – and the 1980 presidential elections. By contrast, in provinces where the indigenous population represented a minority, the number of votes cast increased by only forty-six percent on average.[14]

As the indigenous population became a more important part of the electorate, parties began to woo indigenous voters more aggressively. During the 1980s, however, the main parties such as the Partido Aprista Peruano, commonly known as APRA; Acción Popular (AP); and the Partido Popular Cristiano (PPC), largely eschewed ethnic appeals in favor of class-based, personalistic, and clientelist appeals. Ethnic demands, such as indigenous land and water rights, affirmative action programs, and bilingual education, were largely absent from the party programs and agenda of the main parties.[15] Indeed, the main parties mostly avoided the use of the terms *Indian* or *indigenous* altogether, referring to the indigenous population as *peasants* and seeking to appeal to them as such. Furthermore, the national parties, typically based in Lima, recruited few people with indigenous backgrounds as candidates or for leadership positions within the parties. Less than five percent of congressional

---

[13] Approximately 23.5 percent of the population above eighteen years of age was ineligible to vote in 1978, mainly because of literacy requirements. In some heavily indigenous departments, such as Apurímac, Ayacucho, Huancavelica, Huánuco, and Puno, more than thirty-five percent of the population above eighteen years of age was ineligible to vote (Medina García 1980, 85–6).

[14] The number of people registered to vote rose by 137 percent in majority indigenous provinces and by forty-four percent in minority indigenous provinces between 1978 and 1980. Voting in Peru is compulsory and registration is automatic for those eligible to vote.

[15] See, for example, the platforms of AP, APRA, and the PPC presented in Centro de Investigación de la Universidad del Pacífico (1980).

representatives and less than ten percent of provincial mayors had indigenous last names during the 1980s (Paredes 2008, 12).

Leftist parties, which had a long tradition of organizing among the highlands indigenous peasantry and close ties to indigenous and peasant organizations, did make some ethnic appeals during this period. In its 1985 governing plan, Izquierda Unida (Izquierda Unida 1985, 66) called for the "defense of the rights of Native and Peasant Communities concerning the natural resources on their territory" and the "immediate official recognition of the lands of the peasant and native communities that are still not recognized and the authorization of the corresponding titles."[16] Various leftist parties also called for the protection and teaching of indigenous languages and customs (Centro de Investigación de la Universidad del Pacífico 1980; Izquierda Unida 1985, 125). In addition, the leftist parties recruited people of indigenous extraction for some positions within their parties. Nevertheless, the vast majority of the leaders of the leftist parties were white or mestizo, and these parties focused principally on class-based rather than ethnic appeals.

FUJIMORI'S ETHNIC APPEALS

It was not until the 1990 campaign of Alberto Fujimori that ethnicity became a major issue in a presidential election. Although Fujimori largely avoided explicit ethnic appeals, he benefited from and exploited Peru's ethnic divides (Boggio et al. 1991, 22–3; Carrión 1997, 286–7; Degregori 1991). In the 1990 campaign, supporters of Vargas Llosa, including his spokesperson, questioned how someone of Japanese descent whose parents were not born in Peru could become president (Reyna Izaguirre et al. 2004, 54).[17] As an immigrant, an ethnic minority, and an outsider, however, Fujimori had more in common than did Vargas Llosa with the indigenous in the highlands and the cholo migrants who populated the poor neighborhoods in the cities (Roberts 1995, 94). Fujimori's campaign slogan, "a president like you," took advantage of this, effectively contrasting him to the wealthy, fair-skinned, and aristocratic Vargas Llosa (Carrión 1997, 286–7; Degregori 1991). Fujimori's ticket in 1990 as well as in subsequent elections also included many more dark-skinned people than the traditional parties had typically included, leading Fujimori to describe the 1990 campaign as a contest between "*blanquitos*" and "*un chinito y cuatro cholitos*" (Carrión 1997, 287; Levitsky 1999, 82).[18] Moreover, some of these indigenous people and cholos occupied important places on the ballot. For

---

[16] Another left-leaning party that made ethnic appeals during this period was the Frente Nacional de Trabajadores y Campesinos (FRENATRACA), which was a highly personalistic party based in Puno (Planas 2000, 155–6; Taylor 1987). FRENATRACA, which called for the establishment of a socialist Tahuantinsuyo (the name of the Incan empire), fared well in its base and some neighboring regions, but never established a national presence.

[17] Vargas Llosa denounced the racist statements and actions of some of his supporters. See Reyna Izaguirre et al. (2004, 54) and Vargas Llosa (1994).

[18] Even though Fujimori is of Japanese descent he was popularly referred to as "el chino" or "el chinito."

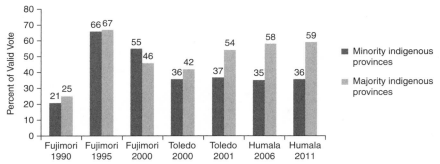

FIGURE 4.1. Mean provincial vote in first round of Peru's presidential elections, 1990–2011.
Source: Oficina Nacional de Procesos Electorales

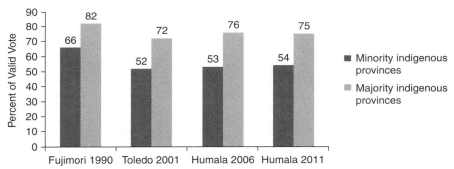

FIGURE 4.2. Mean provincial vote in second round of Peru's presidential elections, 1990–2011.
Source: Oficina Nacional de Procesos Electorales

example, Fujimori's first vice president, Máximo San Román, was a successful, dark-skinned, Quechua-speaking entrepreneur from Cusco, and Fujimori used him extensively in his campaign.[19]

Fujimori's ethnic appeals reaped benefits. As Figures 4.1 and 4.2 show, Fujimori fared particularly well in indigenous areas in the first and second rounds of the 1990 elections. Indeed, during the second round of the 1990 elections he won an astonishing 81.5 percent of the vote in provinces where the majority of the population grew up speaking an indigenous language, as opposed to sixty-six percent in other provinces.[20] Table 4.1 analyzes the extent

[19] San Román later broke with Fujimori and went on to run for president in 2000 as the candidate of the Unión por el Perú, finishing dead last. In the 2006 regional elections, he ran for governor of Cusco as the candidate of the Movimiento Regional Inka Pachakuteq, but came in second.

[20] Fujimori's ethnic appeals in this election were helped by the fact that Vargas Llosa represented an easy target for ethnic as well as class resentment. As one Peruvian woman said: "There is so much racial and social class discrimination that people don't want a cake-eater to govern them" (Boggio et al. 1991, 22).

TABLE 4.1. *The Correlates of the Provincial Vote Share for Selected Peruvian Presidential Candidates, 1990–2006*
(Ordinary Least Squares regression models)

	Constant	Indigenous / Total Population	Poor / Total Households	Summary Statistics
Vote for Fujimori in 1990 1st round	.762*** (.098)	.162*** (.040)	−.672*** (.116)	R² = .216 N = 138
Vote for Fujimori in 1990 2nd round	.592*** (.066)	.217*** (.024)	.053 (.077)	R² = .389 N = 164
Vote for Fujimori in 1995 1st round	.522*** (.066)	.0003 (.025)	.158* (.077)	R² = .026 N = 186
Vote for Fujimori in 2000 1st round	.433*** (.055)	−.173*** (.028)	.155* (.067)	R² = .174 N = 194
Vote for Toledo in 2000 1st round	.554*** (.057)	.161*** (.028)	−.251*** (.068)	R² = .151 N = 194
Vote for Toledo in 2001 1st round	.253*** (.058)	.251*** (.029)	.114 (.069)	R² = .391 N = 194
Vote for Toledo in 2001 2nd round	.339*** (.054)	.295*** (.027)	.173** (.065)	R² = .517 N = 194
Vote for Humala in 2006 1st round	.144** (.053)	.340*** (.026)	.200** (.064)	R² = .594 N = 195
Vote for Humala in 2006 2nd round	.222*** (.054)	.303*** (.027)	.328*** (.065)	R² = .586 N = 195
Vote for Humala in 2011 1st round	.274*** (.073)	.345*** (.036)	.059 (.087)	R² = .401 N = 195
Vote for Humala in 2011 2nd round	.453*** (.052)	.330*** (.026)	.058 (.062)	R² = .541 N = 195

Note: Standard errors in parentheses
* p < .05; ** p < .01; *** p < .001

to which the proportion of the population that grew up speaking an indigenous language and the proportion of households that are poor can explain the provincial-level vote for various presidential candidates between 1990 and 2006.[21] As the table indicates, the proportion of the population that grew up speaking an indigenous language had a statistically significant positive impact on Fujimori's share of the vote in the 1990 elections, even controlling for the size of the poor population in each province.[22] Other things being equal, each

[21] For ease of interpretation, these statistical analyses were performed using Ordinary Least Squares. Using a Tobit model does not appreciably change the results.

[22] For the analyses of the 1990 and 1995 elections, I use data from the 1993 census on the proportion of the population that grew up speaking an indigenous language. I measure the size of the poor population in each province as the proportion of households in the lowest socioeconomic group according to this same census. For the 2000, 2001, and 2006 elections, I use data from the

ten percent increase in the proportion of the population that speaks an indigenous language boosts Fujimori's share of the provincial vote by 1.6 percentage points in the first round and 2.2 percentage points in the second round of the 1990 elections.

Ethnic appeals played a much smaller role in Fujimori's subsequent campaigns, however. Fujimori continued to make symbolic appeals to indigenous people and other ethnic minorities: As president, he often donned a poncho and visited rural highlands communities to inaugurate public works. But these ethnic appeals represented only minor aspects of his campaign strategies, which, as we shall see, focused on more traditional populist and performance-based appeals. Meanwhile, Fujimori's electoral base, which was already fairly heterogeneous in 1990, became even more heterogeneous in subsequent years, as he won broad support among the wealthier and whiter sectors of the population that had supported Vargas Llosa in 1990 (Sulmont Haak 2009). Fujimori remained quite popular in indigenous and poor areas, but he did not fare appreciably better in these areas than in others, as Figures 4.1 and 4.2 illustrate. In fact, Fujimori actually fared worse in majority indigenous provinces than in minority indigenous provinces in the 2000 elections when he faced stiff competition for the indigenous vote from Alejandro Toledo. Moreover, as Table 4.1 shows, once we control for the size of the poor population in each province, the proportion of the provincial population that grew up speaking an indigenous language has no significant impact on Fujimori's share of the vote in the 1995 and 2000 elections.

TOLEDO'S ETHNIC APPEALS

In the 2000 elections, it was Alejandro Toledo, rather than Fujimori, who made extensive ethnic appeals. Toledo, who has strongly indigenous features and whose family came from the indigenous highlands, made his own ethnicity central to his campaigns. Toledo had first used ethnic rhetoric during his unsuccessful 1994–5 campaign for president, pronouncing at one point that "I am a symbol of every one of you ... we are not going to lose this opportunity for the cholos. Our turn has arrived, that is not anti-anybody, but rather pro-us" (Anonymous 1994). He continued to present himself as a cholo during his 2000 and 2001 presidential campaigns and crowds at his 2000 rallies would often chant "*Cholo sí, Chino no!*" (García and Lucero 2004, 11). Toledo also invoked numerous indigenous symbols, wearing indigenous clothing, using the *chakana*, an Incan cross, as the party's logo, and referring to himself as Pachacútec (Barr 2003, 1164; García and Lucero 2008; García

2007 census on the proportion of the population that grew up speaking an indigenous language and the proportion of households in each province that lack a refrigerator. The indigenous proportion variables are highly correlated (Pearson = .989), as are the poor household variables (Pearson = .918). The indigenous proportion and poor household variables are somewhat correlated with each other in 1993 (Pearson = .394) and 2007 (Pearson = .486).

Montero 2001, 77). After the 2001 election, he even held an inauguration ceremony at Machu Picchu, which included some traditional indigenous ceremonies and symbols. Throughout the campaigns, Toledo's Belgian wife, Eliane Karp, also made ethnic appeals, at times in Quechua, on Toledo's behalf. Karp argued that ethnicity did make a difference in the 2000 election, stating that the relationship between Toledo and the electorate was "love at first sight. I can't deny that there is an ethnic factor, a brutal identification [with him]" (Relea 2000, 8).[23]

Toledo also formed alliances with a number of peasant and indigenous organizations, including the Confederación Campesina del Perú, which is the oldest peasant federation operating in Peru. Indeed, the CCP participated to such an extent in his electoral campaign that one leader of the CCP referred to it as the fundamental base of Toledo (interview with Gallo 2008). In addition, he recruited numerous people of indigenous descent to his campaign, including some important indigenous and peasant leaders. According to Paredes (2008, 10), twenty-one percent of the candidates and thirty-eight percent of the people elected to congress from Toledo's party, Perú Posible, had indigenous names. This represented an impressive seventy percent of the total members of congress with indigenous names during the 2001–6 legislative session. Perhaps the most prominent indigenous leader affiliated with his campaign was Paulina Arpasi, the Aymara-speaking secretary general of the CCP from the department of Puno. After she was elected to congress, Arpasi presented herself as the legislature's representative of indigenous people, stating: "I think it is not only necessary that *indígenas* know that they have a representative in the National Congress, it is also very important that the National Congress knows that it has within a representative of the *indígenas*. I will change neither my indigenous dress, nor my constant defense of the rights of the indigenous peoples of Peru" (Quoted in García and Lucero 2004, 173).[24]

Toledo's ethnic appeals helped him considerably in 2000 and, especially in 2001. In both elections, Toledo fared much better in indigenous areas than in non-indigenous areas. In 2000, for example, Toledo won 42.3 percent of the vote in provinces where the majority of the population grew up speaking an indigenous language, whereas he won only 36.2 percent of the vote in other provinces. Toledo might have done even better in indigenous areas if Fujimori had not retained support among the many indigenous and poor people who had benefited from his administration's social programs. In 2001, against weaker competition, Toledo swept indigenous areas, winning 53.9 percent of the vote in majority indigenous provinces in the first round and 71.7 percent in the second round. As Table 4.1 indicates, in 2000 and 2001, the percentage of

---

[23] After becoming president, Toledo appointed Karp as director of a new governmental indigenous institute, the Comisión Nacional de Pueblos Andinos, Amazónicos y Afroperuanos (CONAPA). Karp's tenure as the head of CONAPA was controversial – she was accused of politicizing the institute and trying to control the indigenous movement among other things – and she resigned in 2003 (García and Lucero 2004, 173–4; Pajuelo Teves 2006, 72–80).

[24] Arpasi, however, was later accused by many indigenous leaders of abandoning their cause.

the population that grew up speaking an indigenous language is a statistically highly significant determinant of the provincial vote for Toledo, even controlling for the wealth of the province. Other things being equal, each ten percent increase in the percentage of the population that is indigenous boosts Toledo's share of the provincial vote by 1.6 percentage points in the 2000 elections, 2.5 percentage points in the first round of the 2001 elections, and 3.0 percentage points in the second round of the 2001 elections.

HUMALA'S ETHNIC APPEALS

In the 2006 elections, it was a newcomer to electoral politics, Ollanta Humala, who exploited Peru's ethnic divides most successfully. Many of Humala's ethnic appeals were implicit. His name, his appearance, and his family background conveyed his Andean origins and contrasted him to the other two principal candidates in the 2006 elections, Alan García and Lourdes Flores, who are relatively light-skinned and hail from the coast. Moreover, both Humala's first and last names are Quechua. Indeed, as Humala noted in an interview, he was named after the commander in chief of the armies of Incan leader Pachacuti (Fregosi 2007, 8). Throughout his campaign, Humala also frequently invoked traditional indigenous symbols. The logo of Humala's party, the Partido Nacionalista Peruano, was a traditional Incan clay pot and his campaign rallies and materials often included the rainbow-colored indigenous flag. At campaign rallies, Humala would sometimes don indigenous garb and speak phrases in Quechua.

Humala also sought to appeal to indigenous people and cholos by naming many people of indigenous descent as candidates for important positions. According to Paredes (2008, 11), in 2006 thirteen percent of the congressional candidates of Union por el Perú had indigenous surnames. (Humala ran on the ticket of the UPP because the PNP did not register in time for the elections). By contrast, only six percent of the candidates of APRA, the UPP's main rival in the elections, had indigenous last names. Moreover, many of these indigenous leaders occupied places high on the UPP's ticket which enabled them to be elected to the legislature. For example, Hilaria Supa and María Sumire, two indigenous leaders from Cusco, both won seats in congress representing Humala's ticket, as did Juana Huancahuari, an indigenous peasant leader from Ayacucho. Nevertheless, most of the party's congressional representatives as well as its overall leadership were white or mestizo.

Humala did not forge alliances with many peasant or indigenous organizations prior to the first round of the presidential elections, but some of these organizations, such as the Confederación Nacional Agraria and sectors of Confederación Campesina del Perú, supported him in the second round (interviews with Aguirre 2006, Gallo Carhuachinchay 2008, and Lerner 2006). Humala did strike an alliance with the coca growers, and two of their leaders, Nancy Obregón and Elsa Malpartida, were elected to the Peruvian congress and the Andean parliament, respectively, on Humala's ticket. He also recruited the support of many former soldiers of indigenous descent (Caballero Martín 2006; Panfichi 2006). Humala's brother, Antauro, had helped organize these former soldiers earlier in the decade and many of them subsequently joined Ollanta's campaign.

Humala did not make ethnic demands central to his campaign, but he did include them in his discourse and platform. His governing plan, for example, called for the recognition of Peru as a multicultural country, endorsed multicultural education and the use of indigenous languages in the military and government offices, and demanded the legitimization and incorporation of traditional practices of indigenous medicine and justice (Humala Tasso 2006, 70–1). Humala also frequently denounced the ethnic discrimination and inequalities that still exist in Peruvian society and extolled the virtues of Peru's indigenous population. In one 2006 speech, for example, he noted that during his time in the army he never encountered soldiers with European-origin surnames of wealthy Peruvians but only people with indigenous names: "There was only Huamán, Quispe, Condori … they are the true Peruvian people" (Caballero Rojas 2006).

Like Fujimori and Toledo, Humala was careful to avoid exclusionary ethnonationalist appeals. In Humala's case, however, this task was complicated by the fact that his immediate family members often engaged in ethnonationalist rhetoric. Humala's father, Isak, had developed a radical ethnonationalist ideology dubbed *etnocacerismo*, which proclaimed the superiority of what he called the copper-colored race.[25] In an interview with the *Washington Post*, Isak Humala acknowledged his ethnonationalist views: "We are racists, certainly. We advocate saving the copper race from extinction, disintegration and degeneration." Ollanta's brother, Antauro, had sought to spread this philosophy through his organizing efforts in the highlands of Peru and has also published various articles and books outlining his ideas.[26] Ollanta had previously seemed to endorse this philosophy as well, but during the campaign he sought to distance himself from the more radical and intolerant actions and statements of his family members. Instead, he emphasized the inclusive nature of his campaign, proclaiming in his governing plan that "we represent a historic multicultural movement …" (Humala Tasso 2006, 18). Ollanta presented himself as a nationalist rather than an ethnonationalist. For example, in response to a question about the compatibility of Aymara nationalism and Peruvian nationalism, Humala was unequivocal, stating that, "There is only one nationalism and it should include different nationalities in a single project. Here we cannot speak of different racial identities" (Acevedo and Vilca Arpasi 2007).

Ollanta's father, Isak, and his brother, Antauro, meanwhile, declared their support for another brother, Ulises, who endorsed their ethnonationalist

---

[25] The term *etnocacerismo* makes reference to General Andrés Avelino Cáceres, who led indigenous Peruvian troops against the Chilean military in the War of the Pacific (1879–83).

[26] Antauro Humala's views are spelled out in his books (Humala Tasso 2001, 2007), as well as in an interview with him by Pedraglio and Paredes (2003).

ideology. Ulises ran for president in 2006 as the candidate of a small party, Avanza País, and Antauro ran for congress on the ticket of this same party.[27] As we might expect given the nature of ethnic identity in Peru, Ulises's ethnonationalist rhetoric failed to resonate among Peruvian voters and he won a mere 0.2 percent of the national vote.

Ollanta Humala's inclusive ethnic appeals, by contrast, proved effective. Indeed, Humala fared even better in indigenous areas than Toledo did. In the first round of the 2006 elections, Humala won 58.3 percent of the vote in provinces where a majority of the population grew up speaking an indigenous language, as opposed to only 35.2 percent in other provinces. He did even better in the second round, winning 75.7 percent of the vote in majority indigenous provinces. Humala maintained this strong performance in indigenous areas in the 2011 elections, winning 58.5 percent of the vote in majority indigenous provinces in the first round and 75.1 percent of the vote in these provinces in the second round. As Table 4.1 indicates, the percentage of the population that speaks an indigenous language is a highly statistically significant determinant of the provincial vote for Humala in both 2006 and 2011, even controlling for the level of poverty in the provinces. According to these models, a ten percentage point increase in the proportion of the population that is indigenous would lead to a 3.4 percentage point increase in Humala's share of the vote in the first round of the 2006 elections and a 3.0 percentage point increase in the second round in 2006. Similarly, a ten percentage point increase in the size of the indigenous population would lead to a 3.5 percentage point increase in Humala's share of the vote in the first round of the 2011 elections and a 3.3 percentage point increase in his share of the vote in the second round of these elections.

Survey data show that Humala won the support of members of all the main ethnic groups in Peru in the 2006 elections, but he fared best among people who self-identify as indigenous or grew up in a home where an indigenous language was spoken. According to the 2006 LAPOP survey, in the second round of the elections, Humala won sixty-three percent of the vote of self-identified indigenous people, forty-three percent of the vote of self-identified mestizos, and thirty-one percent of the vote of people who self-identify as white.[28] People who self-identify as mestizo accounted for seventy-eight percent of Humala's

---

[27] By this time, Antauro was in jail because of his leadership of an assault by former soldiers on a police station in Andahuaylas in which four police officers and two former soldiers died. In this protest, Antauro unsuccessfully called for the resignation of President Toledo, the minister of defense, and the head of the army, but he chose to surrender after the police officers were killed. Ollanta claimed to have no knowledge of his brother's actions, but at the time Antauro indicated he was acting on his brother's orders. Ollanta, who was in South Korea at the time, initially released a statement supporting the uprising.

[28] The LAPOP 2006 Peru survey was taken shortly after the election and like most postelection surveys it overstates the support for the winner (García) and understates the support for the runner up (Humala). Whereas 42.5 percent of the survey respondents reported voting for Humala in the second round and 57.5 percent reported voting for García, Humala actually won 47.4 percent of the valid vote and García won 52.6 percent (Carrión et al. 2006, 157).

votes (which is roughly equivalent to their share of the total population), but forty-three percent of these mestizos grew up in a home where an indigenous language was spoken.[29] Overall, Humala won sixty-one percent of the vote of people who grew up in a home where an indigenous language was spoken, as opposed to only thirty-three percent of the vote of people whose parents only spoke Spanish at home. He fared best among those people who had the most exposure to indigenous languages. Humala won seventy-three percent of the vote of those people whose parents only spoke indigenous languages, sixty-eight percent of the vote of those people who reported that an indigenous language was their first language, and fifty-six percent of the vote of those people who reported that an indigenous language was spoken in their household when they were growing up but that it was not their first language. Approximately forty-eight percent of Humala's total votes came from people who grew up in an indigenous language-speaking household, even though they represent only about one-third of the Peruvian population. Thus, the LAPOP data suggest that Humala's ethnic appeals were successful in attracting people of indigenous descent and that these people formed a significant part of his electoral coalition. Nevertheless, his inclusive approach also enabled him to win the support of large numbers of people who neither self-identified as indigenous nor grew up in a home where an indigenous language was spoken.[30]

Humala maintained his dominance of indigenous areas in the 2011 presidential elections. Alejandro Toledo, who was also a candidate in 2011, initially led in polls of the central and southern highlands, but Humala overtook him during the last weeks of the campaign and ended up winning handily in these areas. In the first round of these elections Humala fared best in the heavily indigenous departments of Cusco and Puno where he won more than sixty percent of the vote, but he also won a majority of the valid vote in other departments with large indigenous populations, including Apurímac, Ayacucho, Huancavelica, Madre de Dios, and Tacna. Humala fared even better in the runoff elections, sweeping the indigenous highlands and the Amazon. In Cusco, Puno, Ayacucho, Huancavelica, Madre de Dios, and Tacna he won more than three-fourths of the valid vote in the runoff election. An analysis of individual-level survey data by Muñoz (2011, 12) found that people who grew up speaking Aymara or Quechua were significantly more likely to vote for Humala in the second round, even controlling for a host of other variables. Similarly, according to an analysis by Tanaka, Barrenechea, and Vera (2011, 6), the provincial-level vote for Humala in the first round was highly correlated (Pearson correlation = 0.637) with the percent of the provincial population that grew up speaking an indigenous language. The provincial-level vote for Humala, in fact, was more highly correlated with the percentage of the population that grew up

---

[29] People who self-identify as indigenous constituted only a small portion (nine percent) of all people who voted for Humala because they represent only a small portion (six percent) of the sample.

[30] One survey found that Humala was the most likely of the top three candidates to be perceived as not at all racist (Pontificia Universidad Católica del Perú – Instituto de Opinión Pública 2006, 8).

speaking an indigenous language than it was with the level of poverty in the province or any of the other variables they analyzed.

Humala attracted high levels of support among the indigenous population in 2011, like in 2006, in part because of his indigenous name and highlands origins. Indeed, aside from Toledo, Humala was the only one of the main candidates in the race who was clearly of indigenous descent. Moreover, Humala, in contrast to Toledo, did not represent the political establishment and he campaigned against market-oriented policies, which were unpopular in indigenous areas. Humala also won support in indigenous areas by recruiting numerous indigenous leaders as candidates for key positions. These leaders included Eduardo Kayap, an Awajum leader elected to congress from Amazonas; Hilaria Supa, an indigenous candidate from Cusco elected to the Andean parliament; and Claudia Ccoari, a leader of the CCP in Puno elected to the national legislature (Durand Guevara 2011; Santos and Vilca Arpasi 2011). Ethnic appeals were not the centerpiece of Humala's campaign, but he nevertheless embraced a whole series of traditional indigenous demands. For example, his 2011–16 governing plan decried the traditional exploitation of indigenous people and vowed to "recognize the rights of indigenous peoples, in our conviction and will to construct a more inclusive, just, and democratic country." Humala also frequently employed symbols of indigenous culture from music to clothing in the campaign.

Ethnic appeals thus have played an important role in recent presidential campaigns in Peru. Alberto Fujimori, Alejandro Toledo, and Ollanta Humala have all implicitly or explicitly contrasted their own ethnic heritage with those of their principal rivals in an effort to win support among voters of indigenous descent. They also have invoked indigenous symbols, recruited leaders of indigenous descent, forged ties with indigenous organizations, and embraced some of the demands of the indigenous movement, although they have been careful to avoid exclusionary rhetoric and demands. These inclusive ethnic appeals have helped them attract disproportionate support from indigenous-origin voters. Nevertheless, ethnic appeals have been only one component, and not even the most important component, of their efforts to appeal to the electorate.

POPULIST APPEALS

Populist appeals played an even more important role than ethnic appeals in the electoral campaigns of Fujimori, Toledo, and Humala, helping them to win the support not only of indigenous voters, but of many whites and mestizos as well. Winning the support of self-identified whites and mestizos has been crucial given the fact that they represent more than sixty percent of the Peruvian population according to the 2006 census. Without the support of these voters, none of these candidates would have won the presidency or even come as close as they did.

Fujimori, Toledo, and Humala have used various types of populist appeals to win the support of voters of diverse ethnic backgrounds. All three of them have used personalistic appeals, focusing their campaigns on their personal characteristics and their political independence. They also have all used anti-establishment appeals, denouncing the reigning political elites and parties. In addition, all three candidates have sought to identify themselves with the masses and have directed their appeals principally at the lower classes, which have traditionally provided support for populist candidates. The candidates have varied in the degree to which they have employed nationalist and state interventionist appeals, however. Whereas Humala criticized foreign intervention in Peru and vowed to redistribute income and expand the state's role in the economy, Fujimori and Toledo largely refrained from these traditional populist appeals. Moreover, both Fujimori and Toledo implemented market-oriented policies while in power, which has led many scholars to refer to them as neoliberal populists or neopopulists (Barr 2003; Roberts 1995; Weyland 1999).

FUJIMORI'S NEOPOPULISM

As we have seen, Fujimori sought to portray himself as a man of the people in the 1990 elections, contrasting himself to the aristocratic Vargas Llosa, whom he depicted as the candidate of the wealthy elite (Carrión 1997; Degregori 1991; Roberts 1995). Fujimori surrounded himself with individuals who represented the lower classes and politically and economically marginalized regions. He campaigned extensively in poorer areas and he proposed policies specifically designed to benefit poorer Peruvians, such as proposals to legalize street vendors and to create a bank to lend to businesses in the informal sector (Roberts 1995, 100).

Fujimori also used personalistic appeals extensively. Indeed, his campaigns focused mostly on him rather than his party or platform. In 1990, he barely cobbled together a party in time to compete in the elections and even then he did not put together a detailed governing plan or a complete slate of candidates.[31] Nor did he invest much effort in building a party after he was elected. Instead, he chose to create a new party in each of the subsequent elections in which he competed.

In addition, Fujimori used his dearth of ties to the traditional parties and his lack of a political experience to position himself as an outsider in opposition to the political establishment.[32] Fujimori continued to rail against the political establishment even after becoming president, and in 1992 he went so far

---

[31] Vargas Llosa could not believe that Fujimori was able to rise rapidly in the polls in spite of his lack of preparation. He later wondered who "would vote for an unknown, without a program, without a team for governing, without any political credentials whatsoever, who had hardly campaigned outside of Lima, who had been jury-rigged overnight to serve as a candidate?" (Vargas Llosa 1994, 439).

[32] Fujimori had been dean of an agricultural university, but had never held office previous to being elected president in 1990. He did have some ties to APRA, however, and had served as an adviser on that party's 1985 campaign. In 1990, he first sought to run as a senatorial candidate for Izquierda Unida.

as to carry out a self-coup, closing congress and suspending the constitution. The public, particularly the poorer sectors of the population, largely supported Fujimori's actions and his popularity soared in the wake of the coup.

Fujimori generally avoided traditional economic populist appeals, however. During the 1990 campaign, he did criticize Vargas Llosa's plans to carry out radical economic shock therapy and he proposed some spending programs, but he was vague about what his own economic policies would be. Surprisingly, once in office, Fujimori adopted a sweeping market-oriented reform program that went well beyond what Vargas Llosa had proposed. He slashed government spending and interest rates and devalued Peru's currency. He opened up the Peruvian economy to foreign trade and investment, privatized numerous state enterprises, and deregulated the country's labor and financial markets. Nevertheless, as Roberts (1995) points out, Fujimori's neoliberal policies did not prevent him from using government spending to try to win votes, particularly in poorer areas of the country. In particular, the Fujimori administration manipulated some government social programs, such as the Fondo Nacional de Compensación y Desarrollo, to reward his political supporters and encourage swing voters to support him (Graham and Kane 1998; Schady 2000; Taylor 2001, 6–7).

Fujimori's populist appeals initially paid huge dividends. The 1990 election was largely a clash over personalities, and in one survey that year almost two-thirds of voters mentioned candidate characteristics as the key factors determining their vote, as opposed to only twenty-eight percent who mentioned programs or ideology (Carrión 1997, 285). Fujimori's decision to focus his campaign on his personal characteristics was thus politically fruitful. Indeed, the specific characteristics that Fujimori emphasized – honesty, education, and identification with the people – were among those that Peruvians had cited in surveys as being the most important for a politician (Torres Guzmán 1989, 77–9). In particular, many Peruvians supported Fujimori because they saw him as "closer to the popular classes" in the words of one worker (Boggio et al. 1991, 36–7). Fujimori also benefited from his lack of ties to the traditional parties. By 1990 public opinion had turned heavily against the political establishment after the disastrous administrations of Alan García and Fernando Belaúnde, which had left the economy in ruins and the country in the midst of a violent guerrilla war. According to one survey, more than fifty percent of those people who reported voting for Fujimori in the 1990 elections stated that they chose him because of his political independence (Carrión 1997, 285–6).

After 1990, however, Fujimori's electoral success was based in large part on evaluations of his performance in office rather than his ethnic or populist appeals. Fujimori triumphed in 1995, for example, largely because of his success in overcoming the economic crisis and defeating the Shining Path (Arce 2003; Morgan Kelly 2003; Roberts and Arce 1998; Weyland 2000). By 1993, inflation had declined to 48.6 percent, down from 7,481 percent in 1990, and the economy had begun to grow at a rapid pace, which it would maintain throughout the mid-1990s (Tanaka 1998, 231–2). The capture of the leader of the Shining Path, Abimael Guzmán, in 1992, meanwhile, led to the gradual disintegration of that guerrilla movement. The number of deaths caused by political violence declined from 3,590 in 1984 to eighty-three in 1998 (Arce 2003, 576). These political and economic achievements led to a groundswell of support for Fujimori. According to one poll, thirty-seven percent of the respondents who reported voting for Fujimori in 1995 said that they did so because he had done a good job of governing, while twenty-two percent specifically cited his defeat of terrorism and another seventeen percent referred to his handling of the economy (Apoyo Opinión y Mercado S.A. 1995, 12). At the time of this survey (April 1995), sixty-three percent of all respondents said that they supported Fujimori's economic policies and eighty-two percent said that they approved of his anti-subversive policies. Nevertheless, Fujimori's populist appeals continued to help define his image in the eyes of the voters. During the 1995 electoral campaign, one survey found that fifty-five percent of the respondents identified Fujimori as the candidate who was "closest to people like you," as opposed to only twelve percent who chose his principal rival, former United Nations secretary general Javier Pérez de Cuellar (Schmidt 2000, 107).

TOLEDO'S NEOPOPULIST APPEALS

Alejandro Toledo's populist appeals resembled Fujimori's in a number of ways. Toledo, like Fujimori, tried to present himself as a man of the people. Throughout his campaign, he emphasized his humble origins and his compelling rags-to-riches story: Toledo came from a poor highlands family and had worked as a shepherd and a shoeshine boy before winning a scholarship to attend college in the United States and eventually earning a Ph.D. in educational economics from Stanford University. Like Fujimori, Toledo campaigned extensively in the poorer neighborhoods of Lima, which he toured in his car, dubbed the *cholomobile*. He used his informal, down-to-earth style to establish a rapport with poorer Peruvians. During his 2000 and 2001 campaigns, Toledo also declared that he would be the president of the poor and unveiled numerous social programs designed to help them. For example, he promised to supply health insurance to poor women and children, to create an agricultural bank to provide loans to small farmers, and to improve the sanitation of shantytowns in Lima (Barr 2003, 1165).

Like Fujimori, Toledo ran a highly personalistic campaign that focused mostly on his accomplishments. He created his own party, Perú Posible, and staffed it with his personal allies. Consequently, Perú Posible never developed a coherent national organization and largely disappeared once Toledo finished his term. As president, Toledo did not concentrate and personalize power to the extent that Fujimori did – nor did he bypass existing political institutions to the same degree (Barr 2003, 1166–7). Toledo did present himself as a political outsider, though, and he regularly denounced the political establishment. In Toledo's case, however, the corrupt establishment that he railed against was not the traditional parties, but rather Fujimori's government (Barr 2003, 1165).

Toledo was more of a neopopulist than a traditional populist. He did at times engage in economic populism on the campaign trail. For example, he promised to create a million jobs and to boost the salaries of teachers, health workers, police officers, and other government employees (Barr 2003, 1165–6). Indeed, one of Toledo's campaign slogans was that the T in Toledo stood for *trabajo* or jobs. For the most part, however, he supported the broad outlines of Fujimori's economic model, although he promised to put a human face on market policies. Moreover, as president, he largely stayed within the confines of the market model, even negotiating a free trade agreement with the United States.

The populist appeals of Alejandro Toledo grew steadily more effective over time. Toledo first ran for president in 1995, but his candidacy gained little traction because of Fujimori's overwhelming popularity, and he finished with only 3.2 percent of the national vote. In the 2000 elections, however, Toledo emerged as a major contender after the Fujimori administration successfully discredited the two candidates who were thought to pose the greatest threat to the incumbent: Alberto Andrade, the mayor of Lima, and Luis Castañeda, the former head of the social security system. Unlike Andrade and Castañeda, Toledo had widespread appeal among the poor and voters outside of Lima. Moreover, by the late 1990s, Fujimori's popularity had ebbed somewhat because of growing economic problems and disenchantment with his administration's corruption and disregard for democratic norms. Support for Fujimori's economic policies, for example, dropped from sixty-three percent in April 1995 to thirty-six percent in April 2000 (Apoyo Opinión y Mercado S.A. 2000b, 19).

Nevertheless, Fujimori remained popular among some sectors of the electorate, particularly the poor, because of his earlier political and economic achievements and his considerable spending programs. In a survey by Apoyo (2000a, 29), sixty-four percent of the respondents who supported Fujimori in the first round of the 2000 elections stated that they voted for him because he defeated terrorism, and thirty-one percent mentioned the economic stability he brought the country. Many Fujimori supporters also cited his public works (fifty-four percent), his help to the poor (forty percent), and his help to the neediest towns (twenty-one percent). This reservoir of support, along with his control of the state, helped Fujimori prevail in a closely contested battle. According to the official returns, Fujimori captured 49.9 percent of the valid vote in the first round of the presidential elections, while Toledo won 40.2, but Toledo and many independent observers argued that the Fujimori administration had committed fraud (Bernbaum et al. 2001; Schmidt 2002).[33] The electoral authorities nevertheless certified the results, forcing a runoff election since neither candidate had won fifty percent of the vote. Ten days before the runoff election, however, Toledo withdrew on the grounds that the Fujimori administration had refused to put into place the necessary mechanisms to prevent a repeat of the voter fraud.

---

[33] The extent of fraud in the 2000 elections is the subject of some debate. See Schmidt 2002.

Toledo ran again for president in 2001 after Fujimori's resignation in the wake of various scandals. This time, Toledo won the first round of the elections with 36.5 percent of the vote in spite of a number of personal scandals of his own. Alan García of APRA came in a surprising second place with 25.8 percent of the vote, just ahead of the conservative candidate, Lourdes Flores of Unidad Nacional. García was thought to be a weak opponent because of his disastrous previous administration as president (1985–90), but he was an effective campaigner and possessed a much stronger party organization than Toledo. Nevertheless, Toledo prevailed in the second round with 53.1 percent of the vote.

Toledo's populist appeals helped him considerably in both 2000 and 2001. According to an Apoyo (2000a, 29) survey of the 2000 elections, most voters who supported Toledo cited his personal characteristics, rather than his ideology or party program, as their reason for voting for him in the first round. Sixty percent of his supporters cited his professional preparation as an economist. Others referred to his humble origins: Twenty-six percent, for example, said that they voted for him because he identified with the people, twenty-three percent because he rose up from poverty, and fifteen percent because he was from the provinces. The voters that did refer to his governing program typically mentioned his populist promise to provide jobs. Voters cited similar reasons for voting for Toledo in 2001 (Apoyo Opinión y Mercado S.A. 2001, 9). In that year, however, many voters also said that they supported him because he had defeated the Fujimori dictatorship.

HUMALA'S TRADITIONAL POPULIST APPEALS

Ollanta Humala differed considerably from his predecessors in that he was a populist in the traditional mode who supported redistributive and state interventionist policies. The governments Humala sought to emulate were not those of his immediate predecessors, but rather the populist military regime of Juan Velasco Alvarado. Thus, Humala denounced the free market policies of Fujimori and Toledo. Indeed, the first paragraph of his governing plan declared that:

The systematic application of neoliberalism ... in our country has meant a social fracture without precedents in Peruvian life. On one side there is a gigantic accumulation of wealth and power in a minority of the population, while the other side has experienced a brutal increase in social inequalities and poverty for the large majority of people excluded from the system. (Humala Tasso 2006, 11)

Humala proposed a plan of state-led inward-oriented development that would help redistribute the country's wealth. He vowed to reexamine the privatization of state-owned enterprises that had taken place under Fujimori and to tax the windfall profits of mining companies. He pledged to respect private property, but he argued that in some strategic areas, such as aviation and gas, there should be state participation ("Canal 7 cumplió con presentar a candidatos" 2006).

Humala was an ardent nationalist. He blamed foreign countries and companies for exploiting and impoverishing Peru, and he vowed to defend the "national resources that this [the Toledo] government has given away to transnational companies" (Caballero 2006). Humala also pledged to reexamine Peru's foreign debt commitments as well as the foreign investments made under previous governments, although he was careful to say that he did not oppose foreign investment per se (Sifuentes Alemán 2006). In addition, Humala voiced considerable criticisms of Peru's relationship with the United States, arguing that it was essential to preserve "our autonomy and independence in our relations" (Humala Tasso 2006, 107). He vowed to renegotiate the free trade agreement with the United States signed during the Toledo administration and he promised to bring an end to the forced coca eradication programs that the Peruvian government carried out under U.S. supervision.

Humala's campaign, like those of Fujimori and Toledo, was highly personalistic, and he ran to a large extent on his own biography. Indeed, surveys showed that most voters supported him because of his personal characteristics rather than his party or program (Paredes Castro 2006). His party was little more than a personal electoral vehicle run largely by his friends and allies. This ensured that he was politically independent and fully in command, but it deprived him of the funding and organizational networks that a more institutionalized party might have brought him. It also forced him to seal an alliance with a center-left party, Unión por el Perú, in order to compete in the elections, since he was unable to gather enough signatures to register his own party in time for the contest.

Humala, like Fujimori and Toledo, presented himself as a man of the people. He denounced the wealthy oligarchy, and criticized Toledo for not doing more for the poor (Mäckelmann 2006, 12, 21). He proposed boosting social spending by one percent of GDP in three years in order to reduce chronic malnutrition by fifty percent. And he promised within five years to provide potable water and sanitation to one million people in rural areas and to reduce the number of people living in extreme poverty by a similar amount (Humala Tasso 2006, 96). Humala also proposed various agricultural, employment, and education programs designed to help reduce poverty and generate sustainable development.

In addition, Humala made numerous anti-establishment appeals. A former army commander, Humala had first come to public attention when he, along with his brother, carried out an uprising against Fujimori during the final days of his regime. The military quelled the uprising and imprisoned Humala, but he was freed and pardoned after Fujimori resigned. Humala thus had strong anti-establishment credentials, and he built upon these credentials during his 2006 campaign, railing against the traditional parties, the legislature, and the political class, whom he accused of corruption. He called for a constituent assembly, as in Venezuela, which would overhaul Peru's political institutions. He even proudly embraced the label of the anti-system candidate, declaring: "If the system is corruption, the insensitivity of the political class, the turning over of the country to transnational capital, I feel proud to be anti-system" ("Humala: 'Están formando el partido 'todos contra Ollanta'" 2006).

Humala's populist appeals played an important role in his electoral rise. By late 2005, many Peruvians had long since grown tired of Alejandro Toledo whose approval ratings fell to under fifteen percent in 2005, although they recovered somewhat in early 2006. Humala's anti-establishment credentials and his vehement denunciations of the Toledo government and the traditional parties thus struck a chord with many voters. In an Apoyo (2006b, 3) poll taken shortly after the second round of elections, the two most common responses that supporters of Humala gave to the question of why they voted for him were that he represented a change and that he would combat corruption. Thirty-eight percent of voters provided both of those responses, while another thirty-five percent said that they had voted for him because he was new to politics. Moreover, according to an analysis of data from the 2006 LAPOP survey, Humala fared particularly well among voters critical of the political establishment and Peruvian democracy more generally. In this survey, seventy-two percent of the people who reported voting for Humala in the second round of the elections expressed no or little trust in political parties, as opposed to only fifty-five percent of the people who reported voting for his opponent, Alan García. Similarly, seventy percent of Humala's supporters said that they were dissatisfied or very dissatisfied with the way democracy functioned in Peru, in comparison to only fifty-seven percent of García's supporters. Humala's supporters were also more likely to have participated in protests, to express disapproval of the outgoing government of Alejandro Toledo, and to report that the economy in general and their own economic situation had worsened in the last year.

Humala also won the support of some voters because of his identification with the masses. A postelection poll by the Pontificia Universidad Católica del Perú (2006, 8) found that voters in general felt that Ollanta Humala was the candidate who was closest to the poor, and twenty-three percent of voters in an Apoyo (2006b, 2) survey said that they had voted for him because he understood the problems of the people. Not surprising, Humala fared better among poorer and less educated voters than wealthier and more educated ones. According to the 2006 LAPOP survey, sixty percent of Humala's supporters reported earning less than 600 soles per month, as opposed to fifty percent of García's supporters. And thirty-five percent of Humala's supporters reported having completed nine or fewer years of education, as opposed to twenty-five percent of García's supporters.

Humala's nationalist and state interventionist views also won him some support. For example, eighteen percent of the voters in the Apoyo (2006b, 2) poll said they supported him because he was a nationalist. Similarly, a Catholic University of Peru poll found that voters in general were much more likely to give high marks to Humala than to the other candidates for supporting national interests (Pontificia Universidad Católica del Perú – Instituto de Opinión Pública 2006, 8). Moreover, an analysis of data from the 2006 LAPOP survey shows that Humala drew support disproportionately from people who were on the left or had nationalist and state interventionist views. According to this survey, forty-one percent of Humala supporters identified themselves as left of center, as opposed to nineteen percent of García's supporters.[34] Similarly, only twenty-three percent of Humala's supporters thought they would benefit from the free trade agreement with the United States, in comparison to forty-four percent of García's supporters.[35] Nevertheless, Humala's actual policy proposals do not appear to have played a large role in winning over voters. Indeed, only fifteen percent of voters in the Apoyo poll cited the fact that he had good proposals as their reason for supporting him.[36]

Although Humala fared well among many categories of voters, he ultimately did not win the support of the majority in 2006. Humala won the first round of the elections in April 2006 with 30.6 percent of the valid vote, finishing well ahead of Alan García who, as in 2001, narrowly edged Lourdes Flores for second place. In the second round of the elections, however, García defeated Humala by a margin of 52.6 percent to 47.4 percent. Humala swept the highlands and the Amazon, but he fared less well in Lima and on the coast.

Several factors contributed to Humala's second round defeat in 2006. First, although Humala's stance against market reform may have helped fuel his initial rise in the polls, it hurt him in the second round of the elections. Market-oriented policies have generated greater benefits in Peru than most other Latin American countries. Indeed, between 1991 and 2006, the Peruvian economy grew by 4.7 percent annually, one of the fastest rates in the region. As a result, a relatively large proportion of Peruvians came to support market-oriented policies, although a significant portion of the population opposed them. According to 2006 surveys by Apoyo (2006c, 5; 2006d, 5), fifty-three percent of Peruvians supported the country's free trade agreement with the United States and fifty-one percent opposed the nationalization of gas companies in Peru. Although Humala's nationalist and state interventionist appeals won him support in some sectors of the population, they hurt him with others. In addition, Humala was damaged by his association with Hugo Chávez, the left-wing president of Venezuela who endorsed Humala and repeatedly denounced Alan García. According to a poll by Apoyo (2006a, 1), the vast majority of Peruvians had an unfavorable perception of Chávez and disapproved of his intervention in the campaign.

Equally important, Humala had a number of negative characteristics as a candidate. To begin with, he was a relatively poor public speaker and debater.

[34] I classify as left of center those people who place themselves from one to four on a ten point left–right scale. Many voters (eleven percent of the total) did not know where to place themselves on this scale.

[35] A significant percentage of Humala's supporters, twenty-eight percent, responded that they did not know whether they would benefit from the free trade agreement and another two percent did not respond to the question.

[36] A postelection survey by the Compañía Peruana de Estudios de Mercados y Opinión Pública (2006) provided similar findings.

He was also widely perceived as authoritarian. Indeed, one survey found that forty-two percent of Peruvians classified him as authoritarian and only sixteen percent classified him as democratic, which was by far the worst ratio of any of the top three candidates (Pontificia Universidad Católica del Perú – Instituto de Opinión Pública 2006, 8). The media, his opponents, and various nongovernmental organizations accused him of committing serious human rights violations during the war against the Shining Path and of being complicit in the bloody uprising in Andahuaylas carried out by his brother. Humala's family was also a constant source of embarrassment, although he tried to distance himself from their words and actions. Among the more controversial views expressed by Humala's parents and brothers were calls for the execution of homosexuals and an amnesty for members of the Shining Path. Ultimately, Humala was unable to overcome these obstacles in spite of the relative success of his ethnopopulist appeals.

Table 4.2 presents the results of a logistic regression analysis of the vote for Humala in the second round using individual-level data from the LAPOP 2006 Peru survey. The coefficients represent the maximum likelihood estimates of voting for Humala over García. The results show that having an indigenous linguistic background considerably increases the likelihood of voting for Humala, even when we control for a wide range of other variables, including income, region, and ideology. The variables measuring whether an individual grew up speaking an indigenous language at home and whether the indigenous tongue was his or her first language are both positive and highly statistically significant. This suggests that Humala's ethnic appeals helped him attract a disproportionate level of support from people with indigenous backgrounds.

Interestingly, however, self-identifying as indigenous does not have a significant impact on the likelihood of voting for Humala once the linguistic background of the respondents and other variables are controlled for. This is, no doubt, the case in large part because eighty-seven percent of the Peruvians who self-identify as indigenous in the survey grew up in a home where an indigenous language was spoken. Nevertheless, it is also an indication that Humala's inclusive ethnic appeals were successful in attracting many people who do not self-identify as indigenous. Humala was particularly successful in winning the support of people who self-identify as mestizo. Indeed, the variable measuring whether the respondent is mestizo is positive and falls just short of conventional levels of statistical significance. As the table indicates, he was less successful in winning the support of blacks and mulattos: The coefficient of this variable is negative, although it does not approach statistical significance. Nor was he especially successful in winning the support of whites, which represent the reference category in the model.

Table 4.2 also suggests that Humala's populist appeals paid dividends, helping him win the support of anti-establishment, personalist, nationalist, and state interventionist voters. The variables measuring trust in parties and satisfaction with democracy are negative and statistically significant,

TABLE 4.2. *The Correlates of the Vote for Humala in the Second Round of the 2006 Presidential Elections in Peru*

(Logistic regression analysis using LAPOP 2006 survey)

	Coefficient	Standard error	Significance level
Constant	.373	.577	.518
Indigenous language is maternal language	.681	.305	.026
Indigenous language is second language	.863	.218	.000
Self-identifies as indigenous	.330	.410	.420
Self-identifies as mestizo	.445	.235	.058
Self-identifies as black or mulatto	−.086	.621	.890
Trust in parties	−.127	.054	.019
Satisfaction with democracy	−.249	.124	.045
Participation in protests	.188	.093	.043
Voted based on candidate characteristics	.360	.185	.052
Identifies with leftist ideology	1.197	.174	.000
Monthly income	−.059	.043	.170
Male	.335	.163	.039
Age	−.005	.006	.377
Interested in politics	−.010	.092	.916
Watches news on television	−.114	.103	.266
Believes economy has improved in the last year	−.087	.133	.514
Personal finances have improved in the last year	−.227	.135	.093
Lived principally in the countryside as a child	.530	.196	.007
Resides in Amazon	.595	.332	.073
Resides in Lima	−.574	.275	.037
Resides in southern highlands	−.100	.312	.748
Resides in north	−.126	.281	.653
Nagelkerke R-squared	.283		
N	897		

indicating that people who have little trust in parties and low satisfaction with democracy are more likely to have voted for Humala. Similarly, the coefficient for participation in protests is positive and statistically significant, indicating that people who participated in protests are more likely to have voted for Humala. People who voted based on candidate characteristics are also more likely to have supported Humala, although this variable falls slightly under conventional levels of statistical significance. Finally, leftists, who are typically more critical of foreign intervention in Latin America and support increased state intervention in the economy, are significantly more likely to have voted for Humala.[37] Surprisingly, however, the variable measuring the income of the respondent is statistically insignificant, although it has the expected negative sign. This indicates that poorer voters are not significantly more likely to have voted for Humala once the effect of other variables is controlled.

Relatively few of the control variables are statistically significant. Male voters are significantly more likely to have supported Humala than female voters, but age does not make much of a difference. Nor does interest in politics or the frequency with which respondents watch television news affect the likelihood of voting for Humala. There is also little evidence of retrospective economic voting in the 2006 election: Respondents who thought that the economy had gotten worse in the last twelve months or whose own personal economic situation had deteriorated are not significantly more likely to have voted for Humala once other variables are controlled for. Perhaps most surprising, most of the regional variables are not statistically significant. *Ceteris paribus*, people who live in the Amazon or the southern highlands are not significantly more likely to have voted for Humala, and people who live in the north are not significantly less likely to have voted for Humala. Residents of Lima, however, are significantly less likely to have voted for Humala, whereas people who grew up in the countryside are much more likely to have voted for Humala.

On balance, the logistic regression model presented in Table 4.2 provides support for the argument that Humala's ethnopopulist appeals proved effective in the 2006 elections. These appeals helped Humala win the support of personalist, anti-establishment, nationalist, and state interventionist voters as well as indigenous language speakers more generally. Humala, like ethnopopulist leaders in Bolivia and Ecuador, thus managed to fuse traditional populist constituencies to his indigenous base, although their votes were ultimately not sufficient to deliver him the presidency that year.

Humala ran again for the presidency in 2011 as the candidate of a left-wing alliance called Gana Perú. Throughout much of the campaign, Humala trailed badly in the polls. Indeed, as late as March 2011, he was still in fourth place in most surveys behind Alejandro Toledo; Luis Castañeda, the former mayor of Lima; and Keiko Fujimori, a congresswoman who is Alberto Fujimori's daughter. Humala rose rapidly in the polls during the final weeks of the campaign, however, and on election day (April 10, 2011) he finished first with 31.7 percent of the valid vote, roughly equivalent to his showing in the first round of the 2006 elections. Support for Toledo and Castañeda, meanwhile, declined sharply, enabling Fujimori to finish second with 23.6 percent of the valid vote, which qualified her for the runoff election.

---

[37] Voters who did not think they would benefit from the free trade agreement that Peru signed with the United States were also significantly more likely to have voted for Humala. However, I excluded this variable from the model displayed in Table 4.2 because it includes a large number of nonresponses.

Humala's populist appeals played an important role in his first round electoral victory in 2011. As in 2006, these appeals resonated with many Peruvians who had not enjoyed the benefits of Peru's strong economic growth in the 2000s. Indeed, Humala fared particularly well among poorer and left-of-center voters as well as people who lived in economically marginalized areas of the country (Pontificia Universidad Católica del Perú – Instituto de Opinión Pública 2011). Humala denounced the political establishment throughout the campaign and he was the only one of the major candidates in 2011 to adopt a critical stance toward market-oriented policies. His governing plan argued that "the neoliberal governments of Fujimori, Toledo, and García did not properly increase spending on health and education, lowered salaries and real wages, and generated growth that did not create employment or decent income, and excluded the immense majority of the population of the highlands and tropical regions of the country" (Gana Perú 2010, 6). Humala also talked frequently about redistributing wealth and recovering the country's natural resources, and he vowed to combat corruption and defend the country from foreign exploitation. During one campaign speech, he asked: "Who is afraid of change? Those who have already governed ... who sold the gas of Camisea to foreigners and governed in the most corrupt regime in the last twenty years" (Núñez 2011a).

Yet in 2011 Humala also took steps to moderate his image to win over centrist voters. He hired advisers from the Brazilian Workers Party who persuaded him to shed his red shirts in favor of a suit and tie. He acknowledged that market-oriented policies had brought some benefits and promised that he would respect private property, foreign investments, and the U.S.-Peru free trade agreement. He also backed away from plans to overhaul Peru's constitution, vowed not to seek reelection, and declared himself a strong supporter of freedom of the press and civil liberties. Perhaps most importantly, he sought to distance himself from Hugo Chávez whom he believed had cost him the election in 2006. He warned Chávez not to involve himself in the campaign and declared firmly that "we are not going to turn over Peru to Chávez, we will not follow his model" (Núñez 2011b).

Humala stepped up his efforts to win over centrist voters after the first round of the election. He declared his willingness to dialogue with all sectors of the population and to make concessions in order to unite Peru. He also struck an alliance with Alejandro Toledo and brought in several economists from his team who helped write a new governing plan dubbed "The Road Map" (Levitsky 2011). The new plan, which was considerably more moderate than the original one, emphasized fiscal responsibility, price stability, and the creation of conditions favorable for private investment, in addition to the expansion of social programs. Humala also promised that he would not touch the funds in the private pension system or seek to revise existing trade agreements. In response both Toledo and Mario Vargas Llosa endorsed Humala, and Toledo promised that his party would cooperate with Gana Perú in the legislature.

Humala's efforts to win over centrist voters were helped by the fact that Keiko Fujimori was a polarizing candidate. Although her father's administration had helped defeat the Shining Path and presided over impressive economic growth, it had also been guilty of widespread corruption and abuses of human rights and civil liberties, which ultimately led to the conviction and imprisonment of Alberto Fujimori. Humala suggested that, if elected, Keiko Fujimori would follow in the footsteps of her father, leading to a return of "human rights violations, the persecution of the opposition, and ties to the illegal trafficking of drugs and weapons" ("Peru: carrera ..." 2011). "There may be doubts about me," Humala warned in the final debate. "But on the other side there is proof" (Vergara 2011). Fujimori, moreover, damaged her prospects by failing to distance herself from her father until late in the campaign. Throughout much of the campaign she argued that the Fujimori regime was not a dictatorship and that he was the best president in the history of Peru, although after the first round of the election she apologized for "the errors and offenses" that were committed during his presidency and promised not to pardon him ("Perú: Ollanta Humala ..." 2011).

The runoff election, which was held on June 5, was hotly contested and some preelection polls had Fujimori ahead. Much of the media supported Fujimori, as did the business community. Pedro Pablo Kuczynski and Luis Castañeda, the third place and fifth place finishers in the first round, also endorsed her. On election day, however, Humala emerged victorious with 51.5 percent of the vote. Fujimori won in Lima and on the northern coast, but Humala dominated the Amazon and especially the highlands. As in the first round, indigenous voters, leftists and poor mestizos constituted Humala's main base, but he won the support of enough urban, centrist, and middle class voters to put him over the top. Thus, Humala, too, demonstrated the electoral viability of ethnopopulism.

CONCLUSION

The Peruvian case demonstrates how ethnic proximity may shape ethnic voting behavior in societies in which ethnic mixing is widespread. In recent years indigenous voters in Peru have consistently voted in presidential elections for the viable candidates who are most ethnically proximate to them. Although Fujimori, Toledo, and Humala do not identify as indigenous, people of indigenous descent have viewed these candidates as more ethnically proximate than their main competitors who have typically represented the white Lima elite. They have thus supported them in large numbers.

The Peruvian case also shows that non-indigenous parties can successfully employ ethnopopulist appeals. In Peru, as in Bolivia and Ecuador, ethnopopulist politics has become increasingly the norm. No major indigenous parties have emerged in Peru, but various politicians, including Alberto Fujimori, Alejandro Toledo, and Ollanta Humala, have used ethnic appeals to win the support of indigenous people. They have recruited indigenous candidates, employed indigenous symbols, and embraced indigenous demands, all of which has helped them rack up impressive victory margins in indigenous areas. Fujimori, Toledo, and Humala have used populist appeals even more widely than ethnic appeals, however. They have denounced the political establishment, focused their campaigns on the popular sectors, and presented themselves as the saviors of Peru. These appeals have resonated not just with indigenous people, but also with whites and mestizos, enabling these politicians to build winning electoral coalitions.

None of these politicians or their parties is likely to maintain an enduring hold on the Peruvian electorate, however. Indeed, Fujimori and Toledo have already seen voters of all ethnic backgrounds abandon them en masse and Humala may well experience the same phenomenon. Although the anti-establishment appeals of populist leaders often function well when they are in the opposition, it is much harder for these politicians to win support with anti-establishment rhetoric when they control the government. Moreover, Fujimori, Toledo, and Humala lack the organizational or identity-based ties to voters that are conducive to electoral stability. In the traditional fashion of populist leaders, Fujimori, Toledo, and Humala have neglected to build strong party organizations, preferring instead to develop unmediated personalistic ties to voters. Nor have they developed strong identity-based linkages to indigenous voters and organizations. Thus, there is little reason to expect that they or their parties will continue to thrive well into the next decade.

Ethnopopulism, however, should continue to be an effective electoral strategy in Peru. As long as the indigenous population is economically, socially, and politically marginalized, it is likely to be receptive to ethnopopulist appeals. These appeals, moreover, will also likely continue to resonate among many whites and mestizos who feel that they have not fully enjoyed the benefits of Peru's economic growth.

5

Indigenous Parties outside of the Central Andes

Outside of the central Andes, indigenous parties have had little success.[1] Parties based in the indigenous movement have emerged in a number of nations, but none of these parties have won more than three percent of the national vote.

What explains the poor performance of indigenous parties elsewhere in Latin America? Why have these parties failed to catch on in the manner of the MAS and Pachakutik?

This chapter examines the performance of indigenous parties in Guatemala, Colombia, Venezuela, and Nicaragua: the four Latin American countries with the largest and best-known indigenous parties outside of the central Andes.[2] It contends that institutional factors cannot explain the meager results of indigenous parties in these countries because the institutional environment in three of these four countries was relatively favorable to such parties. As we shall see, in the 1990s Colombia and Venezuela reserved seats in the national legislature for indigenous people, and Nicaragua created an autonomous region in an area of the country with a large population of indigenous people and Afro-Latinos. These measures helped lead to the emergence of the indigenous parties in these countries and gave them a base on which to build, but they were not enough to bring about national-level electoral success.

---

[1] Van Cott (2005, 217) classifies the Alianza Social Indígena in Colombia as a success, even though it has never won more than a tiny fraction of the national vote. According to Van Cott (2005, 217–18), "'successful parties' are those that contest power at the national level or that have a broad geographical coverage of much of the national territory and representation at the national level." This sets a relatively low threshold for party success. Moreover, by this definition, many of the parties that Van Cott categorizes as unsuccessful, such as the Katarista parties in Bolivia and the Movimiento Indígena Amauta Jatari in Ecuador, should be classified as successful since they competed at the national level and, in some cases, even won national level representation.

[2] Indigenous parties have surfaced in a few other countries in Latin America as well, but they have had even less success. In Mexico, for example, an indigenous group in the state of Oaxaca, the Movimiento de Unificación y Lucha Triqui, created a regional political party named the Partido Unidad Popular in 2003. This party, which has been referred to as the first indigenous party in Mexico, managed to elect a candidate to the Oaxaca state legislature in 2004, but has otherwise had little success (Mártinez Sánchez 2004; Valladares de la Cruz 2009).

This chapter argues that indigenous parties have performed relatively poorly outside of the central Andes in part because they have not made widespread populist appeals. None of these parties, for example, emphasized their opposition to neoliberal policies and foreign intervention in their electoral campaigns. Nor did they develop or recruit charismatic leaders able to mobilize diverse sectors of the electorate. Instead, indigenous parties in Guatemala, Colombia, Venezuela, and Nicaragua focused their campaigns in large part on ethnic issues and largely refrained from employing populist rhetoric or policy proposals. Partly as a result, these parties failed to win the support of the traditional populist constituencies, such as urban working class mestizos, that provided extensive backing to the MAS and Pachakutik.

Perhaps even more important, indigenous parties have fared poorly outside of the central Andes because the demographics have been less propitious for them. Indigenous parties in most of Latin America have lacked a sizable and well-organized indigenous base. In Colombia, Nicaragua, and Venezuela, for example, the indigenous population represents only a tiny proportion of the population and the indigenous movement has relatively little clout. Thus, indigenous parties could not make significant electoral inroads in these two countries even with the backing of these countries' indigenous organizations and voters. In Guatemala, the conditions would seem much more propitious for an indigenous party, given that indigenous people represent nearly half of the country's population. Nevertheless, the indigenous movement is relatively weak and fragmented in Guatemala. Moreover, Winaq, the only national indigenous party to emerge in Guatemala to date, has lacked the strong ties to grassroots indigenous organizations that its counterparts in Bolivia and Ecuador enjoyed. As a result, it fared poorly even among indigenous voters.

This chapter begins by discussing why a successful indigenous party has not emerged in Guatemala, the country where the demographics would seem to most favor an indigenous party. It then analyzes the emergence of indigenous parties in Colombia, Venezuela, and Nicaragua and explains why these parties have not managed to expand beyond their narrow base in the indigenous populations. The conclusion speculates on the future prospects for indigenous as well as Afro-Latino parties in the region.

GUATEMALA

Guatemala would appear to have many of the conditions necessary for the success of an indigenous party. To begin with, it has a large indigenous population. According to the 2002 census, thirty-one percent of the population above three years of age first learned to speak in an indigenous language and forty-one percent of the Guatemalan population self-identifies as indigenous (Instituto Nacional de Estadística 2003b, 30–5). Moreover, self-identified indigenous people represent approximately half of the total rural population and constitute a majority in nine of the country's twenty-one departments (Instituto Nacional de Estadística 2003b, 75). Thus an indigenous party in Guatemala could potentially win a sizable share of the vote, a majority in some areas, relying on support from indigenous people alone.

In addition, the high level of dissatisfaction with the traditional parties and political elites in Guatemala should also presumably favor the emergence of an indigenous party. During the 1980s and 1990s, many Guatemalans abandoned the traditional parties and numerous new parties emerged, causing the country to have the second highest level of electoral volatility in Latin America (Madrid 2005a, 6). This dissatisfaction persisted into the 2000s. For example, in a 2005 survey by Latinobarometer, fewer Guatemalans stated that their country had made progress in the fight against corruption or expressed support for the principle of democracy than the citizens of any other country (Corporación Latinobarómetro 2005, 28, 56). The continuing high level of political dissatisfaction in Guatemala makes it a propitious environment for the emergence of new, anti-establishment parties.

Nevertheless, no successful indigenous party has yet emerged in the country. Mayan activists have sought to create various electoral vehicles, but none of these have prospered at the national level. One of the more ambitious efforts was undertaken in 1976 when some indigenous leaders founded an indigenous party, the Frente Integración Nacional (FIN), arguing that: "It is worth the trouble to participate in the next election as subjects of our own history and destiny" (Bastos and Camus 2003, 48). The FIN was originally named the Frente Indígena Nacional, but its founders changed the name under pressure from existing parties and politicians who believed the name would provoke ethnic strife. The leaders of the FIN first negotiated with existing political parties, notably Democracia Cristiana Guatemalteca, in an effort to obtain promises of congressional seats and assistance in legalizing the party. When these negotiations failed, however, the FIN forged an alliance with General Romeo Lucas García and supported his successful candidacy in the March 1978 presidential election. Lucas García promised to help the FIN become a legal political party after the elections as long as it could show that it was ethnically inclusive (Falla 1978, 455). After the election, however, the electoral commission turned down the FIN's application to become a party and the Lucas García regime subsequently persecuted the movement's leaders (Hale 2006, 90). According to one of the movement's leaders, Marcial Maxia, "[Lucas] gave us full support in submitting our application to the Electoral Commission to be recognized as a political party, and then used our lists to identify and kill us, one by one" (Cited in Hale 2006, 90).

A more felicitous experience with electoral competition took place in the department of Quetzaltenango where some Mayan professionals founded an indigenous civic electoral committee named Xel-jú in 1972. Xel-jú won some local offices in the 1970s, but it did not register its first significant breakthrough until 1995 when it elected Rigoberto Quemé as mayor of the departmental capital, Quetzaltenango (Fischer 2001, 93). Xel-jú won in part by reaching out to mestizos and recruiting mestizo candidates (Rasch 2011). Xel-jú won the mayoralty of Quetzaltenango again in 1999 in a close contest, but it finished a distant fourth in 2003 and it has struggled since that time. Other indigenous civic committees in Guatemala have also won some local posts, but none of them have managed to convert themselves into full-fledged political parties or scale up to the national level. Indeed, most indigenous civic committees have not even managed to succeed at the local level. In the 2007 elections, for example, civic electoral committees accounted for only nineteen of the 332 mayors elected in Guatemala, and only two of the mayors elected from the civic committees were indigenous (Asociación de Investigación y Estudios Sociales 2008, 73).

When indigenous people have been elected to local offices, it has typically been as candidates of the traditional parties such as the Democracia Cristiana Guatemalteca, the Partido de Avanzada Nacional, or the Frente Republicano Guatemalteco. Between 1995 and 2007, for example, indigenous people held approximately one-third of Guatemala's 332 mayoral positions, and most of these mayors represented traditional parties (Ceto 2007, 80; Reynolds 2007, 2). Many of the traditional parties have worked hard to recruit prominent indigenous candidates for local offices, including mayoral positions, in rural, highly indigenous municipalities.

The traditional parties have been much slower to recruit indigenous people for national-level posts, however. They have not nominated large numbers of indigenous people as candidates for the national legislature and those candidates they have recruited have typically been placed far down on the parties' lists, thereby reducing their chances of winning. As a result, the percentage of indigenous deputies in the national legislature has remained low, although it did rise from eight percent in the 1986–91 legislature to eleven percent in the 2008–12 legislature (Cupil 2007, 82; Asociación de Investigación y Estudios Sociales 2008, 90–1). Nor have the traditional parties selected many indigenous people for high-level positions in the state bureaucracy. Most presidents have only had one indigenous minister in their cabinets, and the indigenous ministers have usually held less prestigious portfolios (Cojtí Cuxil 2006, 153). Indigenous people have also been mostly absent from leadership positions within the traditional parties. Indeed, they occupied less than ten percent of the seats on the executive committees of the main political parties in 2007 (Mack 2007, 42).

Leftist parties have been somewhat more aggressive about selecting indigenous people for important positions. For example, in 2007 indigenous people represented more than fifty percent of the members of the executive committee of the leftist Unidad Revolucionario Nacional Guatemalteca (URNG) (Cupil 2007, 79–81). Leftist parties have also recruited many indigenous leaders as candidates for the legislature and other national-level positions, but only a handful of these candidates have been elected owing to the meager performance of the left in Guatemala. The left-wing Frente Democrático Nueva Guatemala, for example, nominated an indigenous candidate for the vice presidency in 1995 and the URNG did so in 2003, but neither of these parties fared particularly well in the elections (Hernández Pico 2006). The leftist Alianza Nueva

Nación, meanwhile, nominated Rigoberto Quemé as its presidential candidate in 2003, but Quemé renounced the nomination after a falling out with the party's leader, Pablo Monsanto.

It was not until 2007 that a self-identified indigenous person, human rights activist Rigoberta Menchú, actually ran for president of Guatemala. Menchú created her own political movement, Winaq, to back her candidacy, but she ran as the candidate of Encuentro por Guatemala (EG), a small center-left party. Menchú's candidacy generated considerable media attention because of her status as an indigenous woman and her fame as a winner of the Nobel Peace Prize. Nevertheless, her candidacy failed to take off and in the September 2007 elections she finished a distant seventh with a mere 3.1 percent of the valid vote. Even more surprising, the votes that she received equaled only about half of those won by the EG in the legislative elections.

Menchú's campaign faced a number of important obstacles, including discrimination and a shortage of campaign funds.[3] Indigenous candidates and parties in other countries have managed to overcome these disadvantages in part by relying on the indigenous movement for human and material resources, but by the 2000s, the indigenous movement in Guatemala was a shadow of its former self (Bastos and Brett 2010). Brett (2010, 77–8) argues that with the disintegration of the Coordinación de Organizaciones del Pueblo Maya de Guatemala in the late 1990s, the indigenous movement lost its direction. There were numerous indigenous leaders and organizations, but no umbrella organizations with the ability to coordinate policies and mobilizations. Moreover, in the 2000s the movement became increasingly dominated by elite urban, nongovernmental organizations, rather than mass grassroots associations. One study identifies 328 indigenous organizations in Guatemala, of which the vast majority were based in the capital (Cojtí Cuxil 2010, 103). Thus, by the 2000s the indigenous movement in Guatemala had lost its ability to mobilize people outside of the capital where the bulk of the indigenous population lived.

Menchú, moreover, had only limited influence in most of the country's indigenous communities. In contrast to Evo Morales and the leaders of Pachakutik, Menchú did not preside over a grassroots indigenous movement (Ba Tiul 2007; Falla 2007). Rather, she headed a foundation that was located in the capital and had only a few employees. Thus, in spite of her domestic and international fame, Menchú had little ability to mobilize indigenous people on her behalf. Her party, Winaq, did not provide her with much grassroots support either since it consisted mostly of Mayan intellectuals and nongovernmental organizations from the capital, rather than rural grassroots organizations and leaders (Bastos 2009, 12). Moreover, Menchú failed to win the endorsements or the

---

[3] As an indigenous woman from a poor family, Menchú faced a complex combination of gender, racial, and class biases. Women have been elected president of a number of Latin American countries, such as Argentina, Brazil, Chile, Costa Rica, Nicaragua, and Panama, but these women, unlike Menchú, have been white or light-skinned mestizas and have hailed from the middle or upper classes.

assistance of some of the most important grassroots indigenous or peasant leaders and organizations in the country, such as the Coordinadora Nacional de Organizaciones Campesinas (CNOC). Basilio Sánchez, a leader of the CNOC, said he was reluctant to endorse her because "we never felt her support, she has not gotten close to the social movements" (Ortiz Loaiza et al. 2008, 16). The participants at a hemispheric conference of indigenous communities, the Cumbre Continental de Pueblos y Nacionalidades de Abya Yala, which met in Guatemala in early 2007, also declined to endorse her. Many indigenous leaders and organizations ended up supporting the traditional parties, which used these leaders to attack Menchú's campaign (interview with Pop 2008).

Menchú sought to attract indigenous voters by making frequent ethnic appeals, although she was careful to emphasize the inclusive nature of her movement. She used indigenous clothing, spoke K'iche' on the campaign trail, and declared herself proud to be the first indigenous person to run for president (Figueroa 2007). Like many of the other candidates, she also denounced discrimination, called for education in indigenous languages, and promised more assistance to indigenous communities. Nevertheless, these appeals failed to resonate widely among the indigenous population in part because she lacked ties to local indigenous organizations. Menchú may also have been hurt by her failure to embrace certain causes that have traditionally been important to the indigenous population, such as agrarian reform. Indeed, an analysis of party platforms by the Mirador Electoral found that EG's platform included fewer issues of interest to the indigenous population than that of any of major political party (Mirador Electoral 2007, 5). Many indigenous people also felt that Menchú had distanced herself from them since winning the Nobel Prize. For example, some indigenous people criticized her for not visiting indigenous communities more often and claimed that she had not shared the funds from her prize (Ba Tiul 2007; Falla 2007). As a result, Menchú fared relatively poorly among indigenous voters. Indeed, she won only 4.4 percent of the vote in municipalities where indigenous people represent more than ninety percent of the population (Mirador Electoral 2007, 4).

Menchú was also hurt by her failure to run a populist campaign along the lines of Morales in Bolivia or Hugo Chávez in Venezuela. She did reach out to the urban mestizo population by emphasizing the inclusive and multicultural nature of her campaign, but she failed to employ populist discourse or proposals. In contrast to her counterparts in Bolivia and Ecuador, Menchú did not aggressively denounce the traditional parties and political and economic elites. Nor did she aggressively attack the incumbent government of Oscar Berger. Furthermore, many Guatemalans associated Menchú with the Berger government because she had served as its goodwill ambassador.

Menchú also alienated populist Guatemalans by actively seeking the support of the business community. She met with the leaders of business associations and chose a former head of the country's largest business association, Luis Fernando Montenegro, as her vice presidential candidate. Menchú went so far in this direction that she felt obliged to defend herself from charges that she had allied with the oligarchy (Orellana et al. 2007). Nor did Menchú engage in the nationalist and anti-neoliberal discourse that Morales and other populist leaders have employed (Bastos 2009, 11). Indeed, when Montenegro agreed to become her vice presidential candidate, he did so with the condition that it was not going to be "a campaign against the private sector" (interview with Montenegro 2008). Menchú made good on her word, even endorsing the country's free trade agreement with the United States, albeit with some qualifications ("Menchú Wades into Public Security Debate" 2007, 13).

From the outset, Menchú was wary of embracing any position that smacked of radicalism. During her campaign, she refused to define herself as a leftist and insisted that she had no political ideology, declaring that the left and the right had hurt and divided the country (Falla 2007; Mack 2007, 237). Her decision to forge an alliance with the Encuentro por Guatemala, rather than a more traditional leftist party such as the URNG, exemplified this caution. EG was a moderate center-left party that was based in the urban mestizo middle class and had no ties to the popular sectors. According to the head of EG's legislative delegation, Aníbal García, the party sought to make alliances with all sectors of the population, including the business community. In this way, it was more akin to moderate left parties, such as the Concertación in Chile or the Workers' Party in Brazil, than it was to the parties of Chávez or Morales (interview with García 2008).

Menchu's cautious and centrist approach, however, failed to mobilize disaffected sectors of the population behind her campaign. Menchú won some support in middle class mestizo areas, but she won relatively few votes in the poor urban areas that provided a major source of votes to the Morales and Chávez campaigns. In the end, Menchu's failure to adopt a populist discourse combined with the weakness of her ties to the indigenous population meant that neither mestizos nor indigenous people flocked to her campaign in large numbers.

COLOMBIA

Indigenous parties in Colombia have achieved similarly modest results. Indigenous organizations first participated in national elections in Colombia in 1990 when the country's largest indigenous federation, the Organización Nacional Indígena de Colombia (ONIC), and a regional indigenous group, the Movimiento de Autoridades Indígenas de Colombia (AICO), ran in the elections to form a constituent assembly.[4] The indigenous organizations fared better than expected, winning two seats in the constituent assembly. In addition, a third nonvoting seat was awarded to the indigenous guerrilla movement, Quintín Lame, in a peace accord. The indigenous delegates, along with non-indigenous allies such as the leftist Alianza Democrática M-19, successfully

---

[4] At that time, AICO was known as the Autoridades Indígenas del Suroeste. See Van Cott (2005, 179).

pushed for the inclusion of a wide variety of indigenous rights in the new constitution, including the setting aside of two seats for the indigenous population in the Colombian senate and one seat in the Chamber of Deputies.

These achievements gave the indigenous movement some favorable media attention and provided it with a political base (Van Cott 2000, ch. 3; 2005, 190–1). Their success in the constituent assembly also spurred them to participate in subsequent elections. In 1991, Quintín Lamé, along with the largest regional indigenous federation, the Consejo Regional Indígena del Cauca, formed a political party, the Alianza Social Indígena (ASI) to compete in the elections that year. Other indigenous organizations, such as AICO and ONIC, also opted to participate in the 1991 elections or subsequent contests.

The indigenous parties fared relatively well among indigenous voters and captured a few legislative seats in 1991 and subsequent years. ASI fared the best, reaching its apex in 1998 when it won two unreserved national deputy seats and one unreserved senate seat as well as one of the senate seats reserved for the indigenous population. In addition, ASI won some mayoral, councilor, and regional legislative seats, along with one gubernatorial position during this period. Other indigenous parties also captured some offices. AICO, for example, consistently won one of the senate seats reserved for the indigenous population, and it earned a national deputy seat in 2002 and gubernatorial positions in 2000 and 2003, as well as various mayoral, councilor, and regional legislative seats (Van Cott 2005, 204). ONIC, meanwhile, captured a senate seat in 1991 before withdrawing from electoral competition.

Overall, however, the performance of indigenous parties in Colombia has been decidedly modest, as they have never won more than two percent of the national vote. The meager national-level results of indigenous parties in Colombia stem partly from the small size of the indigenous population in Colombia. According to the 2005 census, the indigenous population represents only 3.3 percent of the total population, although they represent a majority in the departments of Vaupés and Vichada and a sizable proportion of the population in the departments of Amazonas, Cauca, and La Guajira. Moreover, the indigenous movement has little influence and few activists and affiliated organizations outside of indigenous areas, which has made it difficult to campaign in these areas.

The weak performance of indigenous parties outside of indigenous areas has also stemmed from the fact that these parties, unlike their counterparts in Bolivia and Ecuador, have not employed populist strategies very widely or effectively. The indigenous parties have not developed a strong anti-establishment and anti-neoliberal message. Nor have the indigenous parties produced a charismatic leader capable of uniting voters of all ethnicities behind his or her candidacy. To the contrary, the indigenous movement in Colombia remains relatively divided with a plethora of leaders and organizations. Populist strategies might not have been as effective in Colombia as in the central Andes given that Colombian voters have traditionally not been very receptive to outsider parties and populist policies.[5] Nevertheless, had they employed a more populist approach, Colombian indigenous parties, like their counterparts in Bolivia and Ecuador, might well have been able to capture the support of some of the voters fed up with the political establishment and its policies.

Instead, the indigenous parties in Colombia have mostly focused on ethnic issues. They have promoted a variety of ethnic demands from bilingual education to indigenous cultural and territorial rights and they have used ethnic themes, music, and symbols extensively in their campaigns (Laurent 2009, 105). Some indigenous parties have taken steps to reach out to white and mestizo voters (Laurent 2005, 167). The ASI, for example, has forged alliances with some non-indigenous groups, particularly those representing politically excluded groups, and it has recruited some non-indigenous candidates. In 2006, for example, it even recruited Antanas Mockus, the white former mayor of Bogotá, as its presidential candidate. For the most part, however, the indigenous parties have focused their campaigns in indigenous areas and have emphasized ethnic demands. As a result, they have failed to make inroads in most parts of Colombia.[6]

VENEZUELA

Indigenous parties have generated similarly modest results in Venezuela. The indigenous movement first became involved in electoral politics in Venezuela during the late 1990s. Prior to this time, some indigenous leaders had participated in electoral politics, often through traditional parties or leftist parties, but the indigenous movement did not have its own electoral vehicle (Van Cott 2005, 183–4). In 1997, however, the Organización Regional de Pueblos Indígenas de Amazonas, which was the affiliate of the main indigenous federation, the Consejo Nacional Indio de Venezuela (CONIVE) in the state of Amazonas, founded an indigenous party, the Pueblos Unidos Multiétnicos de Amazonas (PUAMA). The indigenous movement created PUAMA partly in order to try to defend the territorial rights of indigenous people in the state of Amazonas, but also because some indigenous leaders felt that the political parties had taken advantage of the indigenous population (Van Cott 2005, 197–8).

PUAMA had little success initially. It participated in elections for the first time in 1998, winning 1.5 percent of the vote in the state of Amazonas and a

---

[5] The two traditional parties, the Partido Liberal Colombiano and the Partido Social Conservador, dominated Colombian politics through the 1990s, typically winning more than ninety percent of the presidential vote and more than sixty percent of the legislative vote. These parties weakened considerably beginning in the early 2000s, but the new parties or movements that have partly supplanted them were headed by former leaders of the traditional parties, such as Alvaro Uribe and Juan Manuel Santos.

[6] Van Cott (2005, 203–4) notes that Colombian indigenous parties have captured a few local posts in non-indigenous areas, such as a councilor position in the city of Bogotá and a seat in the legislature of the department of Antioquía.

post in the state legislative assembly. Another indigenous party, the Movimiento Unido de Pueblos Indígenas (MUPI), that was founded at the same time, fared even worse, winning a mere 0.1 percent of the vote.

The election of Hugo Chávez in 1998 provided the indigenous movement with the opportunity to gain more influence, however. After his election, Chávez convoked a national constituent assembly to rewrite the country's constitution, and reserved three seats in this assembly for indigenous delegates, each of whom represented an affiliate of CONIVE in a different part of the country. In addition, two other indigenous activists managed to win election to unreserved seats in the constituent assembly. The five indigenous delegates, along with their allies, successfully pushed the assembly to include significant indigenous rights in the new constitution, including collective land rights, language rights, and the use of indigenous forms of justice (Van Cott 2003a). The new constitution also set aside three seats in the national legislature for the indigenous population, and reserved one seat in the state legislature and one municipal council position for indigenous people in those states or municipalities that have large indigenous populations. The candidates for these seats could run as representatives of political parties or social organizations, but they had to be indigenous, speak an indigenous language, and have a traditional position of authority in their community or a history of participation in the indigenous movement.

These reserved seats, along with the indigenous movement's ties to the Chávez administration, gave the movement some influence in national politics for the first time. CONIVE, which has been closely allied to Chávez in recent years, has typically managed to get its own candidates elected to the reserved indigenous seats in the national legislature. CONIVE won all three reserved seats in 2000 and 2005, although in 2010 it only captured one of these seats. (The Fundación para la Capacitación e Integración y Dignificación gained one of the seats in 2010 and the Movimiento Indígena Autónomo de Zulia won the other.) In addition, an indigenous representative of CONIVE, Noelí Pocaterra, was elected as the vice president of the national assembly, while another CONIVE leader, Nicia Maldonado, was chosen as the minister for indigenous peoples.

Indigenous parties also have won some open positions in the state of Amazonas where the indigenous represent approximately half of the population. PUAMA, for example, won a nonreserved seat in the national assembly from the state of Amazonas in 2000 as well as three mayoralties and a seat in the Amazonas legislative assembly. In alliance with a left-wing party, Patria Para Todos, PUAMA also won the governorship of the state of Amazonas in 2000. The MUPI, meanwhile, won a seat from Amazonas in the national assembly in the 2005 elections.

Outside of Amazonas, however, the indigenous parties have fared poorly and their share of the national vote has been miniscule. Indigenous parties in Venezuela have encountered limited success for several reasons. First, the indigenous movement is weak or nonexistent outside of a few states. As a result, it has been able to provide little assistance to indigenous parties in most areas of the country. Perhaps even more important, indigenous people represent only a small share of the Venezuelan population. In the 2001 census, only 2.1 percent of the population self-identified as indigenous, and Amazonas was the only state in which the indigenous represented a majority of the population. Indigenous people constitute approximately one-fourth of the population of the state of Delta Amacuro, but the indigenous movement in this state is divided and indigenous parties have had little success there (Van Cott 2005, 182–4). In no other state do indigenous people represent more than five percent of the population.

Given Venezuelan demographics, indigenous parties cannot hope to fare well in national elections relying on the indigenous vote alone. Surprisingly, however, indigenous parties in Venezuela have made few efforts to reach out to whites and mestizos. According to Van Cott (2005, 207), indigenous parties in Venezuela "make no attempt to attract non-Indians, partly because at the local and state levels non-Indians mostly oppose their interests." The indigenous movement and parties have supported Chávez's agenda, but they have mostly concentrated on indigenous issues. As a result, these parties have held little appeal for whites and mestizos.

Although the indigenous movement's alliance with Chávez has provided it with some patronage and policy influence, the alliance has limited the movement's autonomy and potential for growth. Chávez has sought to control the indigenous movement and he has successfully wooed indigenous and mestizo voters with the same combination of ethnic and populist appeals that indigenous parties have used successfully elsewhere. As long as Chávez remains popular it seems unlikely that indigenous-based parties in Venezuela will be able to make inroads in the ethnically mixed urban popular sectors that have provided support for indigenous parties in other countries. Nor does it seem likely that the major indigenous organizations will break with Chávez, given the benefits of their alliance with him. Although a few small indigenous parties, such as Parlamento Indígena Venezuela and Tawala, have allied with the opposition, these parties have typically fared poorly in elections. As a result, indigenous parties in Venezuela appear to have limited electoral prospects for the near future.

NICARAGUA

Indigenous parties in Nicaragua have also failed to expand beyond their narrow base in the indigenous population. The most successful of these parties, Yapti Tasba Masraka Nanih Asla Takanka (YATAMA), which means "Organization of the Children of the Mother Earth" in the Miskitú language, has won important offices in the autonomous region on the coast, but it has not scaled up to the national level. Instead, it has focused on representing the interests of the Miskitú population, which is concentrated on the coast. Nevertheless, it has made alliances with national-level parties which have rewarded it with some cabinet positions and a modicum of national influence.

YATAMA was formed in 1987 by former guerrilla organizations based in the Miskitú population of the Atlantic coast. These guerrilla groups, led by Brooklyn Rivera and Stedman Fagoth, laid down their arms in the late 1980s and converted themselves into an electoral organization in exchange for a pledge by the Sandinista regime to create an autonomous area on the Atlantic coast (Hale 1994; Hooker 2009). The autonomous area consists of two separate regions, the North Atlantic Autonomous Region (RAAN) and the South Atlantic Autonomous Region (RAAS). Both of these regions are self-governed by regional councils composed of forty-five directly elected councilors plus the national assembly representatives from the region. These councils elect a governing board as well as a regional coordinator or governor from among their members.

Elections in the autonomous regions were initially scheduled for early 1989, but because of a hurricane they were rescheduled to coincide with national elections in early 1990. YATAMA fared relatively well in the 1990 elections, winning twenty-three seats in the RAAN and five seats in the RAAS. Moreover, its ally, the Unidad Nicaragüense Opositora (UNO), which won the national elections that year, also captured some seats in the autonomous regions. YATAMA thus had enough votes to dominate the governing board in the RAAN and to elect a member of YATAMA as regional coordinator. In the years that followed, however, it lost ground. In the 1994 elections, for example, YATAMA won only eight seats in the RAAN and five in the RAAS. The party's poor performance in 1994 stemmed partly from its lackluster record of governance in the previous period (Butler 1997, 228–9). Many people on the coast also felt that YATAMA's ally, UNO, which controlled the national government, had done little for the coastal region (González 2008, 213). Equally important, the party was severely divided in 1994. Conflicts with Rivera led Fagoth and his allies to temporarily leave the party and run as candidates of the Partido Liberal Constitucionalista (PLC). As a result, some former YATAMA supporters switched their allegiances to the PLC, which was the big winner of the 1994 elections.

YATAMA fared about the same in the 1998 elections, winning eight seats in the RAAN, but in 2000 it was barred from running altogether. Prior to 2000, YATAMA had participated in elections as a "popular subscription association," but that year Nicaragua passed a new electoral law requiring all organizations to register as a political party in order to compete in elections (Campbell 2007, 504). To register as a party, YATAMA needed to collect three percent of the signatures of all registered voters in the autonomous regions and run candidates in at least eighty percent of the municipalities of the region. In the 2000 elections, YATAMA initially sought to run in alliance with a new party, the Partido de los Pueblos Costeños, but some of the signatures this party collected were ruled invalid. YATAMA then tried to run on its own, but the Supreme Electoral

Council disqualified it on the grounds that it did not have candidates in the requisite number of municipalities. Numerous efforts were made to appeal this ruling, to no avail.[7] As a result, many of YATAMA's supporters boycotted the elections, causing the abstention rate to rise to sixty percent in the autonomous regions, as opposed to approximately forty percent for Nicaragua as a whole (Campbell 2007, 506; González 2008).

In the following years, YATAMA registered as a party and recovered somewhat, winning eleven seats in the RAAN in 2002 and thirteen seats in 2006. The party also forged an alliance with the Sandinistas, which enabled it to gain control of the region's governing board and regional coordinator position. YATAMA initially fared less well in the RAAS where it won only two seats in 2002, but for the 2006 elections it allied with Coast Power, a new Creole-dominated party, which helped it win six seats in the RAAS.

Although YATAMA has been an important political actor in the autonomous region of Nicaragua, especially in the RAAN, since 1990, it has not been able to expand its influence outside of the autonomous regions in part because it is viewed as a party that only represents Miskitú interests. As one research team reported, "YATAMA is perceived as an exclusionary organization" (González 2010, 109–10). YATAMA has traditionally been dominated by Miskitús and it has recruited relatively few non-indigenous people as candidates in the north. Between 1990 and 2010, fifty-nine of the party's sixty-three councilors in the RAAN were Miskitú, while three were Creole and one was Mayangna (González 2010, 104). None were white or mestizo. YATAMA has reached out a bit more in the south where the Miskitús represent a smaller percentage of the population. Indeed, between 1990 and 2010, YATAMA's legislative contingent in the RAAS included ten Miskitús, nine Creoles, and three Mayangna (González 2010, 105). Even in the RAAS, however, YATAMA had no white or mestizo councilors.

Unlike the MAS in Bolivia and Pachakutik in Ecuador, YATAMA has not developed a broad populist platform designed to appeal across ethnic groups. Instead, the party has focused mostly on indigenous interests and demands. YATAMA's most important leader, Brooklyn Rivera, has acknowledged the ethnocentric nature of the party:

We could open ourselves up, and we have done it before, so that non-indigenous candidates participate in our electoral lists, but the other coastal people should count on their own organizations to be capable of representing them. If these organizations don't have the power or capability to represent them, then that should be a preoccupation of those communities, and not of Yatama. To include the rights of other ethnic groups in our struggle could take us away from our principal goal, which is the rights of the indigenous peoples. (González 2010, 111)

YATAMA's exclusionary approach has not prevented it from succeeding in the autonomous region where thirty percent of the population is indigenous,

---

[7] YATAMA eventually took its case to the Inter-American Court of Human Rights, which in 2005 issued a ruling favoring the indigenous party's position.

including forty-five percent of the RAAN (Campbell 2007, 501). But this approach has little possibility of succeeding in the rest of Nicaragua where indigenous people represent only a tiny fraction of the population. Indeed, to date, YATAMA has made no real efforts to compete on the national level.

CONCLUSION

Indigenous parties outside of the central Andes thus have had meager results to date. They have been hindered in part by their failure to adopt the ethnopopulist appeals that have been used effectively by the leaders of the MAS and Pachakutik as well as by various politicians in Peru. Perhaps more important, conditions have been less favorable for indigenous parties outside of the central Andes. In most Latin American countries, the indigenous population is relatively small and the indigenous movement is weak. Indeed, Guatemala is the only Latin American country outside of the central Andes where indigenous people represent more than ten percent of the total population. Moreover, in Guatemala, as we have seen, the indigenous movement is fragmented and demobilized.

As a result, prospects do not appear to be good for the rise of indigenous parties outside of the central Andes. Although indigenous parties may exercise influence in states, provinces, or municipalities where indigenous people represent a large share of the population, they are less likely to succeed at the national level where the indigenous population represents a small fraction of the electorate. Indigenous parties in some countries may be able to overcome the absence of a large indigenous base in some cases by reaching out to whites and mestizos through populist appeals, as Pachakutik did in Ecuador. But these parties are likely to face tough competition for populist constituencies from the many non-indigenous parties that have also employed these strategies in recent years.

The prospects for the emergence of strong Afro-Latino parties in the region also appear relatively limited in the near term even though people of African descent represent a large proportion of the population in some Latin American countries, such as Brazil, Colombia, the Dominican Republic, and Venezuela. According to one widely cited study by the United Nations – Economic Commission for Latin America and the Caribbean (CEPAL), the black and mulatto population of Latin America and the Caribbean total approximately 146 million, including seventy-five million in Brazil (Hopenhayn and Bello 2001, 23).[8] Other estimates suggest that the region's Afro-Latino population is considerably smaller, some put it as low as thirty-five million, but even the

---

[8] The high numbers in the CEPAL study stem in part from the fact that the study uses inflated estimates of the size of Afro-Latino population for some countries like Colombia and Venezuela. The CEPAL study, for example, estimates the Afro-Colombian population at thirty-one million and the Afro-Venezuelan population at seventeen million, which would mean that Afro-Latinos represent approximately three-quarters of the total population of each of these countries.

lower estimates suggest that Afro-Latinos represent a significant share of the population in some countries and are certainly large enough to support an Afro-Latino party (Monge Oviedo 1992, 19; Oakley 2001, 3).

One of the main obstacles to the rise of Afro-Latino parties in the region is the absence of racial or ethnic consciousness among people of African descent. The 1993 census in Colombia, for example, found that only 1.2 percent of the population self-identified as black, even though most sources suggest that Afro-Colombians represent anywhere from eight to twenty-six percent of the total population (Sánchez and García 2006). Similarly, in Brazil, only six percent of the population identified as black in the 2000 census, although scholars have argued that at least half of the population is of African origin.[9] Latin Americans of African descent have declined to identify as black, mulatto, or Afro-Latino in part because of social prejudices against people of African descent. Widespread acceptance of the ideology of racial democracy, which suggests that race is largely irrelevant in Latin America because of the long history of race mixing in the region, has also inhibited racial consciousness in the region (Paschel and Sawyer 2008, 198–9).[10]

Another obstacle to the rise of Afro-Latino parties is the relative weakness of the Afro-Latino movement. Although Afro-Latino organizations have grown in recent years, they do not have the organizational scope and density that the indigenous movement enjoys in countries such as Bolivia and Ecuador.[11] Afro-Latino organizations, for example, have not demonstrated an ability to carry out nationwide protests or to shut down their nations' capitals, as the indigenous movement has done in some countries. Nor have they established strong national federations that bring together numerous local organizations.

The absence of racial consciousness and the relative weakness and fragmentation of the Afro-Latino movement has impeded the formation of Afro-Latino parties. Very few Afro-Latino parties have arisen to date and those parties that have emerged have fared poorly. The Alianza Social Afrocolombiana, for example, competed in the 2010 presidential elections in Colombia, but it won only one-tenth of one percent of the national vote.

Nevertheless, there are several reasons why we might expect the prospects for Afro-Latino parties to improve over time. First, it seems unlikely that the political, social, and economic marginalization of the Afro-Latino population will disappear anytime soon, which will provide a strong motive for

---

[9] In the 2000 Brazilian census, another thirty-nine percent of the population identified as *pardo*. The term *pardo*, which translates as *grey* or *brown*, does not clearly denote blackness or African origin.

[10] The absence of a distinctive language may also have impeded ethnic or racial consciousness among many Afro-Latinos. Where Afro-Latino communities are separated from the rest of their population by a different language, as in some of the English-speaking communities of Central America, they have typically had a stronger racial identity, and they have been more successful in lobbying for political rights (Hooker 2008).

[11] For surveys of Afro-Latino movements in the region, see Paschel and Sawyer (2008), Hoffman (2010), Oakley (2001), and Wade (1997).

Afro-Latinos to organize politically. Afro-Latinos, like indigenous people, are disproportionately poor and they have lower life expectancies, fewer years of schooling, and less access to housing and healthcare than the rest of the population (Bailey 2009; Oakley 2001; Ribando Seelke 2008; Telles 2004). They also suffer from frequent discrimination. This marginalization and discrimination mean that the Afro-Latino population has significant grievances which political entrepreneurs could use to mobilize them.

Second, it is likely that Afro-Latino social movements will strengthen over time. These movements have grown steadily in recent decades, thanks in part to support from international development agencies, and there is ample reason to expect this growth to continue (Paschel and Sawyer 2008; Ribando Seelke 2008). As Afro-Latino movements become stronger, they might well form parties, just as indigenous social movements did. Third and finally, it is also quite possible that racial identities in Latin America will become stronger over time. The expansion of Afro-Latino social movements should promote greater racial consciousness in the region, and so, too, should the spread of race-conscious state policies. Increased racial consciousness, in turn, will provide greater opportunities for partisan mobilization.

Any Afro-Latino parties that do emerge, like their indigenous counterparts, will need to be inclusive in order to attract support. Exclusionary appeals would not only alienate whites, but also Afro-Latinos of mixed descent or with racially ambivalent identities. Moreover, given the relatively low salience of race in the region, it is unlikely that Afro-Latino parties could be successful by relying on ethnic or racial appeals alone. Afro-Latino parties, like indigenous parties, might find traditional populist strategies particularly effective in winning support across ethnic lines, particularly given that the Afro-Latino population, like the indigenous population, is typically poor and politically disenchanted. Indeed, in the long run, ethnopopulism may turn out to be as effective a strategy for the Afro-Latino parties as it has been for indigenous movements.

6

Indigenous Parties and Democracy in the Andes

The emergence of powerful indigenous parties in Latin America has been greeted by some observers with trepidation. National security analysts in Washington and elsewhere have feared that such movements will be a breeding ground for extremist, anti-capitalist, and racially exclusionary ideas ("A political awakening" 2004, 37; Madrid 2005b; Oppenheimer 2003, 16A). Peruvian novelist and Nobel laureate Mario Vargas Llosa has gone so far as to argue that Latin American indigenous movements have disturbing elements that "appeal to base instincts, to the worst instincts of people, like distrust of people who are different" (Olmos 2003). These attitudes, he suggests, "sooner or later will drag us to barbarism." Indeed, there is an extensive academic literature that suggests that ethnic parties lead to ethnic conflict and the breakdown of democracy.

What impact has the rise of indigenous parties in Latin America had on democracy in the region? Have indigenous parties led to ethnic conflict and exclusion or have they deepened democracy in the region, as some of their supporters would expect?

This chapter examines the impact of the two most important indigenous parties in Latin America: the Movimiento Unidad Plurinacional Pachakutik in Ecuador and the Movimiento al Socialismo in Bolivia. It focuses mostly on the latter, however, because the MAS has had the most experience governing. The MAS won various mayoralties beginning in 1995, became the country's largest opposition party in 2002, and captured the presidency in 2005. Pachakutik, like the MAS, has won numerous mayoralties and a significant number of seats in the legislature since the mid-1990s, but it has not held the Ecuadorian presidency, although it did briefly participate in the government of Lucio Gutiérrez (2003–5). Pachakutik and the MAS have arguably had an important impact on democracy at the municipal level as well as at the national level. Nevertheless, this study focuses mostly on the national-level policies of these parties because of the relatively limited data available on the parties' records of municipal governance.[1]

---

[1] For analyses of the municipal-level policies of the MAS, Pachakutik, and other indigenous parties in Latin America, see Cameron (2010) and Van Cott (2009).

The MAS and Pachakutik have not only used ethnic and populist appeals to win support, they have also employed ethnic and populist policies in governing. This chapter argues that the ethnic policies and appeals of these parties have had a mostly positive impact on democracy. The ethnic policies and appeals have helped boost political participation and support for democracy among indigenous people, and they have helped increase indigenous political influence and representation. The two parties have also sought to reduce ethnic inequality and discrimination and promote greater respect for indigenous culture and practices, which should help deepen democracy in these countries in the long run.

By contrast, the populist rhetoric and policies of the two parties – specifically their personalistic, anti-establishment, and plebiscitarian tendencies – have had a negative impact on democracy. The Morales administration, in particular, has undermined horizontal accountability and the rule of law by concentrating power, weakening the existing political institutions, and attacking the media and the political opposition. Morales's anti-democratic behavior has little in common with traditional indigenous political norms, which tend to emphasize power sharing and consensus building. It has much more in common with the practices of non-indigenous populist leaders such as Hugo Chávez and Rafael Correa.

The impact of the rise of indigenous parties on democracy in the Andes is thus decidedly mixed, and it is likely to remain so in the future. In the following pages, I explore these arguments in more detail. The first section discusses why existing theories of ethnic parties expect such parties to destabilize democracy and lead to ethnic polarization. It argues that indigenous parties in Latin America have not had the destabilizing effects predicted by theorists of ethnic parties in large part because the ethnic landscape in Latin America has encouraged such parties to seek support across ethnic lines. The second section explains why the indigenous parties' ethnic profile and policies have had positive effects on democracy. The third section, by contrast, shows how the parties' populist policies and rhetoric have undermined democracy. The conclusion discusses what impact indigenous parties might have on democracy in the future.

ETHNIC PARTIES AND DEMOCRACY

Much of the existing literature on ethnic parties argues that they have a profoundly negative impact on democracy (Horowitz 1985; Rabushka and Shepsle 1972; Sisk 1996). According to these scholars, the pernicious effect of ethnic parties stems in part from their tendency to engage in ethnic outbidding. As we have seen, ethnic parties often try to mobilize co-ethnics by appealing to ethnic prejudice and resentment and by exaggerating the threat represented by other ethnic groups. These appeals worsen ethnic polarization, increase the likelihood of ethnic violence, and make it difficult for moderate leaders and multiethnic parties to subsist. As Horowitz (1985, 291) put it: "[B]y appealing to electorates in ethnic terms, by making ethnic demands on government, and by bolstering the influence of ethnically chauvinistic elements within each group, parties that begin by merely mirroring ethnic divisions help to deepen and extend them."

According to these theorists, ethnic parties also tend to undermine democracy when they take power. Rabushka and Shepsle (1972, 86) argue that when ethnic parties take power "a sense of communal self-preservation leads to efforts to manipulate the machinery of the state in order to secure and maintain communal advantage." To strengthen their hold on power, ethnic parties will manipulate electoral rules, use state resources in their political campaigns, and harass or intimidate the opposition. Once in power, ethnic parties may also favor co-ethnics in the provision of state goods and services. Such favoritism exacerbates ethnic polarization and reduces support for government institutions. It may also lead to violent resistance. With little chance of defeating the dominant ethnic group at the ballot box, minority ethnic groups sometimes resort to violence in order to protest policies or try to take power.[2] Violent resistance, however, will typically provoke further repression and other authoritarian measures from the dominant ethnic group.

Some scholars have challenged these claims, however, arguing that ethnic parties may help bring about democratic stability or deepening under certain conditions (Birnir 2007; Chandra 2005; Madrid 2005b; Van Cott 2005). Chandra (2005, 236), for example, argues that ethnic parties may sustain democracy where the existing political institutions "encourage the politicization of ethnic divisions and induce proliferation of multiple ethnic majorities." Birnir, meanwhile, argues that ethnic identities and parties may promote party system stability in new democracies by providing a "stable but flexible information shortcut for political choices" (Birnir 2007, 9). She maintains that ethnic groups and parties are only likely to become intransigent where they are denied access to government (Birnir 2007).

As Chandra (2005) points out, the predictions laid out in much of the literature on ethnic parties are based in part on primordialist assumptions about ethnic identification and attitudes. These theorists assume that ethnic identification is singular and fixed and that voters will only support the parties that identify with their ethnic group. The fluidity of ethnic identities in Latin America, however, makes it feasible for ethnic parties to win support across ethnic lines. Ethnic parties in Latin America have therefore typically refrained from making exclusionary appeals and reached out to members of other ethnic groups.

For this reason, the rise of indigenous parties in the region has not had the dire effects on ethnic relations that many scholars would have predicted (Madrid 2005b). Contrary to the expectations outlined in the literature on ethnic parties, the emergence of indigenous parties in Latin America has not

---

[2] According to Horowitz (1985, 298), "there is a certain fixity that sets in where parties are ethnically based that is conducive either to stalemate or to fears of permanent domination. The ascriptive predictability of party outcomes fosters conflict."

led to the disappearance of multiethnic parties. Indeed, all of the main parties in the region, including the MAS and Pachakutik, are multiethnic, and none of the major parties have engaged in ethnic outbidding or exclusionary appeals. Although indigenous leaders have at times made ethnonationalist statements, most of the leaders of indigenous parties have emphasized their parties' openness and have avoided ethnonationalist policies and behavior. Nor has the emergence of indigenous parties led to a significant worsening of ethnic polarization in the region. Bolivia has become increasingly polarized between supporters and opponents of the Morales administration in recent years, but the polarization is more ideological and regional than ethnic in nature.

Various scholars have argued that the rise of indigenous movements and parties has actually had a positive impact on democracy in the region. Lucero (2008, 189), for example, maintains that "indigenous movements represent a democratizing force in contemporary Latin America. ..." Yashar (2005, 300), meanwhile, has written that remarkably, "the recent politicization of ethnic cleavages in Latin America has not unleashed ethnic conflict but has led to an explicit effort to accommodate a diverse ethnic population and a more plural form of democracy." Finally, Van Cott (2005, 235) suggests that: "On balance, the emergence of ethnic parties in South America has been positive for democratic institutions in the region. ..." The following section discusses the main contributions of indigenous parties to deepening democracy in the region. As the subsequent section makes clear, however, these benefits must be weighed against the very negative effects of the indigenous parties' populist tendencies.

ETHNIC REPRESENTATION

Indigenous people have traditionally been marginalized politically as well as socially and economically in the Andes. Most indigenous people in the Andes are poor and lack the resources to contribute to political campaigns or causes. They also typically have lower levels of education than non-indigenous people and live in rural areas far from the national centers of power. Until the 1990s, indigenous people rarely occupied important political posts or positions of influence in the region. The leadership of political parties, government ministries and agencies, and most powerful interest groups was almost exclusively white and mestizo. Indigenous people served at times in important positions in the ministry of agriculture or rural development or in agencies dedicated to the indigenous population, but they generally did not have a significant presence in other government agencies. Nor did many indigenous people serve in elected positions prior to the 1990s. Small, rural municipalities sometimes had indigenous mayors or councilors, but the elected leaders of the larger cities tended to be overwhelmingly white and mestizo.

The political exclusion of the indigenous population prior to the 1990s was particularly noticeable in national legislatures. The traditional parties would rarely nominate indigenous people as congressional candidates, and when they did they typically placed them far down on their party lists where they had little chance of getting elected. In Ecuador only one indigenous leader served in the legislature in the 1980s and only a handful did in the 1990s, excluding those representing Pachakutik. A few indigenous leaders served in the Bolivian legislature in the 1980s, but they represented small indigenous parties based in the Aymara population. Even in the 1990s, the traditional parties in Bolivia failed to incorporate many indigenous leaders, although the Movimiento Nacionalista Revolucionario did choose an Aymara leader, Victor Hugo Cárdenas, as its vice presidential candidate in 1993. Indeed, as late as the 1997–2002 congress, the traditional parties in Bolivia had no indigenous senators and only one indigenous deputy (Albó 2002, 95; Madrid 2005a, 12).

It was not until the emergence of indigenous parties in the mid-1990s that indigenous people came to occupy numerous positions of influence in the region. Unlike the traditional parties, the indigenous parties nominated numerous indigenous leaders as candidates for important political posts, and many of these candidates were elected. The increased number of indigenous authorities was particularly noticeable at the local and regional levels. In Ecuador, Pachakutik won eleven mayoralties and twenty-nine municipal councilor positions in 1996, twenty-seven mayoralties and thirty-five municipal councilor positions in 1998, and twenty-three mayoralties and eighty-four municipal councilmember positions in 2000 (Van Cott 2005, 127). Pachakutik also captured five provincial prefect (governor) positions in 1998 and 2000, and six in 2004 (Van Cott 2005, 127). Most of these positions were won by indigenous leaders, although Pachakutik's white and mestizo candidates also captured some important local posts.

The rise of the MAS in Bolivia, along with the passage of a decentralization law that created several hundred mostly rural municipalities, led to the election of numerous indigenous mayors and council members in that country as well. In the 1995 municipal elections, the predecessor of the MAS, the IU/ASP, won ten mayoralty positions and fifty-four municipal councilor positions (Van Cott 2005, 86). As Chapter 2 discussed, the IU/ASP split in two before the 1999 municipal elections, with the faction controlled by Alejo Véliz winning four mayoralties and twenty-three municipal councilor positions and the faction controlled by Evo Morales, which became known as the MAS, gaining ten mayoralties and seventy-nine municipal councilor positions (Van Cott 2005, 86). The MAS's real breakthrough, however, came in the 2004 elections when it finished first in 101 municipalities, winning eighty-nine mayoralties and 454 councilmember positions. The MAS built on this impressive performance in the 2010 elections, finishing first in 229 municipalities and winning more than one thousand councilmember positions.

The MAS also has demonstrated its strength in departmental elections in Bolivia, winning three of the nine prefectural positions in 2005 and six of nine in 2010. Not all of the MAS's local officeholders have been indigenous. Indeed, over time the MAS elected an increasing number of whites and mestizos, particularly in urban municipalities or for department-wide positions.[3] Nevertheless, the MAS has continued to field many more indigenous candidates than the other main parties and, as a result of its success, indigenous people now hold a wide variety of important local and regional offices in Bolivia.

With the rise of indigenous parties, many more indigenous people also gained important national-level offices. In Ecuador, Pachakutik elected eight national legislators in 1998, fourteen in 2002, and six in 2006. Two-thirds of Pachakutik's national legislative delegation in 1996 and 1998 was indigenous, but this proportion fell to one-half in 2002 before rising to five-sixths in 2006. Some of Pachakutik's indigenous legislators occupied important positions in the Ecuadorian congress: Nina Pacari, for example, was elected the second vice president of the Ecuadorian congress in 1998. The rise of Pachakutik also enabled indigenous people to gain access to important positions in the state bureaucracy. After his 2002 election, Lucio Gutiérrez rewarded Pachakutik for its support by granting it control of four ministries, including the ministry of foreign relations, headed by Pacari, and the ministry of agriculture, held by Luis Macas. Pachakutik's political appointees were forced to resign when the party broke with Gutiérrez less than a year after his election. Gutiérrez, however, quickly appointed other indigenous leaders, such as Antonio Vargas, to top posts in order to try to retain support among the indigenous population. This policy has continued under Rafael Correa. Correa has had a tempestuous relationship with Pachakutik and CONAIE, but he has recruited indigenous candidates and appointed indigenous leaders to high-profile posts in order to win support in indigenous areas. Thus, even though Pachakutik has lost ground in recent years, many indigenous people continue to hold important positions in government.

The rise of the MAS in Bolivia has enabled indigenous people to occupy important national-level political positions in that country as well. Indeed, with the election of Evo Morales in 2005, a self-identified indigenous person became president of Bolivia for the first time. Morales, moreover, brought many indigenous people into top policymaking positions in the executive branch. Indigenous leaders, for example, have served as minister of foreign relations, minister of justice, and minister of education under Morales. Indigenous people now also represent a large share of the legislature in Bolivia. The MAS only elected four national legislative deputies in 1997, all of whom were indigenous. In 2002, however, it elected twenty-seven deputies and eight senators; in 2005, it elected seventy-two deputies and twelve senators; and in 2009, it elected eighty-two deputies and twenty-six senators.[4] Although the proportion of the MAS's deputies and senators who are indigenous has declined, approximately

[3] Approximately three-quarters of the IU's mayors and council members in 1995 were of indigenous or peasant origin (Albó 2002, 85). Numerous indigenous and peasant mayors were also elected by other parties that year, especially the Movimiento Bolivia Libre, a small leftist party.

[4] Another indigenous party in Bolivia, the Movimiento Indígena Pachakutic, elected six indigenous deputies in 2002.

half of them in recent years have been indigenous, and they have occupied important leadership roles in the senate, the chamber of deputies, and the constituent assembly. Other parties also have recruited more indigenous candidates in recent years in order to compete more effectively with the MAS in indigenous areas. In the 2002 elections, for example, the Movimiento de Izquierda Revolucionaria elected eight indigenous leaders, including Elsa Guevara, to congress, while the Nueva Fuerza Republicana elected another eight indigenous representatives, including Alejo Véliz. Nevertheless, the vast majority of indigenous senators and deputies in recent years have belonged to the MAS.

The MAS has even gone so far as to ensure ethnic representation in certain state institutions by mandating it in the new constitution. According to Article 206 of the constitution, at least two of the members of the Supreme Electoral Tribunal and at least one of the members of each of the departmental electoral tribunals must be of indigenous or peasant origin. The new constitution also calls for the creation of legislative seats specifically for the indigenous population, and the Morales administration has established seven of these seats. By constitutional mandate, these legislators are to be elected from rural, heavily indigenous districts situated in departments where the indigenous population represents a minority of the total population. The new constitution does not set aside any ministries for the indigenous population, but it does recommend that the president respect "plurinational character and gender equity in the composition of the cabinet." In addition, Article 234 of the new constitution requires that public servants speak at least two of the country's official languages, which should favor the indigenous population since indigenous languages are now among the country's official languages.

Thus, in both Bolivia and Ecuador, the rise of indigenous parties has enabled indigenous people to gain greater representation in government. Indigenous parties have recruited numerous indigenous candidates, they have set aside positions for indigenous people, and they have appointed many indigenous people to top policymaking posts. In addition, the rise of indigenous parties has led non-indigenous parties to try to recruit more indigenous leaders in order to compete more effectively in indigenous areas. As a result, indigenous people now occupy many more important elected and appointed positions than they did previously both at the national and local level.

POLITICAL PARTICIPATION

The rise of indigenous parties also has encouraged greater political participation by the indigenous population. Indigenous people have participated in various ways. Many indigenous people have attended rallies or protests organized by the indigenous parties. Unlike the traditional parties in Bolivia and Ecuador, the MAS and Pachakutik have ties to numerous grassroots organizations, which they are able to use to mobilize people for demonstrations as well as elections. The MAS, for example, encouraged its supporters to carry out protests in support of the agrarian reform law as well as its constitutional reform proposals. Indigenous people also have participated in various party decision making forums. Both Pachakutik and the MAS hold regular assemblies and congresses to help select the parties' candidates as well as their policy priorities. These forums bring together large numbers of indigenous leaders and representatives. A more select group of indigenous leaders has participated in the executive committees of Pachakutik and the MAS or in the Coordinadora Nacional para el Cambio (CONALCAM), an organization the Morales administration created to coordinate the government's actions with the social movements that support it. A number of Pachakutik and MAS mayors also have devised mechanisms to encourage popular participation in municipal planning (Cameron 2010; Van Cott 2009).

The rise of indigenous parties also has led to greater participation of indigenous people in elections. Traditionally, voter turnout was lower in indigenous areas than in non-indigenous areas in Bolivia and Ecuador for a number of reasons (Madrid 2005b, 168; Ticona Alejo et al. 1995; Wray 1996). First, indigenous people tend to live disproportionately in rural areas, and they often have to travel long distances to vote. Indigenous people also tend to be less educated and at times do not speak or read Spanish. As a result, they may have more difficulty understanding the ballot and seeking assistance with voting procedures (Aguilar 2005; Wray 1996). Indigenous people are also less likely to have the identity cards necessary to vote in part because such documents are neither widespread nor essential in rural areas. The 1992 Bolivian census found that in rural areas only fifty-three percent of men and only thirty-eight percent of women above fifteen years of age possessed identity documents (Ticona Alejo et al. 1995, 184). Finally, and perhaps most important, the failure of the traditional parties to recruit indigenous candidates or address indigenous movement demands may also have dampened voter turnout among indigenous people.

The rise of indigenous parties has helped overcome these problems. The candidates and platforms of indigenous parties have inspired enthusiasm among indigenous voters, which has encouraged them to turn out in greater numbers. The indigenous parties also have worked hard to reduce barriers to voting for indigenous people. Pachakutik, for example, pushed for the expansion of voting centers in indigenous areas and for the delivery of more identity cards in poor, rural communities (interviews with Cabascango 2005, Pacari 2005). It also lobbied for the translation of electoral materials and advertising into indigenous languages and for the inclusion of more indigenous people on the local electoral boards, and it worked with various indigenous organizations on electoral training and education programs (interview with Cabascango 2005).

The MAS has similarly promoted voter turnout in indigenous areas. The MAS has asked the electoral authorities to open more voting centers in rural areas and to keep these voting centers open later (interviews with Nuñez 2004 and Torrico 2004). Leaders of the MAS have also sought to expand the voter registration periods and to create programs that distribute identity cards to the population free of charge (interviews with Nuñez 2004, Peredo 2004, and

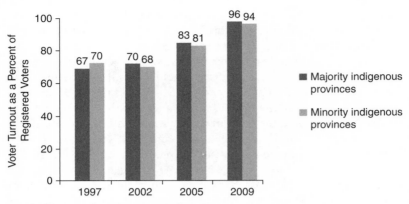

FIGURE 6.1. Voter turnout in Bolivia, 1997–2009.
Source: Corte Nacional Electoral

Torrico 2004). Most recently, the government also pushed to lower the voting age to sixteen so that the party's youthful supporters will be eligible to vote.

These efforts have helped boost voter turnout in the last decade. In Bolivia, the number of votes cast in elections has risen sharply since the emergence of the MAS. According to data from the National Electoral Court, the total number of voters in presidential elections increased by thirty-four percent between 1997 and 2005.[5] By contrast, the number of voters did not rise at all between 1985 and 1993, prior to the emergence of the MAS. Voter turnout as a percentage of registered voters in Bolivia also has increased significantly in recent years, particularly in indigenous areas.[6] As Figure 6.1 indicates, in 2009 voter turnout as a percentage of registered voters was ninety-six percent in provinces where a majority of the population learned to speak in an indigenous language as opposed to ninety-four percent in provinces where the majority of the population learned to speak in Spanish. By contrast, in 1997, it was only sixty-seven percent in municipalities where the majority of the population learned to speak in an indigenous language and seventy percent in municipalities where a majority of the population learned to speak in Spanish.[7]

[5] According to the National Electoral Court, the total number of voters increased from 1.731 million in 1993 to 2.321 million in 1997, 2.994 million in 2002, 3.102 million in 2005, and 4.859 million in 2009. See Casanova Saínz (2003, 176). The number of voters rose particularly sharply between 1993 and 1997 and between 2005 and 2009 in part because the minimum voting age was reduced in 1997 and again in 2009.

[6] Data on voter turnout as a percentage of registered voters in Bolivia are not strictly comparable over time because the requirements for registering and the reliability of the voter registry varied considerably from election to election.

[7] Estimates of voter turnout as a percentage of the voting age population also suggest that there has been a significant increase in turnout in recent years, although these sources vary somewhat on the extent of the increase (see Casanova Saínz 2003, 176; Institute for Democracy and Electoral Assistance 2010). According to data from the National Electoral Court, the number of voters as a percent of the voting age population rose from 56 percent in 1997 to 64 percent in

In Ecuador, voter turnout in presidential elections also rose sharply in indigenous areas after the emergence of Pachakutik. Between 1992 and 2002, the number of votes cast in counties where the indigenous population represents a majority rose by eighty-four percent, as opposed to fifty percent in counties where self-identified indigenous people represent a minority. After the decline of Pachakutik, voter turnout in indigenous areas dipped sharply, however. Between 2002 and 2006, the number of votes cast declined by twenty-five percent in majority indigenous counties, while it rose by two percent in minority indigenous counties. Voter turnout measured as a percentage of registered voters also rose sharply in indigenous areas during the heyday of Pachakutik, climbing from sixty-five percent in 1992 to eighty-five percent in 2002 in counties where the indigenous represent a majority.[8] By contrast, in counties where the indigenous population represents a minority, turnout as a percentage of registered voters increased by a much smaller amount, rising from sixty-nine percent to seventy-six percent during this period. Thus, in both Bolivia and Ecuador, the rise of indigenous parties helped reverse the gap in voter turnout between indigenous and non-indigenous areas.

SATISFACTION WITH AND SUPPORT FOR DEMOCRACY

The rise of the MAS also has led to an increase in support for, evaluations of, and satisfaction with democracy in Bolivia. High levels of approval for Morales, in particular, seem to have led to this increase since it occurred shortly after Morales was elected president. Whatever the cause, significantly more Bolivians, especially indigenous people, now express satisfaction with democracy, classify Bolivia as somewhat or very democratic, and express support for the principle of democracy. Ecuador also has witnessed an increase in support for and satisfaction with democracy in recent years, but the timing of that increase suggests that it was a result of the election of Rafael Correa, not the rise of Pachakutik. Moreover, in Ecuador, support for and satisfaction with democracy did not increase more quickly among indigenous people than non-indigenous people.[9]

Prior to the election of Evo Morales, Bolivia had one of the lower rates of satisfaction with democracy in the hemisphere. According to the Latin Barometer

---

2002 before leveling off at 61 percent in 2005. Turnout as a percent of the voting age population has risen particularly sharply in provinces where a majority of the population learned to speak in an indigenous language, climbing from 44 percent in 1997 to 54 percent in 2002 before declining slightly to 51 percent in 2005. By contrast, in provinces where a majority of the population learned to speak in Spanish, turnout as a percentage of the voting age population has scarcely changed in the last decade, climbing slightly from 55 percent in 1997 to 58 percent in 2002, but then dropping back down to 55 percent in 2005.

[8] In Ecuador, as in Bolivia, the quality of data on voter registration varies considerably over time. Unfortunately, no provincial-level data were available on voter turnout as a percentage of the voting age population.

[9] This section is based on the author's analyses of LAPOP and Latin Barometer survey data.

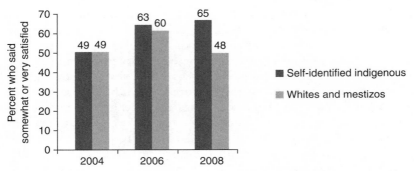

FIGURE 6.2. Satisfaction with democracy in Bolivia, 2004–2008.
Source: LAPOP 2004, 2006, and 2008 Bolivia surveys

surveys, in 2005 Bolivia ranked twelfth out of eighteen Latin American countries in terms of the degree of satisfaction with democracy (Corporación Latinobarómetro 2005, 58). Satisfaction with democracy in Bolivia began to increase after the election of Evo Morales later that year, however. The percentage of Bolivians who reported that they were somewhat satisfied or very satisfied rose from twenty-four percent in 2005 to forty-one percent in 2007 and fifty percent in 2009, according to the Latin Barometer surveys. Surveys carried out by the Latin American Public Opinion Project identified a similar initially upward trend, although LAPOP reports that democratic satisfaction tailed off subsequently. According to these surveys, the percentage of Bolivians who were satisfied or very satisfied with democracy rose from forty-nine percent in 2004 to sixty-one percent in 2006, before dropping to fifty-two percent in 2008.

As Figure 6.2 indicates, satisfaction with democracy has risen particularly rapidly among indigenous people in Bolivia. LAPOP surveys found that in 2008, sixty-five percent of self-identified indigenous people reported being satisfied or very satisfied with democracy, up from forty-nine percent in 2004. By contrast, only forty-eight percent of whites and mestizos reported being satisfied or very satisfied with democracy in 2008, which was slightly lower than in 2004.[10] Similarly, according to Latin Barometer surveys, forty-eight percent of people whose mother tongue was indigenous said they were somewhat or very satisfied with democracy in 2007, up from twenty-four percent in 2005. Satisfaction with democracy rose by a smaller amount among those people whose maternal language was Spanish, climbing from twenty-four percent to thirty-eight percent during this period.

The percentage of Bolivians who believe that their country is democratic also rose considerably in the wake of Morales's election. Latin Barometer surveys asked interviewees to rank how democratic their country was on a scale of one to ten with one being not at all democratic and ten being totally democratic.

[10] The gap in LAPOP surveys between indigenous and non-indigenous people in terms of satisfaction with democracy is also quite large if indigenous status is measured by language rather than self-identification.

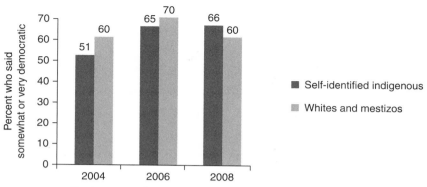

FIGURE 6.3. Evaluations of democracy in Bolivia, 2004–2008.
Source: LAPOP 2004, 2006, and 2008 Bolivia surveys

In 2005, only thirty-five percent of Bolivians ranked their country as fairly or totally democratic (answers six to ten on the ten point scale), but by 2007 forty-nine percent of Bolivians did. LAPOP surveys had similar findings: In 2004, fifty-nine percent of Bolivians ranked their country as very or somewhat democratic, but in 2006 this figure rose to sixty-nine percent, before dropping to sixty-one percent in 2008.

Evaluations of Bolivian democracy by indigenous people rose by a particularly large amount during this period, as Figure 6.3 indicates. According to Latin Barometer surveys, only twenty-eight percent of people whose mother tongue was indigenous ranked Bolivia as fairly or totally democratic in 2005, whereas thirty-nine percent of people whose maternal language was Spanish did. By 2007, however, sixty-five percent of people whose mother tongue was indigenous ranked Bolivia as fairly or totally democratic, as opposed to only fifty percent of people whose maternal language was Spanish. LAPOP surveys, meanwhile, found that the percentage of self-identified indigenous people with positive evaluations of Bolivian democracy grew from fifty-one to sixty-six percent between 2004 and 2008. The percentage of mestizos and whites with positive evaluations of Bolivian democracy, meanwhile, rose from sixty percent in 2004 to seventy percent in 2006, before returning to the sixty percent level in 2008.

Bolivians have also expressed greater support for the principle of democracy since the election of Morales. According to Latin Barometer polls, the percentage of Bolivians who agreed or strongly agreed with the statement that "democracy may have problems, but it is the best form of government" rose from sixty-eight percent in 2005 to eighty-one percent in 2007 and remained at that high level in 2009. LAPOP surveys also have revealed an increase in support for democracy in Bolivia. LAPOP asks people to rank on a scale from one to seven the extent to which they agree with the statement that "democracy may have problems but it is better than any other form of government." According to the LAPOP surveys, only sixty-one percent of Bolivians agreed

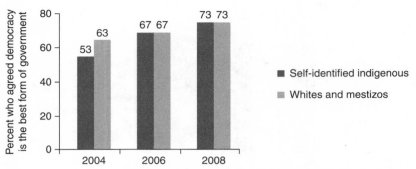

FIGURE 6.4. Support for the principle of democracy in Bolivia, 2004–2008.
Source: LAPOP 2004, 2006, and 2008 Bolivia surveys

somewhat or a lot (answers five to seven on the seven point scale) with this
statement in 2004, but by 2006, sixty-seven percent agreed with the statement,
and by 2008 seventy-three percent did.

As Figure 6.4 indicates, support for democracy rose more quickly among
indigenous people than it did among whites or mestizos during this period.
LAPOP found that in 2004 only fifty-three percent of self-identified indigenous
people agreed or strongly agreed that democracy was the best form of government, but by 2008, seventy-three percent of them did. The percentage of whites
and mestizos who agreed or strongly agreed that democracy was the best form
of government also rose, but by a smaller amount, climbing from sixty-three
percent in 2004 to seventy-three percent in 2008. Latin Barometer surveys also
detected a relatively large increase in support for democracy among indigenous people in recent years. In the 2005 Latin Barometer survey, only fifty-nine
percent of Bolivians whose mother tongue was an indigenous language agreed
that democracy was the best system of government, but by 2007 this figure had
jumped to seventy-nine percent. By contrast, during the same period, support
for democracy rose from seventy-two percent to eighty-two percent of those
Bolivians whose maternal language was Spanish.

Thus support for, satisfaction with, and evaluations of democracy have risen
considerably in Bolivia since the election of Evo Morales. This is particularly
true for people of indigenous descent. Self-identified indigenous people and
indigenous language speakers now typically evaluate Bolivian democracy more
favorably, express greater satisfaction with it, and report higher support for
the principle of democracy than do self-identified whites or mestizos or people
whose maternal language is Spanish. Skeptics might argue that the increase
in satisfaction with and support for democracy is meaningless because it sim-
ply reflects approval of the Morales administration rather than genuine satisfaction with or support for democratic principles. Nevertheless, the mere fact
that the indigenous population feels greater attachment to and support for the
national government has benefits for democracy. As we have seen, the indigenous population has traditionally been politically marginalized and disaffected,

which has led it to participate in anti-systemic protests and other actions that undermine democracy.

Ecuador also has experienced a rise in support for and satisfaction with democracy in recent years, but these increases were not consistently higher among indigenous people than non-indigenous people. Moreover, the timing of the increase suggests that it is principally a result of the election of Rafael Correa in 2006, rather than the rise of Pachakutik. Indeed, the increase in support for and satisfaction with democracy in Ecuador coincided with the decline of Pachakutik. According to Latin Barometer surveys, the proportion of Ecuadorians who said that they were satisfied or very satisfied with democracy rose from only fourteen percent in 2005 to thirty-five percent in 2007, before dipping slightly to thirty-three percent in 2009. LAPOP surveys registered a similar increase. In the 2006 LAPOP survey, only twenty-five percent of Ecuadorians said that they were satisfied or very satisfied with democracy, but in 2008, fifty-seven percent of Ecuadorians did. Surveys by LAPOP and Latin Barometer report similar increases in the percentage of people who rate Ecuador as somewhat or very democratic and who agree or strongly agree that democracy is the best form of government. In each case, however, the increase took place after Correa's election, during a period in which Pachakutik was in decline. Moreover, neither survey finds the increase to be consistently stronger among indigenous people. This suggests that the emergence of indigenous parties alone is not sufficient to boost support for or satisfaction with democracy among indigenous people. Rather, support for and satisfaction with democracy is only likely to increase significantly among indigenous people where the indigenous parties actually hold power at the national level.

ETHNIC POLICIES

In the last decade, the MAS and Pachakutik have pushed various policies to reduce ethnic inequalities and discrimination and encourage greater respect for indigenous traditions. These policies may strengthen democracy in the long run by reducing ethnic resentments and promoting the socioeconomic advancement and incorporation of the indigenous population. Such policies are only likely to bolster democracy to the extent they are effective in achieving their aims, but there is some preliminary evidence from Bolivia that the indigenous population has benefited from the MAS's policies.

Since the Morales administration took office in early 2006, it has enacted a wide range of pro-indigenous policies and programs. Many of these policies have not specifically targeted indigenous people, but they have nevertheless benefited them disproportionately. This has been the case, for example, with the Morales administration's literacy programs, which taught more than eight hundred thousand people to read between 2006 and 2008 (Movimiento al Socialismo 2009, 35–6). Indigenous people constitute a large majority of the illiterate population in Bolivia and thus they have been the main beneficiaries of these programs. The Bono Juana Azurduy program, which makes small payments to pregnant women and children under two years of age who see the doctor regularly, and the Bono Juancito Pinto, which pays families to keep their kids in school, also have disproportionately benefited the indigenous population because it is younger and has higher birth rates than the non-indigenous population. Indigenous people, who live disproportionately in rural areas, also have benefited from the Morales administration's agrarian reform program. This program redistributed almost a million hectares of land and provided the titles to twenty-six million hectares of land between 2006 and 2009 (Movimiento al Socialismo 2009, 26).

The Morales administration also has introduced many programs and policies that specifically seek to promote indigenous culture, eliminate discrimination, and improve the socioeconomic standing of indigenous people. The government, for example, has tightened the laws against job discrimination and increased the penalties for violations. The Morales administration also has sought to expand the teaching of indigenous languages, culture, and history in the education system, although these efforts have met some resistance especially in non-indigenous areas. In addition, the government's new constitution recognizes the country as plurinational and makes the indigenous flag, the *wiphala*, one of Bolivia's national symbols. It also recognizes various indigenous tongues as official languages and requires that the central government and the department governments use at least two official languages.

The new constitution also grants numerous rights to the indigenous peoples of Bolivia. These include the right to collective land ownership, the right to benefit from the exploitation of natural resources in their territories, as well as collective rights to indigenous knowledge and practices. Perhaps the most important of the collective rights is the right to territorial autonomy and self-governance, including the right to elect their leaders through traditional methods and the right to use traditional forms of justice. Article 26 stipulates that indigenous communities have the right to "elect, designate, and nominate their representatives ... according to their norms and procedures." Article 192 of the new constitution, meanwhile, specifies that "the State will promote and strengthen indigenous-peasant justice" and that "all public authorities and people will accept the decisions of the indigenous-peasant jurisdictions." In order to exercise territorial autonomy and self-governance, indigenous communities have to first vote for it and as of 2010, eleven largely indigenous municipalities had done so.

It is far too early to make a definitive assessment of the impact of these policies, but some preliminary results are encouraging. Illiteracy, infant mortality, and extreme poverty have all declined under the Morales administration, and the rural poor's share of national income has significantly increased (Movimiento al Socialismo 2009, 38). Moreover, as a result of the Morales administration's policies, indigenous languages and practices now have greater official standing, indigenous leaders have increased authority, and indigenous people have greater rights and protection from discrimination.

Critics of some of these policies have objected that the granting of special rights to a certain class of citizens is problematic for democracy. They have argued that indigenous communities that use traditional forms of justice or self-governance might violate individual rights or marginalize women from the political process. The new constitution, however, specifically stipulates that indigenous municipalities must respect individual rights and guarantees and it grants the Plurinational Constitutional Tribunal and Supreme Electoral Tribunal the authority to monitor and sanction any violations. In addition, according to Article 210 of the new constitution, the Supreme Electoral Tribunal is charged with guaranteeing that the electoral processes in the indigenous municipalities are democratic and that there is equal participation of men and women. It is too early to tell whether these constitutional stipulations will be rigorously enforced, but the MAS has at least made some efforts to recruit female candidates for important offices. After his 2009 reelection, Morales announced the appointment of a cabinet that was fifty percent female. Women, for example, were appointed to lead the ministry of justice as well as the ministry of rural development. In addition, nearly half of the MAS's senators and almost a quarter of the MAS's deputies in the 2010–15 legislature are female, which are slightly larger proportions than those of the other parties in Bolivia. Pachakutik has also placed women in important positions, most notably Nina Pacari, but they have typically represented only a small fraction of Pachakutik's leadership contingent.

Pachakutik, in contrast to the MAS, has only had limited opportunities to enact national-level policies because it has not held power at the national level, except for the eight months in 2003 that it was allied with the government of Lucio Gutiérrez. Nevertheless, the party has helped enact pro-indigenous policies through its work in the legislature and constituent assembly. In the 1997–8 constituent assembly, for example, Pachakutik successfully inserted language into the new constitution recognizing indigenous peoples and nationalities, describing Ecuador as pluricultural and multiethnic, and granting indigenous people a range of collective rights, including the right to education in indigenous languages and the right to use traditional indigenous justice (Andolina 2003, 747–8; Collins 2006, 295–6). In the legislature, meanwhile, Pachakutik helped enact the Parish Council Laws of 2000, which created a new level of local government in rural areas. This law helped empower indigenous people by shifting power from central and municipal authorities to the rural communities (Collins 2006, 280). Legislators from Pachakutik also have presented numerous other bills that have sought to benefit the indigenous population. These include legislation seeking to create an indigenous development fund and extend official recognition of indigenous languages and forms of justice (Collins 2006, appendix). Although these bills have not typically passed, they have drawn attention to these issues and some of their ideas have been incorporated in subsequent policy initiatives and legislation. Thus, Pachakutik's advocacy of indigenous demands appears to have had a positive impact on Ecuadorian democracy to date, albeit a modest one.[11]

POPULIST CHALLENGES TO DEMOCRACY

Whereas the ethnically oriented policies of the MAS and Pachakutik have had a mostly positive impact on democracy, the indigenous parties' populist tendencies have had clearly negative effects. As discussed in Chapter 1, I characterize leaders, movements, and parties as populist if they are personalistic, anti-establishment, and focused on mobilizing the masses. Each of these tendencies can be harmful to democracy if taken too far. Excessively personalistic leadership may concentrate power and undermine institutions and horizontal accountability. Aggressively anti-establishment rhetoric and policies may lead to social and political polarization and even violate the rule of law. Mass mobilizations may enable populist leaders to intimidate or overwhelm the opposition or bring about cycles of protests that destabilize the country.

As we have seen, Pachakutik has demonstrated various populist tendencies. Although Pachakutik is not a personalistic party, it has waged personalistic presidential campaigns and supported personalistic candidates, namely Freddy Ehlers in 1996 and 1998 and Lucio Gutiérrez in 2002. As president, Gutiérrez, initially with the support of Pachakutik, governed in a highly personalistic manner and made various efforts to gain control of independent institutions like the judiciary and the electoral tribunal (Montúfar 2008). These efforts, which were initially successful, undermined horizontal accountability in Ecuador. In addition, the leaders of Pachakutik have engaged in extensive anti-establishment rhetoric and behavior. Pachakutik has consistently criticized the traditional parties and elites and sought to block the policies they favor. It also has proposed various nationalist and state interventionist policies designed to redistribute wealth and end foreign intervention. Because Pachakutik has typically been in the opposition, it has only had limited success in enacting these policies, however. Nevertheless, its rhetoric and behavior have contributed to the high levels of political polarization in Ecuador.

Perhaps most problematic, Pachakutik has supported and participated in mass mobilizations that have undermined Ecuador's fragile democracy. The indigenous movement played a prominent role in the protests that overthrew Ecuadorian president Abdalá Bucaram in 1997 and his successor, Jamil Mahuad, in 2000. Although most legislators from Pachakutik did not participate directly in these protests, they did lend support to them in various ways. In the case of Bucaram, for example, Pachakutik voted with a majority of the legislature to remove him from the presidency on grounds of insanity, a move that most independent observers viewed as unconstitutional. The indigenous movement did not play much of a role in the protests that led to the overthrow

---

[11] For a contrary view, see Mijeski and Beck (2011) especially ch. 7.

of Gutiérrez in 2005, but legislators from Pachakutik voted with the majority of the legislature to remove him from the presidency on the dubious grounds that he had abandoned his post. Although these actions were politically popular, they destabilized Ecuadorian democracy.

The MAS has demonstrated even stronger populist tendencies. Morales has aggressively attacked the traditional political and economic elites in Bolivia as well as the media, the church, and foreign interests. He has sought to concentrate power in his own hands by usurping authority, overhauling the country's existing political institutions, and neutralizing leaders that he views as a threat. Morales has frequently used mass mobilizations and other plebiscitarian strategies to achieve his aims. He has consolidated his power through elections, intimidated the opposition through mass protests and rallies, and advanced his policy goals through plebiscites and referendums. As a result, Morales, like his populist counterparts in Ecuador and Venezuela, has compromised horizontal accountability, undermined respect for the rules of the game, and created a highly polarized and volatile political environment.

The MAS's anti-establishment orientation has been noticeable both in its rhetoric as well as in many of the policies it has established. The Morales administration has presented itself as the defender of the Bolivian people and it has depicted the political opposition, foreign interests, and even domestic institutions, like the church, the media, and the judiciary as elitist enemies of progress and social justice. The MAS's Manichaean us-versus-them approach to politics has frequently led it to forego negotiation and compromise in favor of conflict and imposition.

Many of the MAS's attacks have focused on the country's traditional political and economic elites. In its early years, the MAS typically railed against the traditional parties, which it denounced as corrupt and self-serving organizations. The disintegration of these parties and the emergence of significant opposition to Morales in Santa Cruz and the other lowlands departments led the leadership of the MAS to refocus its energies on the latter, which have pushed for greater autonomy from the central government. In the words of one scholar, "the government has been strengthening a mental map that divides in a simple form the centralist patriots and the autonomist oligarchs" (Barié 2007, 8). According to Morales, the elites in Santa Cruz and elsewhere "want autonomy for the bourgeoisie, for the rich and not for the people" (Barié 2007, 8). Morales and other leaders of the MAS have often used harsh language in denouncing the opposition. Morales, for example, once denounced Manfred Reyes Villa, the former prefect of Cochabamba and his leading opponent in the 2009 elections, as "anti-democratic, subversive, and racist" ("Reyes Villa demands that Morales resign" 2007, 8).

The Morales administration has not hesitated to launch criminal charges against leaders of the political opposition or other people it views as its enemies. The government has filed criminal charges against numerous past presidents, including Gonzalo Sánchez de Lozada, Jorge Quiroga, Eduardo Rodríguez, and Carlos Mesa, as well as other important opposition figures such as Reyes Villa; Mario Cossío, the prefect of Tarija; Rubén Costas, the prefect of Santa Cruz; Ernesto Suárez, the prefect of Bení; Leonel Fernández, the former prefect of Pando; and Victor Hugo Cárdenas, the former vice president. The crimes with which they have been charged run the gamut from human rights violations to corruption and treason. At least some of these charges appear to be politically inspired. Moreover, the Morales administration appears to be overly quick to condemn the people it has charged. Indeed, it recently proposed a law that would prevent anyone charged with a crime from taking office, although members of the opposition and the media objected that these provisions were unconstitutional ("New 'Plurinational' State" 2010, 4).

The MAS has frequently used mass mobilizations to intimidate the political opposition and advance its policy aims. The social movements that make up the MAS, such as the coca growers' unions, have a long history of carrying out social protests, including roadblocks, the occupation of land and buildings, and other aggressive measures. These protests have continued during the Morales administration. Supporters of the MAS, for example, carried out protests to put pressure on the legislature to enact the new constitution and pass agrarian reform legislation. In both cases, critics complained that the mobilizations prevented some opposition legislators from attending the deliberations. Supporters of the MAS also used social protests to try to pressure opposition prefects to resign. In the department of Cochabamba, MAS supporters went so far as to set fire to the governor's palace, forcing the opposition prefect to flee. Supporters of the MAS are not the only actors in Bolivia to use mass mobilization as a political weapon, however. Opponents of the MAS also have engaged in, at times, violent protests in order to put pressure on the government.

As Chapter 2 discussed, the leaders of the MAS, like traditional populists, have often employed nationalist and anti-imperialist rhetoric. The MAS's 2002 platform, for example, recounts a history of Bolivian subjugation to external powers, arguing that: "Bolivia fell first into the claws of the English, and then passed to the Yankees and into the dominion of transnational companies from Europe, North America and East Asia, and its servants, the World Bank, the International Monetary Fund, and the World Trade Organization. The Creole Oligarchy served and serves as its faithful internal ally ..." (Movimiento al Socialismo 2002, 5). The MAS has sought to reverse this history of domination by adopting an independent foreign policy and taking a tough line against transnational companies that do business in Bolivia. During its first term, the Morales administration nationalized ten firms and forced foreign gas companies to renegotiate their contracts with the country. The Morales administration also adopted an often belligerent attitude toward the United States, which it has repeatedly accused of funding opposition groups and seeking to destabilize Bolivian democracy. In late 2008, Morales expelled the U.S. ambassador, Philip Goldberg, saying that "we do not want people here who conspire against democracy" (Mathis 2009, 1). The United States retaliated by expelling the Bolivian ambassador to the United States and suspending Bolivia's trade preferences, which led Bolivia, in turn, to ban the U.S. Drug Enforcement Administration from the country. As of mid-2011, relations had not been normalized in spite of some movement in that direction.

The MAS also has attacked domestic institutions, such as the Catholic Church and the media, which it has accused of being in league with the opposition. The church has angered the MAS by resisting some of its policies such as the new constitution and its proposed education reforms. In July 2006 Education Minister Felix Patzi called the church an ally of the oligarchy that had dominated the country for 500 years (U.S. Department of State 2007). Morales, meanwhile, has objected to the church's interference in politics and its ties to the opposition. Morales also has been highly critical of the media, referring to it on more than one occasion as his "number one enemy." Santos Ramírez, a former MAS senator, has argued that "the strongest, the most radical, the most racist opposition to the MAS comes from the media. How can this be explained? It can be explained by asking: who are the owners of the television stations with a national presence, of the radios, of the newspapers? They are exactly those people who yesterday had political and economic power in their hands" (Harnecker et al. 2008, 169). Much of the media has, in fact, been highly critical of Morales. Indeed, a survey of opinions expressed in the nation's six major dailies undertaken by a well-known journalist at the end of 2006 revealed a clear bias against the government (Van Cott 2007). In order to counter this bias, the Morales administration has sought to develop alternative media sources, such as a network of community-based radio stations.

Morales also has sought to strengthen his hold on power and weaken competing sources of authority by overhauling the country's existing political institutions through the constitutional reform process. The new constitution strengthened Morales in a number of different ways. First, it permitted Morales to run for reelection, enabling him potentially to stay in power until 2020. Article 168 of the new charter allows the president to serve two consecutive five-year terms and Morales had initially argued that his first term did not count toward this limit since it took place under the previous constitution. The opposition bitterly opposed this idea, however, and in the negotiations over the constitutional reform that took place in late 2008, Morales agreed not to stand for reelection in 2014. Nevertheless, after he was reelected in 2009, Morales began to backtrack from this commitment, and sectors of the MAS expressed the desire to keep him in power as long as possible. According to Gerardo García, the vice president of the MAS: "This has been our objective since the foundation of the political instrument. The sectors [of the MAS] consider that Evo Morales should stay in power for 50 years or more if possible" ("Morales Prepares" 2007, 3).

The new constitution also expanded the size of the legislature in order to help the MAS gain control of it. During the Morales administration's first term, the senate was in the hands of the opposition, which repeatedly stymied the government's initiatives. Even though in 2005 the MAS had won by large margins in five out of nine departments, it only captured two out of the three seats in each department. The opposition, by contrast, won two out of three seats in three departments and all three seats in the fourth, which gave it a narrow majority in the senate. The new constitution, however, increased the number of senators to be elected from each department from three to four. By expanding the number of seats allocated in each department, the MAS hoped to be able to win at least three out of the four senate seats in the departments where it was strong, while picking up enough seats in the departments where it was weaker to eke out a majority. As it turned out, the MAS fared even better in the 2009 elections than it expected, winning all four senate seats in La Paz, Oruro, and Potosi, three out of four in Chuquisaca and Cochabamba, and two out of the four seats in the departments of Beni, Pando, Santa Cruz, and Tarija. Had the 2009 elections used the previous rules for apportioning seats, the MAS would have won a slightly lower proportion of seats in the senate, although it still would have gained a majority.

The new constitution also enabled the Morales administration to strengthen its control of the judiciary. Beginning early in his first term, Morales sought to coax members of the traditionally conservative judiciary to resign by criticizing them vociferously and reducing their salaries. These efforts were partly successful in that numerous justices did resign, but the Morales administration and the legislature could not come to an agreement on their replacements. As a result, the work of various judicial institutions, such as the constitutional tribunal, ground to a halt. This impasse, however, was broken by the passage of the new constitution, which called for the direct election of members of the judiciary. This meant that the Morales administration no longer had to seek legislative approval of judges. Moreover, in early 2010, the legislature, which by that time was controlled by the MAS, passed a law allowing Morales to appoint temporary magistrates until new ones could be elected. As a result, the Morales administration has been able to select judges who are more to its liking.

The Morales administration also has sought to gain control of traditionally non-partisan institutions, such as the National Electoral Court (CNE). During the 2005 elections, Morales extensively criticized the National Electoral Court and after taking power he replaced the president and some other members of the CNE with figures believed to be more sympathetic to the MAS. The MAS then eliminated the CNE in the new constitution creating a new electoral authority, the Supreme Electoral Tribunal (TSE). The TSE is composed of seven members, only one of whom is directly appointed by the president. The remaining six members must be chosen with a two-thirds vote of the legislature, but because the MAS now controls more than two-thirds of the legislature, it can appoint members who are sympathetic to its aims.

The Morales administration also has used various methods to gain control over or weaken the departmental governments. During Morales's first term, the opposition held six out of the nine prefectural positions, and the opposition prefects led the resistance to the central government's policies. The MAS, however, managed to pass legislation to allow a recall referendum on all of the prefectural positions (as well as the president). It then managed to recall two of the opposition prefects. The MAS also sought to undermine the departmental governments by enacting a tax reform measure that deprived them of many of their resources. It also granted greater autonomy to municipalities, regions, and indigenous communities in the new constitution, thereby creating a potential local counterbalance to departmental authority.

Thus, the Morales administration has managed to weaken the opposition and concentrate power considerably during its tenure. The government's populist policies have undermined horizontal accountability, generated widespread protests, and created growing political polarization. As a result, they have undermined Bolivian democracy. Pachakutik's populist tendencies have had a less dramatic impact because it has typically been in the opposition, but some of its actions have nevertheless destabilized Ecuadorian democracy and contributed to social and political polarization in that country.

CONCLUSION

This chapter has argued that the emergence of indigenous parties in Latin America has had a mixed impact on democracy in the region. On the positive side, the main indigenous parties have not engaged in ethnic outbidding or the exclusionary types of behaviors that much of the literature on ethnic parties outlined. To the contrary, both the MAS and Pachakutik have actively recruited white and mestizo candidates and have developed broad and inclusive platforms. Moreover, the rise of these two parties has helped increase indigenous political participation and representation in both countries and has boosted support for and satisfaction with democracy among indigenous people in Bolivia. These two parties may also help reduce ethnic inequalities and discrimination and enhance respect for indigenous culture and traditions in the long run.

On the negative side, the populist tendencies of Pachakutik and especially the MAS have weakened democracy in various ways. The efforts of Evo Morales to concentrate power and subvert the opposition have undermined horizontal accountability and the rule of law in Bolivia, and Pachakutik's support of extra-constitutional efforts to overthrow sitting presidents has weakened democratic stability and the rule of law in Ecuador. In addition, the harsh anti-establishment rhetoric and policies of the two parties have contributed to growing political polarization in both countries.

One would hope that in the future indigenous parties might eschew or at the very least tone down their populist rhetoric and policies, but, unfortunately, there are strong incentives for indigenous parties to engage in such behavior. Ethnopopulist appeals and policies have proved effective at generating support, particularly among marginalized sectors of the population. Because they represent a traditionally excluded group, indigenous parties have obvious reasons to employ anti-establishment rhetoric and policies. Moreover, the leaders of these parties have argued that it is necessary for them to concentrate power in order to carry out the sweeping changes that they envision. As a result, indigenous parties are likely to continue to employ populist rhetoric and policies that undermine democracy in the region.

7

Conclusion

Although ethnic parties are commonplace in much of the world, there is still little consensus on what leads them to emerge and thrive. Scholars have proposed theories that focus on a wide range of explanatory variables, from institutional factors to primordial ties. These theories shed much light on the recent emergence of indigenous parties in Latin America, but they cannot explain why some of these parties have fared well while others have performed poorly. Nor can they explain why some indigenous parties in the region were able to win support across ethnic lines.

This study has argued that the successful indigenous parties in Latin America have won by combining inclusive ethnic and populist appeals. They have wooed indigenous voters by recruiting indigenous candidates, maintaining strong ties with indigenous organizations, invoking indigenous symbols, and adopting traditional indigenous demands. These appeals have worked particularly well where the indigenous population is relatively large, well-organized, and ethnically conscious.

The successful parties, however, have not relied on indigenous votes alone. They have also reached out to white and mestizo voters by emphasizing their inclusive nature, recruiting white and mestizo candidates, and forging ties to urban mestizo-dominated groups. Populist rhetoric and proposals have played a key role in the efforts of these parties to win the support of voters of all ethnicities. The successful indigenous parties have focused their campaigns on the lower classes, denounced the traditional parties and elites, and presented their own leaders as the saviors of their countries. They have also vigorously opposed market-oriented policies and foreign intervention, and vowed to redistribute wealth to the poor. These populist appeals have been effective in large part because disenchantment with the existing political elites and their policies has been quite high in the region, particularly among the poorer sectors of the population.

The ethnic landscape of Latin America has made an inclusive approach feasible. *Mestizaje* has blurred the boundaries between ethnic groups in the region and reduced ethnic polarization, making it easier for parties to win support across ethnic lines. Nevertheless, *mestizaje* has not eliminated ethnic attachment or ethnic discrimination in the region, and the continuing high levels of ethnic identification, discrimination, and inequality in Latin America have helped make the success of the indigenous parties possible. Indeed, many Latin Americans of indigenous descent have voted for the indigenous parties because of these parties' ethnic appeals and their efforts to combat ethnic inequality and discrimination.

Indigenous parties are not the only parties that have successfully employed ethnopopulist appeals in the region. Some mestizo-led parties have also won high levels of support among indigenous voters as well as whites and mestizos by employing a combination of inclusive ethnic and populist appeals. The mestizo-led parties have not typically emphasized ethnic demands as much as the indigenous parties, but they have recruited numerous indigenous candidates, forged ties to indigenous organizations, and utilized various indigenous symbols. These appeals have helped them win a disproportionate share of indigenous voters.

Latin American voters have often favored candidates and parties of ethnic groups that are proximate to their own. As a result, the indigenous parties have fared best among self-identified indigenous voters and indigenous mestizos, and least well among whites and mestizos who do not come from indigenous backgrounds. Some mestizo-led parties, meanwhile, have fared well among self-identified indigenous voters and indigenous mestizos by nominating presidential and legislative candidates who either self-identify as indigenous or are clearly of indigenous descent. Ethnic proximity has thus shaped the vote for both indigenous and mestizo-led parties in the region.

These findings have a number of important implications for theories of ethnic politics and populism, which I explore in the following pages. The chapter is organized as follows. The first section examines the implications of my arguments for the literature on ethnic parties. The second section discusses the contributions of the book to theories of populism. The final section identifies some promising areas for future research.

IMPLICATIONS FOR THEORIES OF ETHNIC POLITICS

The findings of this book suggest that the nature of ethnic identification and inter-ethnic relations in each country shapes the effectiveness of different kinds of ethnic appeals and mediates the impact that ethnic parties have on ethnic conflict and democracy. As Chapter One discussed, much of the literature on ethnic parties has argued that such parties succeed by mobilizing their base through exclusionary appeals. This literature has argued that ethnic parties have little chance of earning votes from members of other ethnic groups, so they must focus their efforts on winning the support of co-ethnics. They do this by exaggerating the threat represented by other ethnic groups and appealing to ethnonationalist sentiments. As a result, ethnic parties tend to increase the likelihood of ethnic conflict and undermine democracy.

These arguments are based upon primordial assumptions about ethnicity, however. They assume that people have a single ethnic identity and that ethnic attachments are strong and stable. They also assume that ethnic polarization is high enough that most people would not consider voting for a political party created to represent a different ethnic group.

A significant body of research has questioned the validity of these assumptions, however. Various scholars, dubbed *constructivists*, have shown that individuals typically have multiple ethnic identities that change over time. Numerous studies have also demonstrated that societies vary considerably in terms of the degree of ethnic polarization.

This book argues that where ethnic polarization is low and ethnic identities are multiple and fluid, ethnic parties that employ a more inclusive strategy will be more successful than those that use an exclusionary strategy. A low level of ethnic polarization and fluid, multiple ethnic loyalties permit ethnic parties to win support across ethnic lines, but only if these parties use inclusive strategies. Exclusionary strategies will typically not resonate with voters in societies with low levels of ethnic polarization and will alienate many individuals with fluid or multiple ethnic loyalties.

Ethnic parties that employ inclusive strategies are likely to have a much more positive impact on ethnic relations and democracy than ethnic parties that adopt exclusionary strategies. Inclusive ethnic parties will typically seek to defuse ethnic tensions by avoiding ethnonationalist rhetoric and policy proposals and recruiting people of various ethnicities for leadership positions. These parties will tend to lose votes if there is a worsening of ethnic tensions and they therefore have incentives to dampen rather than exacerbate ethnic conflict.

Theorists of ethnic parties thus need to take into account the preexisting nature of ethnic identification and inter-ethnic relations in formulating hypotheses about how ethnic parties will behave and what impact they will have on ethnic conflict and democracy. In particular, they need to take into account well-documented findings by constructivist scholars about the fluidity and complexity of ethnic boundaries (Chandra 2001).

Some recent studies of ethnic parties have explicitly incorporated constructivist assumptions about ethnicity (Chandra 2004, 2005; Posner 2005; Wilkinson 2006). These studies have assumed that individuals have multiple ethnic identities, but these scholars have typically focused on the different ethnic category sets that people belong to, such as race, religion, and language. This literature has argued that under some circumstances people may identify with their religious group, but under other circumstances they may identify with their racial or linguistic group.

In this study, however, I have pointed out that where ethnic mixing is widespread individuals may identify with different ethnic groups in the same category set. For example, a woman with Indian and Spanish ancestry may identify as both indigenous and caucasian or she may identify with some sort of intermediary category such as mestizo.

Widespread ethnic mixing thus tends to blur ethnic boundaries. The presence of numerous ethnically mixed individuals makes it more difficult for people to distinguish clearly between different ethnic groups and to sort individuals into discrete ethnic categories. In ethnically mixed societies, individuals may therefore vote on the basis of ethnic proximity – that is, they may vote for candidates or parties from ethnic groups that they resemble or feel closer to, rather than voting only for candidates or parties from their own ethnic group.

Ethnic mixing also tends to reduce ethnic polarization. Individuals who have family members on both sides of an ethnic divide will be less likely to have animosity toward either of those groups than individuals whose ancestors come from a single side of the divide. Ethnically mixed individuals thus may serve as a buffer group that reduces societal ethnic tensions. This makes it easier for ethnic parties to win support across ethnic lines and encourages them to adopt inclusive electoral strategies.

Ethnic mixing in Latin America has been widespread and in most countries of the region, people of mixed descent now represent the largest single group. The high level of *mestizaje* in the region has reduced ethnic polarization and blurred ethnic boundaries, although it has not eliminated ethnic inequality and discrimination. This has made it possible for ethnic as well as non-ethnic parties to win support across ethnic lines. As a result, inclusive parties, including inclusive ethnic parties, have been far more common and successful in the region than exclusionary ones. Not all of the inclusive ethnic parties in the region have succeeded, but their track record has certainly been better than that of the exclusionary parties. Thus, an ethnically inclusive approach has been a necessary but not a sufficient condition for ethnic party success in Latin America.

Outside of Latin America, the level of ethnic mixing has varied widely. In Europe, intermarriage between members of certain ethno-regional groups is commonplace, which has reduced ethnic polarization and blurred ethnic boundaries. This has made it feasible for some European ethno-regional parties to win support across ethnic and regional lines. For example, various ethno-regional parties, such as the Scottish National Party and the Party of Wales (Plaid Cymru) in Great Britain, or the Lega Nord in Italy, have broadened their policy platforms and wooed voters outside of their ethnic and regional base (Tronconi 2005, 142–3).

In other countries, however, intermarriage across the lines of the major ethnic cleavage(s) in the society has been relatively rare. This is the case, for example, in the deeply divided societies examined by Horowitz (1985) and Rabushka and Shepsle (1972), such as Malaysia, Sri Lanka, Kenya, Uganda, Guyana, and Trinidad and Tobago. According to Horowitz (1985, 62), "rates of exogamy for severely divided societies typically run below 10 percent of all marriages, and probably lower if only unions between the most-conflicted groups are counted." The low rate of intermarriage in these societies helps maintain clear and stable ethnic boundaries and ensures that ethnic polarization remains high. Ethnic parties in these societies therefore have had little hope of winning support from members of other ethnic groups. Instead they typically have sought to mobilize members of their own ethnic group through exclusionary ethnonationalist appeals that have worsened ethnic polarization and undermined democracy.

Thus, ethnic mixing has important electoral consequences. Ethnic parties in ethnically mixed societies will often behave differently from ethnic parties in societies that are not ethnically mixed, and they will typically have a different impact on ethnic polarization and democracy. Ethnic mixing is not the only determinant of the behavior of ethnic parties or the level of ethnic polarization and ethnic fluidity in a society, but it is an important one. (Moreover, it is important to remember that the level of ethnic mixing in a society is a consequence as well as a cause of the degree of ethnic polarization and ethnic fluidity.) Surprisingly, however, relatively little research to date has been carried out on the electoral consequences of ethnic mixing.

It seems likely that ethnic mixing would shape other forms of political and organizational behavior as well. Horowitz (1985, 7) maintains that in ethnically polarized societies, "strong ethnic allegiances permeate organizations, activities, and roles to which they are formally unrelated." Labor unions, business associations, and other societal organizations become organized along ethnic lines and defend only the interests of co-ethnics. By contrast, in societies with high levels of *mestizaje*, we would expect most organizations from social movements to government agencies to be ethnically inclusive. These organizations should not only incorporate members of various ethnic groups, but they should also typically refrain from adopting ethnonationalist or exclusionary policies and demands.

Ethnic mixing should also typically reduce ethnic conflict. Indeed, the high level of *mestizaje* in Latin America is presumably one explanation for the low level of ethnic violence in the region. People of mixed descent will often serve as a moderating force and help to defuse ethnic tensions in ethnically mixed societies. In these societies, ethnic parties will typically seek support across ethnic lines and they will refrain from demonizing members of other groups in order to mobilize co-ethnics. As a result, they are less likely to prompt or exacerbate ethnic violence. The preponderance of multi-ethnic organizations in ethnically mixed societies, meanwhile, may help reduce the likelihood of ethnic conflict by increasing inter-ethnic social capital and making people of different ethnic groups more aware of their common interests.

To be sure, ethnic mixing also has some negative consequences. It may lead, for example, to the disappearance of certain traditions, cultures, and populations. *Mestizaje* in Latin America, for example, has reduced the number of indigenous language speakers and led to the marginalization or disappearance of some indigenous customs and ways of life. Ethnic mixing may also coexist with high levels of ethnic discrimination and inequality, as it does in Latin America.

Nevertheless, it is clear that ethnic mixing has some important benefits for political systems as well. Thus, the literature on ethnic politics needs to take into account the level of ethnic mixing in societies in making predictions about how ethnicity shapes political outcomes. The degree of ethnic mixing in a society influences both the degree of ethnic polarization and the nature of ethnic identification, which in turn shape a variety of kinds of political behavior. In ethnically mixed societies, we should therefore expect politics to take very different forms than in unmixed societies.

IMPLICATIONS FOR THEORIES OF POPULISM

This book has also sought to make theoretical and conceptual contributions to the study of populism. One of the principal problems bedeviling the literature on populism has been disagreements about its meaning. This book defined *populism* as a campaign and governing strategy in which a personalistic leader seeks to mobilize the masses in opposition to the elites. Other recent studies have proposed somewhat similar definitions, and it is my hope that this study will contribute to an emerging consensus on the meaning of populism (Barr 2009; Canovan 1999; Carrión 2009; Roberts 2006).

The definition of populism employed in this book has a number of advantages. First, it recognizes that populism is a complex and multifaceted concept. The definition used here draws on various characteristics that have been emphasized by scholars, rather than seeking to boil populism down to a single essential characteristic. Second, my definition does not limit the applicability of the term to governing parties or movements. It focuses not just on a party's policies, but also on a party's appeals – that is, what they do to attract voters. Third, the definition is broad enough to include numerous movements that scholars have characterized as populist from Peronismo in Argentina to Fujimorismo in Peru. It does not limit the term to a certain historical period or a particular economic strategy. At the same time, the concept used here allows for the identification of specific subtypes of populism, which have been prevalent in particular periods or areas. I identified several subtypes, including traditional populism, neoliberal populism, and ethnopopulism.

This study has focused to a large degree on ethnopopulism. It defines *ethnopopulism* as a campaign and governing strategy that combines ethnic and populist appeals and/or policies. Ethnopopulism is a relatively recent phenomenon in Latin America. As various scholars have argued, populist movements in the region were traditionally based largely in the urban mestizo lower classes (Conniff 1982; Drake 1982). Although these movements sometimes incorporated rural indigenous people, they were led by whites or mestizos, and they largely refrained from making ethnic demands. As a result, ethnic appeals have been viewed as marginal to or even incompatible with populism in the region.

This book has shown not only that ethnic and populist appeals are compatible, but that they can be an effective campaign strategy. Some indigenous parties have successfully reached out to traditional populist constituencies, especially lower class urban mestizos, by employing personalist, anti-establishment, and redistributive as well as ethnic appeals. Similarly, some mestizo-led movements have won the support of indigenous voters by employing ethnic as well as populist appeals. That ethnic and populist appeals could be effectively combined in Latin America should not be surprising. Populism has traditionally been highly flexible ideologically, and its anti-establishment orientation and focus on lower class concerns have understandably appealed to members of politically and economically marginalized ethnic groups.

The findings of this book shed light not only on the rise of ethnopopulism but on the resurgence of populism more generally in the region. Populist movements of all stripes have gained ground in Latin America in recent years in large part because of rising disenchantment with the traditional parties and their market-oriented economic policies. Populist leaders have capitalized on this disenchantment by attacking the traditional parties and their domestic and international allies. They have presented themselves as the saviors of their countries and they have vowed to fight corruption and to govern in the name of the poor. Many populist leaders have also pledged to bring an end to the "long night of neoliberalism" and to reassert their countries' sovereignty over natural resources.

Yet there are important reasons to question how long these populist movements will endure. Historically, populist movements in Latin America have often proved short-lived. Many populist parties have found that their anti-establishment appeals are more effective when they are in the opposition than when they are forced to govern. Support for populist parties in power typically depends in large part on performance-based criteria, such as their ability to deliver economic and social goods and populist politicians or parties that have failed to deliver on their promises have seen their electoral support evaporate (Conniff 1982, 20; Drake 1982; Kaufman and Stallings 1991; Weyland 2001). Perhaps most important, populist parties are often unstable in part because they tend to invest little in organizations. Instead, they rely heavily on personalistic linkages to voters, which have proven fragile, particularly in the event of the death or political downfall of their leaders (Weyland 2001, 13).

There are some reasons why we might expect the current generation of ethnopopulist parties to be more stable than previous populist movements, however. Some of the ethnopopulist parties are rooted in strong indigenous movements that provide the parties with a solid grassroots base. Furthermore, the ethnic linkages that these parties have established with voters may prove more enduring than the personalistic, clientelistic, and performance-based linkages that populist parties have traditionally maintained with the electorate. Indeed, various studies have found that electoral volatility tends to be lower in countries with high levels of ethnic diversity in part because of the identity-based ties that ethnic parties often establish with voters in these countries (Alonso 2008; Bartolini and Mair 1990; Birnir 2007). Some of the indigenous parties that have emerged in the last two decades have demonstrated staying power. The MAS, for example, has steadily increased its share of the electorate since its emergence in the mid-1990s. Pachakutik also demonstrated a great deal of electoral stability during its first decade of existence. Nevertheless,

Pachakutik encountered problems beginning in 2006 when it moved in a more ethnonationalist direction, and the MAS too has begun to see its popularity wane. Moreover, the mestizo-led ethnopopulist parties that have emerged have failed to create strong party organizations or establish significant ethnic linkages to voters, which calls into question their long-term prospects. Thus, it remains to be seen whether ethnopopulist parties will turn out to be more enduring than other types of populist parties.

It is also premature to assess the impact of indigenous parties on democracy in the region, particularly given that only one indigenous party has held power at the national level. Nevertheless, the preliminary results are not terribly encouraging. As Chapter Six discussed, the democratic deficiencies of the indigenous parties stem not from their ethnic agenda but rather from their populist tendencies. Indeed, the ethnic policies of the MAS and Pachakutik have actually deepened Latin American democracies in some ways. Indigenous parties have improved the representation of indigenous people in the halls of power, and they have boosted indigenous political participation and support for democracy. Indigenous parties also have helped enact various policies designed to improve the socioeconomic standing of the indigenous population, which may indirectly strengthen Latin American democracies by making them more ethnically inclusive.

The populist tendencies of Pachakutik and the MAS have undermined democracy, however. The MAS, in particular, has concentrated too much power in its leader, who has bypassed and manipulated institutions designed to guarantee horizontal accountability. The anti-establishment rhetoric and behavior of the MAS have been equally problematic. Not only has it denounced the media, the church, and the political opposition in harsh terms, but it has also brought criminal and civil charges against key opposition figures. The MAS has also used mass mobilizations and plebiscites to consolidate power and to intimidate the opposition. Unfortunately, these actions may end up outweighing any positive effects that the MAS's ethnically inclusive policies have had on democracy in the region.

A FUTURE RESEARCH AGENDA

This book has left a number of important areas for future research. To begin with, further study is needed on variance in ethnic identification across individuals, ethnic groups, and nations, and how that variation shapes voting and other forms of political participation. The impact of ethnic or racial mixing on ethnic identification and political behavior is a particularly promising area for future research. We also need further analysis of the extent to which evaluations of ethnic proximity shape voting and other types of political activity. This study has demonstrated that ethnic identification, ethnic mixing, and ethnic proximity have all shaped the behavior of voters and parties within Latin America, but further research is needed to see how such variables shape political behavior outside of the region.

To facilitate such research, we will need to develop better sets of questions about ethnic identification and ascription. Census and survey data typically measure whether individuals identify with an ethnic group, but they do not measure the strength and stability of those attachments, or whether such individuals also identify with other ethnic groups. Nor do such surveys typically assess whether and why individuals view some ethnic groups as ethnically proximate and others as ethnically distant. Some of these data will not be easy to collect, but if we fail to do so we implicitly accept primordialist assumptions about the singularity and stability of ethnic identification.

Future research will also need to explore what other factors shape the kinds of appeals ethnic parties employ. This study has argued that parties are more likely to employ inclusive ethnic appeals in societies where ethnic polarization is low and ethnic identification is multiple and fluid. Even in these societies, however, not all ethnic parties are inclusive. Nor have all ethnic parties adopted exclusionary appeals in societies where ethnic polarization is high and ethnic identification is singular and stable. It is likely that both agency and structure play an important role in shaping the strategies employed by ethnic parties, but further research is needed to understand what factors are most important to their decision making processes.

Finally, we need further research on the impact of ethnic parties, especially indigenous parties, on democracy. In the long run, indigenous parties in Latin America will be judged not on their electoral achievements, but on what they do once in power. Indigenous parties have not been around for a very long time and only in Bolivia have they truly held power at the national level. Nevertheless, their record of governance to date raises some concerns. Indigenous parties have promised to create more just societies in which all citizens live well. It will be left to future researchers to decide whether such parties will be remembered more for advancing the cause of ethnic equality or succumbing to the perils of populism.

Bibliography

Interviews Cited

Aguinaga, Carlos. 2007. Author interview with former president of Supreme Electoral Tribunal. Quito, July 5.

Aguirre, Walter. 2006. Author interview with member of the Political Committee of the Partido Nacionalista Peruano. Lima, July 14.

Atamaint, Shiram Diana. 2007. Author interview with Pachakutik deputy. Quito, June 27.

Babar, Hugo. 2007. Author interview with president of Datanálisis. Quito, July 2.

Barrera, Augusto. 2005. Author interview with former secretary of social dialogue and planning, Ministry of the Presidency. Quito, July 19.

Burbano, Ghandi. 2007. Author interview with former member of Supreme Electoral Tribunal. Quito, July 3.

Cabascango, José María. 2005. Author interview with indigenous leader and former member of Supreme Electoral Tribunal. Quito, July 19.

Calapucho, Efrén. 2005. Author interview with CONAIE leader. Quito, July 19.

Carvajal Donoso, Hugo. 2004. Author interview with MIR senator. La Paz, July 19.

Díaz, Ricardo. 2007. Author interview with MAS senator. La Paz, August 17.

Gallo Carhuachinchay, Renán. 2008. Author interview with member of the National Council of the Confederación Campesina del Peru. Lima, June 10.

Garay, Luis. 2004. Author interview with director of polling firm Apoyo. La Paz, July 27.

García, Aníbal. 2008. Author interview with the national deputy and head of the legislative delegation of Encuentro por Guatemala. Guatemala City, August 7.

García, Gerardo. 2007. Author interview with vice president of the MAS. La Paz, August 20.

García Linera, Alvaro. 2004. Author interview with vice president of Bolivia. La Paz, July 25.

Huascar, Antolín. 2006. Author interview with president of the Confederación Nacional Agraria. Lima, July 21.

Huber, Ludwig. 2008. Author interview with professor at the Instituto de Estudios Peruanos. Lima, June 10.

Ilaquiche, Raúl. 2007. Author interview with Pachakutik deputy. Quito, June 28.

Lajo, Javier. 2008. Author interview with former coordinator of Conferencia Permanente de los Pueblos Indígenas del Perú. Lima, July 19.

Lazarte, Jorge. 2004. Author interview with Bolivian political scientist and former member of the National Electoral Court. La Paz, August 2.

Lerner, Salomón. 2006. Author interview with adviser to Ollanta Humala. Lima, July 12.

Miranda, Patricio. 2007. Author interview with Pachakutik deputy. Quito, July 3.

Montenegro, Luis Fernando. 2008. Author interview with the 2007 vice presidential candidate of Encuentro por Guatemala. Guatemala City, August 7.

Núñez, Dionisio. 2004. Author interview with MAS deputy. La Paz, July 23.

Pacari, Nina. 2005. Author interview with former Pachakutik deputy and minister of foreign relations. July 18.

Palacín, Miguel. 2008. Author interview with general coordinator of the Coordinadora Andina de Organizaciones Indígenas and former head of CONACAMI. Lima, June 12.

Peredo, Antonio. 2004. Author interview with legislator and former vice presidential candidate of the MAS. La Paz, July 22.

Pop, Alvaro. 2008. Author interview with the head of the 2007 Misión Indígena de la Observación Electoral. Guatemala City, August 6.

Quiroga, Luis Alberto. 2004. Author interview with director of polling firm Encuestas y Estudios. La Paz, August 2.

Quishpe, Salvador. 2007. Author interview with Pachakutik deputy. Quito, July 9.

Quispe, Felipe. 2004. Author interview with leader of the MIP. La Paz, July 29.

Ramírez, Santos. 2007. Author interview with MAS senator. La Paz, August 21.

Rivera Cusicanqui, Silvia. 2004. Author interview with Bolivian sociologist. La Paz, July 16.

Sucuzhañay, Carlos. 2007. Author interview with Pachakutik deputy. Quito, June 28.

Talahua, Gilberto. 2007. Author interview with Pachakutik national coordinator. Quito, July 5.

Torres, Javier. 2008. Author interview with former director of the Servicios Educativos Rurales. Lima, July 19.

Torres, Ramses. 2007. Author interview with Pachakutik deputy and chief of legislative delegation. Quito, July 5.

Torrico, Gustavo. 2004. Author interview with MAS deputy. La Paz, July 22.

Tuesta, Fernando. 2008. Author interview with former director of the Oficina Nacional de Procesos Electorales. Lima, June 11.

Vilca, Paulo. 2008. Author interview with analyst of Servicios Educativos Rurales. Lima, June 12.

Villca, Lino. 2007. Author interview with MAS senator. La Paz, August 15.

Zurita, Leonilda. 2007. Author interview with secretary for External Relations of MAS. La Paz, August 20.

References

"7 de cada 10 bolivianos se ven mestizos." 2009. *La Razón*, March 3. [Cited March 10, 2010]. Available from: http://www.la-razon.com/index.php?edition_a=1&fecha=2009–03–03.

Acevedo, Angela, and Paulo Vilca Arpasi. 2007. "La clase política no representa a nadie." *Cabildo Abierto,* May.

Aguilar, Josefina. 2005. *Observación electoral intercultural: elecciones seccionales Ecuador 2004.* Quito: Ediciones Abya-Yala.

Albó, Xavier. 1991. "El retorno del indio." *Revista Andina* 9 (2): 299–321.

1993. *Y de Kataristas a MNRistas?: la sorprendente y audaz alianza entre aymaras y neoliberales en Bolivia.* La Paz: Unitas/Cedoin.

2002. "Bolivia: From Indian and Campesino Leaders to Councillors and Parliamentary Deputies." In *Multiculturalism in Latin America*, ed. R. Seider. New York: Palgrave MacMillan: 74–102.

Alenda Mary, Stéphanie. 2002. "CONDEPA y UCS, fin del populismo?" *Opiniones y Análisis* 57: 47–83.

Alonso, Sonia. 2008. "Enduring Ethnicity: The Political Survival of Incumbent Ethnic Parties in Western Democracies." In *Controlling Governments: Voters, Institutions, and Accountability*, eds. J. M. Maravall and I. Sánchez Cuenca. New York: Cambridge University Press: 82–104.

Alvarez, Michael R., and Jonathan Nagler. 1998. "When Politics and Models Collide: Estimating Models of Multiparty Competition." *American Journal of Political Science* 42: 55–96.

Andolina, Robert James. 1999. Colonial Legacies and Plurinational Imaginaries: Indigenous Movement Politics in Ecuador and Bolivia. Dissertation, Dept. of Political Science, University of Minnesota, Minneapolis.

2003. "The Sovereign and Its Shadow: Constituent Assembly and the Indigenous Movement in Ecuador." *Journal of Latin American Studies* 35: 721–50.

Andrade, Susana. 2003. "Gobiernos locales indígenas en el Ecuador." *Revista Andina* 37: 115–36.

Anonymous. 1994. *Caretas* November 10, 35.

Apoyo Opinión y Mercado S.A. 1995. "Informe de Opinión." April.

2000a. "Informe de opinión." April.

2000b. "Informe especial del SAE: Encuesta nacional extraordinaria." April 30.

2001. "Informe de opinión." May.

2006a. "Opinión data: Resumen de encuestas a la opinión pública." 6 (73), May 8.

2006b. "Opinión data: Resumen de encuestas a la opinión pública." 6 (77) June 18.

2006c. "Opinión data: Resumen de encuestas a la opinión pública." 6 (76), May 28.

2006d. "Opinión data: Resumen de encuestas a la opinión pública." 6 (74) May 15.

Arce, Moisés. 2003. "Political Violence and Presidential Approval in Peru." *The Journal of Politics* 65 (2): 572–83.

Aroca Medina, Javier. 1999. *Los pueblos indígenas de la frontera amazónica: Simbolizan el verdadero canto de amistad entre Perú y Ecuador* [accessed July 13, 2008]. Available from http://webserver.rcp.net.pe/convenios/coppip/Aroca1.html.

Asociación de Investigación y Estudios Sociales. 2008. *Guatemala: Informe Analítico del Proceso Electoral 2007.* Guatemala: ASIES.

Asociación Interétnica de Desarrollo de la Selva Peruana. 2009. *¿Cómo estamos organizados?* [cited July 16, 2009]. Available from http://www.aidesep.org.pe/index.php?id=2,0,0,1,0,0.

Ba Tiul, Máximo. 2007. "Movimiento Winaq, la Controversia: Ni a la Izquierda Ni a la Derecha." Guatemala: FLACSO.

Báez Rivera, Sara, and Víctor Bretón Solo de Zaldívar. 2006. "El enigma del voto étnico o las tribulaciones del movimiento indígena: Reflexiones sobre los resultados de la primera vuelta electoral (2006) en las provincias de la sierra." *Ecuador Debate* 69: 19–36.

Bailey, Stanley R. 2009. *Legacies of Race: Identities, Attitudes, and Politics in Brazil.* Stanford: Stanford University Press.

Barié, Cletus Gregor. 2007. "Bolivia: Cuánta revolución cabe en la democracia?" *FRIDE Comentario*: 1–14.

Barr, Robert R. 2002. Between Success and Survival: Devolution and Concentration in Latin America. Dissertation, Dept. of Government, University of Texas at Austin.

   2003. "The Persistence of Neopopulism in Peru? From Fujimori to Toledo" *Third World Quarterly* 24 (6): 1161–78.

   2006. "Indigenous Populism in Latin America." Paper delivered at Annual Meeting of the American Political Science Association, August 31–September 3, 2006, Philadelphia.

   2009. "Populists, Outsiders and Anti-Establishment Politics." *Party Politics* 15 (1): 29–48.

Barrera Guarderas, Augusto. 2001. *Acción colectiva y crisis política: El movimiento indígena ecuatoriano en la década de los noventa.* Quito: Ediciones Abya-Yala.

Barrera Guarderas, Augusto, ed. 2004. *Entre la utopía y el desencanto: Pachakutik en el gobierno de Gutiérrez.* Quito: Editorial Planeta.

Barth, Fredrik, ed. 1969. *Ethnic Groups and Boundaries.* Boston: Little, Brown and Company.

Bartolini, Stefano, and Peter Mair. 1990. *Identity, Competition, and Electoral Availability: The Stabilisation of European Electorates, 1885–1985.* New York: Cambridge University Press.

Bastos, Santiago. 2009. "Guatemala: los límites de la política multicultural tras la tierra arrasada." Paper delivered at Congress of the Latin American Studies Association, June 11–14, 2009, Rio de Janeiro, Brazil.

Bastos, Santiago, and Roddy Brett, eds. 2010. *El movimiento maya en la década después de la paz (1997–2007).* Guatemala City: F&G editores.

Bastos, Santiago, and Manuela Camus. 2003. *Entre el mecapal y el cielo: Desarrollo del movimiento maya en Guatemala.* Guatemala: FLACSO.

Beck, Scott H., and Kenneth J. Mijeski. 2001. "Barricades and Ballots: Ecuador's Indians and the Pachakutik Political Movement." *Ecuadorian Studies / Estudios ecuatorianos* 1.

   2006. "How to Lose by Winning: The Ecuadorian Indigenous Movement after the 2002 Elections." Paper delivered at Congress of the Latin American Studies Association, March 15–18, 2006, San Juan, Puerto Rico.

Becker, Marc. 2008. *Indians and Leftists in the Making of Ecuador's Modern Indigenous Movements* Durham: Duke University Press.

Belote, Linda Smith, and Jim Belote. 1984. "Drain from the Bottom: Individual Ethnic Identity Change in Southern Ecuador." *Social Forces* 63 (1): 24–50.

Benavente, Claudia. 2008. "Evo Morales, hijo del pueblo y primer presidente indígena." In *Los Tele-presidentes: cerca del pueblo, lejos de la democracia*, ed. O. Rincón. Bogotá: Friedrich Ebert Stiftung: 55–66.

Bernbaum, Marcia, Rafael López Pintor, and Cynthia Sanborn. 2001. *Transparencia: Civil Society Observes Peru's Controversial 2000 Elections.* Lima: Asociación Civil Transparencia.

Betz, Hans-Georg. 1994. *Radical Right-Wing Populism in Western Europe.* Basingstoke: Macmillan.

   2001. "Exclusionary Populism in Austria, Italy, and Switzerland." *International Journal* 56 (3): 393–420.

Birnir, Jóhanna Kristín. 2004. "Stabilizing Party Systems and Excluding Segments of Society?: The Effects of Formation Costs on New Party Foundation in Latin America." *Studies in Comparative International Development* 39 (3): 3–27.

2007. *Ethnicity and Electoral Politics*. New York: Cambridge University Press.

Birnir, Jóhanna Kristín, and Donna Lee Van Cott. 2007. "Disunity in Diversity: Party System Fragmentation and the Dynamic Effect of Ethnic Heterogeneity on Latin American Legislatures." *Latin American Research Review* 42 (1): 99–125.

Blancas Bustamante, Carlos. 2005. "La Ley de Partidos Politicos: Análisis jurídico." *Elecciones* 5: 105–23.

Boggio, María Rosa, Fernando Romero, and Juan Ansión. 1991. *El pueblo es así y también asá: Lógicas culturales en el voto popular*. Lima: Instituto Democracia y Socialismo.

Bohrt Irahola, Carlos, and Silvia Chávez Reyes. 2002. *Elecciones 2002: Resultados y transformaciones*. La Paz: FUNDEMOS.

"Bolivians Love Evo: Want Closer Ties with the U.S." 2006. *Latin American Weekly Report*, May 23, 16.

Brett, Roddy. 2010. "De movimiento indígena a complejidad política: La evolución de las políticas indígenas 1996–2007." In *El movimiento maya en la década después de la paz (1997–2007)*, eds. S. Bastos and R. Brett. Guatemala City: F&G Editores: 55–92.

Bruhn, Kathleen. 1997. *Taking on Goliath: The Emergence of a New Left Party*. University Park: Penn State University Press.

Brysk, Alison. 2000. *From Tribal Village to Global Village: Indian Rights and International Relations in Latin America*. Stanford: Stanford University Press.

Burbano de Lara, Felipe. 2005. "La producción de lo étnico y la descomposición de la nación: El caso del Ecuador." In *Movimiento indígena en América Latina: Resistencia y proyecto alternativo*, eds. F. Escárzaga and R. Gutiérrez. Mexico City: Gobierno del Distrito Federal: 237–65.

Butler, Judy. 1997. "The Peoples of the Atlantic Coast." In *Nicaragua without Illusions*, ed. T. Walker. Wilmington: Scholarly Resources: 219–234.

Buvinić, Mayra, and Jacqueline Mazza, eds. 2004. *Social Inclusion and Economic Development in Latin America*. Washington: Inter-American Development Bank.

Caballero, Gerardo. 2006. "Ollanta Humala intenta subir de nuevo." *El Comercio*, March 12.

Caballero Martín, Victor. 2006. "En busca del voto rural." *Quehacer* (159): 35–41.

Caballero Rojas, Gerardo. 2006. "Ollanta Humala niega ser autoritario y que busque enfrentar a peruanos." *El Comercio*, April 6.

Cabieses, Hugo. 2004. "Peru's Cocaleros on the March." *NACLA Report on the Americas*: 10–13.

Calderón, Fernando, and Eduardo Gamarra. 2004. *Crisis y reforma de los partidos en Bolivia*. La Paz: Programa de las Naciones Unidas para el Desarrollo (PNUD).

Cameron, John D. 2010. *Struggles for Local Democracy in the Andes*. Boulder: First Forum Press.

Campbell, Maia Sophia. 2007. "The Right of Indigenous Peoples to Political Participation and the Case of YATAMA V. Nicaragua." *Arizona Journal of International and Comparative Law* 24 (2): 499–540.

"Canal 7 cumplió con presentar a candidatos." 2006. *El Comercio*, March 4.

Canessa, Andrew. 2006. "Todos Somos Indígenas: Towards a New Language of National Political Identity." *Bulletin of Latin American Research* 25 (2): 241–63.

Canovan, Margaret. 1999. "Trust the People! Populism and the Two Faces of Democracy." *Political Studies* (47): 2–16.

Carlsen, Laura. 2007. "Bolivia – Coming to Terms with Diversity: An Interview with Álvaro García Linera, Vice President of Bolivia." In *Americas Policy Program Special Report*, Nov. 16.

Carrión, Julio. 1997. "La opinión pública bajo el primer gobierno de Fujimori: ¿De identidades a intereses?" In *Los enigmas del poder: Fujimori 1990–1996*, ed. F. Tuesta Soldevilla. Lima: Fundación Friedrich Ebert: 277–302.

2009. "The Persistent Attraction of Populism in the Andes." In *Latin American Democracy: Emerging Reality or Endangered Species*, eds. R. L. Millett, J. S. Holmes, and O. J. Pérez. New York: Routledge: 233–51.

Carrión, Julio, Patricia Zárate, and Mitchell A. Seligson. 2006. *The Political Culture of Democracy in Peru: 2006*. Nashville: Latin American Public Opinion Project.

Casanova Saínz, Mauricio. 2003. "Análisis de la estadística sobre abstencionismo electoral en las elecciones nacionales." In *Participación y abstención electoral en Bolivia*, ed. C. Toranzo Roca. La Paz: Friedrich Ebert Stiftung – Instituto Latinoamericano de Investigaciones Sociales: 149–81.

Centro de Investigación de la Universidad del Pacífico. 1980. *Peru 1980: Elecciones y planes de gobierno*. Lima: Centro de Investigación de la Universidad del Pacífico.

Ceto, Pablo. 2007. "Formas propias de organización indígena y su relación con los partidos políticos." In *Multiculturidad y partidos políticos: Estudios sobre organización y participación de los pueblos indígenas*. Guatemala: Organización de los Estados Americanos: 71–102.

Chandra, Kanchan. 2001. "Cumulative Findings in the Study of Ethnic Politics." *APSA-CP* 12 (1): 7–11.

2004. *Why Ethnic Parties Succeed: Patronage and Ethnic Head Counts in India*. New York: Cambridge University Press.

2005. "Ethnic Parties and Democratic Stability." *Perspectives on Politics* 3 (2): 235–52.

2006. "What is Ethnic Identity and Does It Matter?" *Annual Review of Political Science* 9: 397–424.

2011. "What is an Ethnic Party?" *Party Politics* 17 (2): 151–69.

Chandra, Kanchan, and Steven Wilkinson. 2008. "Measuring the Effect of 'Ethnicity.'" *Comparative Political Studies* 41 (4/5): 515–63.

Chiriboga, Manuel, and Fredy Rivera. 1989. "Elecciones de enero 1988 y participación indígena." *Ecuador Debate* 17: 181–221.

Clark, A. Kim. 1998. "Race, 'Culture,' and Mestizaje: The Statistical Construction of the Ecuadorian Nation, 1930–1950." *Journal of Historical Sociology* 11 (2): 185–211.

Clark, A. Kim, and Marc Becker, eds. 2007. *Highland Indians and the State in Modern Ecuador*. Pittsburgh: University of Pittsburgh Press.

Cleary, Matthew R. 2000. "Democracy and Indigenous Rebellion in Latin America." *Comparative Political Studies* 33 (9): 1123–53.

"Cocaleros intentan volver a unirse." 2006. *El Comercio*, July 16, A24.

Cojtí Cuxil, Demetrio. 2006. "Agendas políticas indígenas y respuestas estatales: Los pueblos indígenas en la democracia y estado guatemaltecos (1985–2005)." In *La Inclusión de los Pueblos Indígenas en los Partidos Políticos*. Guatemala: Organización de los Estados Americanos: 143–79.

2010. "La educación superior indígena y su relación con el movimiento y liderazgo indígenas." In *El movimiento maya en la década después de la paz (1997–2007)*, eds. S. Bastos and R. Brett. Guatemala City: F&G Editores: 93–133.

Collier, David, and James E. Mahon. 1993. "Conceptual 'Stretching' Revisited: Adapting Categories in Comparative Analysis." *American Political Science Review* 87 (4): 845–55.

Collins, Jennifer N. 2001. "Opening Up Electoral Politics: Political Crisis and the Rise of Pachakutik." Paper delivered at Congress of the Latin American Studies Association, Sept. 6–8, 2001, Washington, DC.

2006. Democratizing Formal Politics: Indigenous and Social Movement Political Parties in Ecuador and Bolivia, 1978–2000. Dissertation, Dept. of Political Science, University of California, San Diego.

Compañia Peruana de Estudios de Mercados y Opinión Pública S.A.C. 2006. "Estudio de opinión pública." Lima: CPI, May.

Conaghan, Catherine M. 2011. "Ecuador: Rafael Correa and the Citizen's Revolution." In *The Resurgence of the Latin American Left*, eds. S. Levitsky and K. M. Roberts. Baltimore: The Johns Hopkins University Press: 260–82.

Confederación Nacional Agraria. 2008. CNA, [accessed July 9, 2008]. Available from http://www.cna.org.pe/.

Conniff, Michael. 1982. "Toward a Comparative Definition of Populism." In *Latin American Populism in Comparative Perspective*, ed. M. Conniff. Albuquerque: University of New Mexico Press: 3–30.

Coordinadora Andina de Organizaciones Indígenas. n.d. *Plan estratégico: Tejiendo sueños de integración de los pueblos andinos*. Lima: CAOI.

Córdova C., Ángel Polibio. 1999. *Estudios & datos: Ecuador en perspectiva*. Quito: Ediciones CEDATOS.

Corporación Latinobarómetro. 2005. "Latinobarómetro Report 2005." Santiago: Corporación Latinobarómetro.

Corte Nacional Electoral. 1958. *Informe anual*. La Paz: CNE.

2006. "Resultados Elecciones Generales y de Prefectos 2005." La Paz: CNE.

Cupil, Jaime. 2007. "Las demandas de los pueblos indígenas a la política partidaria: El caso de Guatemala." In *La inclusión de los pueblos indígenas en los partidos políticos*. Guatemala: Organización de los Estados Americanos: 69–98.

Dalton, Russell L., Scott C. Flanagan, and Paul Allen Beck, eds. 1984. *Electoral Change in Advanced Industrial Democracies: Realignment or Dealignment?* Princeton: Princeton University Press.

Darlic Mardesic, Vjekoslav. 1987. *Estadísticas Electorales del Ecuador, 1978–1987*. Quito: Instituto Latinoamericano de Investigaciones Sociales.

Dary, Claudia, ed. 1998. *La construcción de la nación y la representación ciudadana en México, Guatemala, Perú, Ecuador y Bolivia*. Guatemala: FLACSO.

Davila Puño, Julio. 2005. *Peru: Gobiernos locales y pueblos indígenas*. Lima: Grupo de Trabajo Racimos de Ungurahui.

de la Cadena, Marisol. 2000. *Indigenous Mestizos: The Politics of Race and Culture in Cuzco, Peru, 1919–1991*. Durham: Duke University Press.

de la Torre, Carlos. 2000. *Populist Seduction in Latin America: The Ecuadorian Experience*. Athens, Ohio: Ohio University Center for International Studies.

2004. "Polarización populista y democracia en Ecuador." *Diálogo Político* 21 (2): 89–113.

2006. "Eleiçòes e perspectivas pós-eleitorais no Equador." *Cadernos Adenauer* 7 (4): 67–83.

de la Torre, Carlos, and Catherine Conaghan. 2009. "The Hybrid Campaign: Tradition and Modernity in Ecuador's 2006 Presidential Election." *International Journal of Press/Politics* 14 (3): 335–52.

Degler, Carl N. 1971. *Neither Black Nor White: Slavery and Race Relations in Brazil and the United States.* New York: Macmillan.

Degregori, Carlos Iván. 1991. "El aprendiz de brujo y el curandero chino: Etnicidad, modernidad y ciudadanía." In *Demonios y redentores en el nuevo Perú: Una tragedia en dos vueltas*, eds. C. I. Degregori and R. Grompone. Lima: Instituto de Estudios Peruanos: 71–142.

Dirección General de Estadística y Censos. 1950. *Censo Demográfico 1950.* La Paz: Dirección General de Estadística y Censos.

Dornbusch, Rudiger, and Sebastian Edwards, eds. 1991. *The Macroeconomics of Populism in Latin America.* Chicago: University of Chicago Press.

Dow, Jay K., and James W. Endersby. 2004. "Multinomial Probit and Multinomial Logit: A Comparison of Choice Models for Voting Research." *Electoral Studies* 23.

Downs, Anthony. 1957. *An economic theory of democracy.* New York: Harper.

"Dr. Luis Macas: Barreré a los corruptos del Congreso." 1996. *Kipu* 26: 66.

Drake, Paul. 1982. "Conclusion: Requiem for Populism?" In *Latin American Populism in Comparative Perspective*, ed. M. L. Conniff. Albuquerque: University of New Mexico Press: 217–45.

Dunning, Thad, and Lauren Harrison. 2010. "Cross-cutting Cleavages and Ethnic Voting: An Experimental Study of Cousinage in Mali." *American Political Science Review* 104 (1): 21–39.

Durand Guevara, Anahí. 2005. "El movimiento cocalero y su (in)existencia en el Perú. Itinerario de desencuentros en el río Apurímac." *Bulletin de L'Institut Français d'Études Andines* 34 (1): 103–26.

2006. "Revaloración étnica y representación política: Los casos de INTI y MINCAP de Lircay, Huancavelica." In *Peru: El problema agrario en debate – SEPIA XI,* eds. J. Iguíñiz, J. Escobal, and C. I. Degregori. Lima: SEPIA: 541–82.

2011. "Tan lejos, tan cerca: Movimientos sociales, conflictividad y el último proceso electoral." *Revista Argumentos* 5 (2): 23–33.

"El evismo ensalza a Evo en el poder." 2006. *La Razón*, August 5.

"El presidente ideal." 2002. *Sente*, February, 16–17.

"En la emancipación de los pueblos, Evo es sustituible." 2006. *La Razón*, August 5.

Escobar, Gabriel. 1996. "Indians of Ecuador Coalescing in Quest for Political Power." *The Washington Post*, July 23, A12.

Esteva-Fabregat, Claudio. 1995. *Mestizaje in Ibero-America.* Tucson: University of Arizona Press.

"Evo sacudió el sistema político y empoderó a los indígenas." 2006. *La Razón*, August 5.

Falla, Ricardo. 1978. "El movimiento indígena." *Estudios Centroaméricanos* 33 (356/357): 437–61.

2007. "Rigoberta Menchú: A Shooting Star in the Electoral Sky." *Revista Envío*, 312, July.

Felbab-Brown, Vanda. 2006. "Trouble Ahead: The *Cocaleros* of Peru." *Current History*: 79–83.

Fernández Fontenoy, Carlos. 2000. "Sistema político, indigenismo y movimiento campesino en el Perú." In *Los movimientos sociales en las democracias andinas*, eds. J. Massal and M. Bonilla. Quito: FLACSO: 193–211.

Figueroa, Oscar. 2007. "Pronunció discurso en idioma K'iche'." *La Prensa Libre*, July 30.

Fischer, Edward F. 2001. *Cultural Logics and Global Economies: Maya Identity in Thought and Practice.* 1st ed. Austin: University of Texas Press.

Frank, Erwin, Ninfa Patiño, and Marta Rodríguez, eds. 1992. *Los políticos y los indígenas.* Quito: Ediciones Abya-Yala.

Fregosi, Renée. 2007. "Interview de Nadine et Ollanta Humala." *Cahiers de Amérique Latine* (50): 7–18.

Freidenberg, Flavia. 2003. *Jama, caleta y camello: Las estrategias de Abdalá Bucaram y el PRE para ganar las elecciones.* Quito: Corporación Editora Nacional.

Freidenberg, Flavia, and Manuel S. Alcántara. 2001. *Los dueños del poder: Los partidos políticos en Ecuador (1978–2000).* Quito: FLACSO.

Freyre, Gilberto. 1959. *New World in the Tropics: The Culture of Modern Brazil.* New York: Alfred A. Knopf.

Gálvez Vera, José Luis. 2002. "Las encuestas en la campaña electoral: Tendencias y resultados." *Opiniones y Análisis* 57: 9–46.

Gana Perú. 2010. "La Gran Transformación – Plan de Gobierno 2011–2016." Lima: Gana Perú.

García Linera, Alvaro. 2005. "The Indigenous Movements in Bolivia." *Diplomacy, Strategy & Politics* 1 (3): 12–30.

García, María Elena, and José Antonio Lucero. 2004. "'Un País Sin Indígenas?' Rethinking Indigenous Politics in Peru." In *The Struggle for Indigenous Rights in Latin America,* eds. N. Postero and L. Zamosc. Portland: Sussex Academic Press: 158–88.

2008. "Exceptional Others: Politicians, Rottweilers, and Alterity in the 2006 Peruvian Elections." *Latin American and Caribbean Ethnic Studies* 3 (3): 253–70.

García Montero, Mercedes. 2001. "La década de Fujimori: Ascenso, mantenimiento y caída de un líder antipolítico." *América Latina Hoy* (28): 49–86.

González, Miguel. 2008. Governing Multi-ethnic Societies in Latin America: Regional Autonomy, Democracy, and the State in Nicaragua, 1987–2007. Dissertation, Dept. of Political Science, York University.

2010. "Los indígenas y los 'étnicos': Inclusión restringida en el Régimen de Autonomía en Nicaragua." In *Política e identidad afrodescendientes en México y América Central,* ed. O. Hoffman. Mexico City: Instituto Nacional de Antropología e Historia: 93–128.

Goodin, Robert E. 1975. "Cross-Cutting Cleavages and Social Conflict." *British Journal of Political Science* 5 (4): 516–19.

Graham, Carol, and Cheikh Kane. 1998. "Opportunistic Government or Sustaining Reform? Electoral Trends and Public Expenditure Patterns in Peru, 1990–1995." *Latin American Research Review* 33 (1): 67–104.

Greene, Shane. 2006. "Getting over the Andes: The Geo-Eco-Politics of Indigenous Movements in Peru's 21st Century Inca Empire." *Journal of Latin American Studies* 38: 327–54.

Grefa, Valerio. 1996. "El triángulo del Pachakutik." In *Por el camino del arco iris.* Quito: Agencia Latinoamericana de Información: 51–8.

Grijalva, Agustín, ed. 1992. *Vote sabiendo: Lo que ofrecen los partidos y los candidatos.* Quito: Corporación Editora Nacional.

Grofman, Bernard, and Arend Lijphart, eds. 1986. *Electoral Laws and their Political Consequences.* New York: Agathon Press.

Guerrero Cazar, Fernando, and Pablo Ospina Peralta. 2003. *El poder de la comunidad: Ajuste estructural y movimiento indígena en los Andes ecuatorianos.* Buenos Aires: Consejo Latinoamericano de Ciencias Sociales.

Guevara, Klével. 1996. "Una campaña de corazón." In *Por el camino del arco iris*. Quito: Agencia Latinoamercana de Información: 95–9.

Gunther, Richard, and Larry Diamond. 2003. "Species of Political Parties: A New Typology." *Party Politics* 9 (2): 167–99.

Gurr, Ted Robert. 1993. *Minorities at Risk: A Global View of Ethnopolitical Conflicts*. Washington: U.S. Institute of Peace.

"Gutiérrez dice sí al capital foráneo para el petróleo." 2002. *El Comercio*, October 30.

Hale, Charles R. 1994. *Resistance and Contradiction: Miskitu Indians and the Nicaraguan State, 1894–1987*. Stanford, CA: Stanford University Press.

  2006. *Más que un Indio = More than an Indian: Racial Ambivalence and Neoliberal Multiculturalism in Guatemala*. 1st ed. Santa Fe, NM: School of American Research Press.

Hall, Gillette, and Harry Anthony Patrinos, eds. 2006. *Indigenous Peoples, Poverty and Human Development in Latin America, 1994–2004*. New York: Palgrave Macmillan

Hanchard, Michael George. 1999. *Racial Politics in Contemporary Brazil*. Durham [NC]: Duke University Press.

Harmel, Robert, and John D. Robertson. 1985. "Formation and Success of New Parties: A Cross-National Analysis." *International Political Science Review* 6 (4): 501–23.

Harnecker, Marta, Federico Fuentes, and Santos Ramírez. 2008. *MAS-IPSP: Instrumento político que surge de los movimientos sociales*. Caracas: Centro Internacional Miranda.

Hawkins, Kirk Andrew. 2010. *Venezuela's Chavismo and Populism in Comparative Perspective*. New York: Cambridge University Press.

Healy, Kevin. 1991. "Political Ascent of Bolivia's Peasant Coca Leaf Producers." *Journal of Interamerican Studies and World Affairs* 33 (1): 87–120.

Hernández Pico, Juan. 2006. "Could 'Evo' Happen in Guatemala?" *Revista Envío* 301.

Hoffman, Odile, ed. 2010. *Política e identidad: Afrodescendientes en México y América Central*. Mexico City: Instituto Nacional de Antropología e Historia.

Hooker, Juliet. 2008. "Afro-descendant Struggles for Collective Rights in Latin America: Between Race and Culture." *Souls* 10 (3): 279–91.

  2009. *Race and the Politics of Solidarity*. New York: Oxford University Press.

Hopenhayn, Martín, and Alvaro Bello. 2001. "Discriminación étnico-racial y xenofobia en América Latina y el Caribe." In *Serie políticas sociales* 47. Santiago: CEPAL.

Horowitz, Donald L. 1985. *Ethnic Groups in Conflict*. Berkeley: University of California Press.

  1991. *A Democratic South Africa?: Constitutional Engineering in a Divided Society*. Berkeley: University of California Press.

Htun, Mala. 2004. "Is Gender like Ethnicity? The Political Representation of Identity Groups." *Perspectives on Politics* 2 (3): 439–58.

Huber, Ludwig. 2008. "La representación indígena en municipalidades peruanas: Tres estudios de caso." In *Ejercicio de gobierno local en los ámbitos rurales: Presupuesto, desarrollo e identidad*, eds. R. Grompone, R. Hernández Asensio, and L. Huber. Lima: Instituto de Estudios Peruanos: 175–272.

Hug, Simon. 2001. *Altering Party Systems: Strategic Behavior and the Emergence of New Political Parties in Western Democracies*. Ann Arbor: University of Michigan Press.

Humala Tasso, Antauro. 2001. *Ejército peruano: Milenarismo, nacionalismo y etnocacerismo.* Lima: Instituto de Estudios Etnogeopolíticos.

2007. *Etnonacionalismo, izquierda y globalidad (visión etnocacerista).* 2nd edition Lima: Ediciones Antaurpi.

Humala Tasso, Ollanta. 2006. *Ollanta uniendo al Perú: Plan de gobierno 2006–2011.* Villa El Salvador: Partido Nacionalista Peruano.

"Humala: "Están formando el partido 'todos contra Ollanta.'" 2006. *El Comercio,* March 23.

Hurtado, Javier. 1986. *El Katarismo.* La Paz: Hisbol.

Ianni, Octavio. 1975. *La formación del estado populista en América Latina.* Mexico City: Era.

Ibarra, Alicia. 1992. *Los indígenas y el estado en el Ecuador.* Quito: Ediciones Abya-Yala.

Ibarra, Hernán. 2002. "El triunfo del Coronel Gutiérrez y la alianza indígena militar." *Ecuador Debate* 57: 21–33.

Institute for Democracy and Electoral Assistance. 2010. *Voter Turnout: Bolivia,* [accessed July 26, 2010]. Available from http://www.idea.int/vt/country_view.cfm?id=29.

Instituto de Estudios de Iberoamérica y Portugal. 2003. "Estudio 47: Bolivia – encuesta a diputados bolivianos, 2002–2007." In *Elites parlamentarias latinoamericanas:* Universidad de Salamanca.

Instituto Interuniversitario de Iberoamérica. 2006. "Estudio 62: Bolivia – encuesta a diputados bolivianos, 2006–2010." In *Élites parlamentarias iberoamericanas.* Salamanca: Universidad de Salamanca.

Instituto Nacional de Estadística. 2003a. *Bolivia: Características sociodemográficas de la población.* La Paz: INE.

2003b. *Características de la población y de los locales de habitación censados.* Guatemala: INE.

Instituto Nacional de Estadística e Informática. 1994. *Censo Nacional Agropecuario.* INEI, [accessed July 9, 2008]. Available from http://www.inei.gob.pe/web/resulta-docenso.asp.

2007. *Estado de la población peruana: Indocumentación y grupos étnicos.* Lima: INEI.

"Interview with Luis Macas." 2003. In *Contemporary Indigenous Movements in Latin America,* eds. E. Langer and E. Muñoz. Wilmington: Scholarly Resource Books.

"Is this the New Evo Morales?" 2007. *Latin American Special Report,* July 7.

Izquierda Unida. 1985. *Plan de gobierno de Izquierda Unida: Peru 1985–1990 síntesis.* Lima: Izquierda Unida.

Jiménez Pozo, Wilson, Fernando Landa Casazola, and Ernesto Yáñez Aguilar. 2006. "Bolivia." In *Pueblos indígenas, pobreza y desarrollo humano en América Latina: 1994–2004,* eds. G. Hall and H. A. Patrinos. Bogota: Banco Mundial: 45–73.

Kalyvas, Stathis N. 1996. *The Rise of Christian Democracy in Europe.* Ithaca, NY: Cornell University Press.

Kaufman, Robert R., and Barbara Stallings. 1991. "The Political Economy of Latin American Populism." In *The Macroeconomics of Populism in Latin America,* eds. R. Dornbusch and S. Edwards. Chicago: University of Chicago Press: 15–43.

Keck, Margaret E. 1992. *The Workers' Party and Democratization in Brazil.* New Haven: Yale University Press.

King, Gary, Michael Tomz, and Jason Wittenberg. 2000. "Making the Most of Statistical Analyses: Improving Interpretation and Presentation." *American Journal of Political Science* 44: 347–61.

Kitschelt, Herbert. 1988. "Left-Libertarian Parties: Explaining Innovation in Competitive Party Systems." *World Politics* 40 (2): 194–234.

Knapp, Gregory. 1987. *Geografía quichua de la sierra del Ecuador*. Quito: Abya-Yala.

"La desintegración de Pachakutik continua." 2005. *El Comercio*, December 23.

"La imagen del Presidente no es elaborada, es espontánea." 2006. *La Razón*, November 5.

Laclau, Ernesto. 2005. *On Populist Reason*. New York: Verso.

Lago, Ignacio, and Ferran Martínez. 2011. "Why New Parties?" *Party Politics* 17 (1): 3–20.

Laitin, David D. 1998. *Identity in Formation: The Russian-speaking Populations in the Near Abroad*. Ithaca: Cornell University Press.

Larrea, Carlos, and Silvia Sommaruga. 1984. "Participación electoral, abstención y consistencia de los resultados electorales de la elección presidencial." In *1984: El Ecuador en las urnas*, ed. L. Verdesoto Custode. Quito: Editorial El Conejo: 233–49.

Laurent, Virginie. 2005. "Una década de movilización electoral indígena en Colombia: Entre la consolidación y la incertidumbre." In *Participación política, democracia y movimientos indígenas en los Andes*. La Paz: Fundación PIEB: 165–76.

2009. "Movimiento indígena y retos electorales en Colombia: Regreso de lo indio para una apuesta nacional." *Elecciones* 8 (9): 87–114.

Lawson, Kay and Peter H. Merkl. 1998. *When Parties Fail: Emerging Alternative Organizations*. Princeton: Princeton University Press.

León Guzmán, Mauricio. 2003. "Etnicidad y exclusión en el Ecuador: Una mirada a partir del Censo de Población de 2001." *Iconos* 17: 116–32.

León, Jorge. 2005. "Los pueblos indígenas y su participación gubernamental en Ecuador, 2002–2003." In *Participación política, democracia y movimientos indígenas en los Andes*. La Paz: Instituto Francés de Estudios Andinos: 11–38.

Levitsky, Steven. 1999. "Fujimori and Post-Party Politics in Peru." *Journal of Democracy* 10 (3): 78–92.

2011. "A Surprising Left Turn." *Journal of Democracy* 22 (4): 84–94.

Levitsky, Steven, and Kenneth M. Roberts. 2011. "Introduction: Latin America's Left Turn: A Framework for Analysis." In *The Resurgence of the Latin American Left*, eds. S. Levitsky and K. M. Roberts. Baltimore: The Johns Hopkins University Press: 1–28.

Leyes de elecciones, partidos políticos y reglamentos. 1991. Quito: Corporación de Estudios y Publicaciones.

Lijphart, Arend. 1977. *Democracy in Plural Societies: A Comparative Exploration*. New Haven: Yale University Press.

Lipset, Seymour Martin. 1959. "Some Social Requisites of Democracy: Economic Development and Political Legitimacy." *American Political Science Review* 53 (1): 69–105.

Lipset, Seymour Martin, and Stein Rokkan. 1967. "Cleavage Structures, Party Systems, and Voter Alignments." In *Party Systems and Voter Alignments: Cross-National Perspectives*, eds. S. M. Lipset and S. Rokkan. New York: The Free Press: 1–64.

Lluco, Miguel. 2005. "Acerca del Movimiento de Unidad Plurinacional Pachakutik-Nuevo País." In *Movimiento indígena en América Latina: Resistencia y proyecto alternativo*, eds. F. Escárzaga and R. Gutiérrez. Mexico City: Gobierno del Distrito Federal: 119–32.

López, Santiago. 2005. "Partidos desafiantes en América Latina: Representación política y estrategias de competencia de las nuevas oposiciones." *Revista de Ciencia Política* 25 (2): 37–64.

Lucero, José Antonio. 2008. *Struggles of Voice: The Politics of Indigenous Representation in the Andes*. Pittsburgh: University of Pittsburgh Press.

"Lucio y las elecciones." 2002. *Sente* 16, May, 40–3.

"Luis Macas es el candidato de Pachakutik a la Presidencia." 2006. *Kipu* 47: 375–6.

Macdonald Jr., Theodore. 2002. "Ecuador's Indian Movement: Pawn in a Short Game or Agent in State Reconfiguration." In *The Politics of Ethnicity*, ed. D. Maybury-Lewis. Cambridge: David Rockefeller Center for Latin American Studies, Harvard University: 170–97.

Mack, Luis Fernando. 2007. "La participación política de los grupos étnicos de ascendenscia mayense: Algunas reflexiones." In *Multiculturidad y partidos políticos: Estudios sobre organización y participación de los pueblos indígenas*. Guatemala: Organización de los Estados Americanos: 11–69.

Mäckelmann, Mathias. 2006. "Perú 2006: Comunicación política y elecciones." *Diálogo Político* 23 (2): 11–34.

Madrid, Raúl L. 2005a. "Ethnic Cleavages and Electoral Volatility in Latin America." *Comparative Politics* 38 (1): 1–20.

   2005b. "Indigenous Parties and Democracy in Latin America." *Latin American Politics and Society* 47 (4): 161–79.

   2005c. "Indigenous Voters and Party System Fragmentation in Latin America." *Electoral Studies* 24 (4): 689–707.

   2008. "The Rise of Ethnopopulism in Latin America." *World Politics* 60 (3): 475–508.

   2010. "The Origins of the Two Lefts in Latin America." *Political Science Quarterly* 125 (4): 587–609.

   2011. "Ethnic Proximity and Ethnic Voting in Peru." *Journal of Latin American Studies* 43 (2): 267–97.

Mainwaring, Scott, Ana María Bejarano, and Eduardo Pizarro Leongómez, eds. 2006. *The Crisis of Democratic Representation in the Andes*. Stanford, CA: Stanford University Press.

Mainwaring, Scott P. 2006. "State Deficiencies, Party Competition, and Confidence in Democratic Representation in the Andes." In *The Crisis of Democratic Representation in the Andes*, eds. S. P. Mainwaring, A. M. Bejarano, and E. Pizarro Leongómez. Stanford, CA: Stanford University Press: 295–345.

Mainwaring, Scott, and Timothy Scully, eds. 2003. *Christian Democracy in Latin America: Electoral Competition and Regime Conflicts*. Stanford, CA: Stanford University Press.

Marenghi, Patricia, and Manuel Alcántara Sáez. 2007. "Los partidos étnicos de América del Sur: Algunos factores que explican su rendimiento." In *Pueblos indígenas y política en América Latina*, ed. S. Martí i Puig. Barcelona: Bellaterra-CIDOB: 57–101.

Martínez Sánchez, Francisco. 2004. "El primer partido político indígena de México." *Derecho y Cultura* 13: 103–16.

Massal, Julie. 2005. *Les mouvements indiens en Equateur: Mobilisations protestaires et démocratie*. Paris: Editions Karthala.

Mateos Díaz, Araceli, and Manuel Alcántara Sáez. 1998. *Los diputados ecuatorianos: Actitudes, valores y percepciones políticas.* Quito: PASGD.

Mathis, William. 2009. "U.S.-Bolivian Relations: Halting an Avalanche." Washington: Council on Hemispheric Affairs.

Maybury-Lewis, David, ed. 2002. *The Politics of Ethnicity: Indigenous Peoples in Latin American States.* Cambridge, MA: David Rockefeller Center for Latin American Studies, Harvard University.

Mayorga, René Antonio. 2005. "Bolivia's Democracy at the Crossroads." In *The Third Wave of Democratization in Latin America,* eds. S. P. Mainwaring and F. Hagopian. New York: Cambridge University Press: 149–78.

Medina García, Oswaldo. 1980. *Perú (1978–1980): Análisis de un momento político* Lima: C'est Editorial.

Meguid, Bonnie M. 2008. Institutional Change and Ethnoterritorial Party Representation at the European Level. Paper delivered at the conference on European Identities? Regionalism, Nationalism and Religion, October. London, UK.

Mejía Acosta, J. Andrés. 2002. *Gobernabilidad democrática: Sistema electoral, partidos políticos y pugna de poderes en Ecuador, 1978–1998.* Quito: Fundación Konrad Adenauer.

"Menchú Wades into Public Security Debate." 2007. *Latin American Weekly Report,* March 22.

Mijeski, Kenneth J., and Scott H. Beck. 2011. *Pachakutik and the Rise and Decline of the Ecuadorian Indigenous Movement.* Athens: Ohio University Press.

Mirador Electoral. 2007. "La participación indígena en el proceso electoral Guatemala 2007: Una tarea inconclusa." Guatemala.

Molina B., Ramiro, and Xavier Albó. 2006. *Gama étnica y lingüística de la población boliviana.* La Paz: Programa de las Naciones Unidas para el Desarrollo.

Monge Oviedo, Rodolfo. 1992. "Are We or Aren't We?" *NACLA Report on the Americas* 25 (4): 19.

Montúfar, César. 2008. "El populismo intermitente de Lucio Gutiérrez." In *El retorno del pueblo: Populismo y nuevas democracias en América Latina,* eds. C. de la Torre and E. Peruzzotti. Quito: FLACSO: 267–298.

"Morales Prepares Ground to Rule Until 2018." 2007. *Latin American Weekly Report,* April 12, 3.

Moreno Morales, Daniel, Eduardo Córdova Eguivar, Vivian Schwarz Blum, Mitchell A. Seligson, Gonzalo Vargas Villazón, and Miguel Villarroel Nikitenko. 2008. *The Political Culture of Democracy in Bolivia, 2008.* Nashville: Latin American Public Opinion Project.

Morgan Kelly, Jana. 2003. "Counting on the Past or Investing in the Future? Economic and Political Accountability in Fujimori's Peru." *The Journal of Politics* 65 (3): 864–80.

Mörner, Magnus. 1967. *Race Mixture in the History of Latin America.* Boston: Little, Brown and Company.

Movimiento al Socialismo. 2002. *Programa de gobierno: Territorio, soberanía, vida.* La Paz: Movimiento al Socialismo.

    2009. *2010–2015 Programa de gobierno: Bolivia, país líder.* La Paz: Movimiento al Socialismo.

Movimiento Unidad Plurinacional Pachakutik – Nuevo País. 1998. "Declaración de principios ideológicos." Quito: MUPP-NP.

Mudde, Cas. 2007. *Populist Radical Right Parties in Europe.* Cambridge, UK; New York: Cambridge University Press.

Mudde, Cas, and Cristobal Rovira Kaltwasser. 2010. "To the Right, To the Left? Populism in Europe and Latin America Compared." Paper delivered at Annual Meeting of the American Political Science Association, September 2–5, 2010, Washington, DC.

Muñoz-Pogossian, Beatriz. 2008. *Electoral Rules and the Transformation of Bolivian Politics: The Rise of Evo Morales*. New York: Palgrave MacMillan.

Muñoz Chirinos, Paula. 2011. "Más allá de la campaña." *Opinión & Análisis* 2: 9–16.

Mustillo, Thomas J. 2007. Entrants in the Political Arena: New Party Trajectories During the Third Wave of Democracy in Latin America. Dissertation, Dept. of Political Science, University of North Carolina, Chapel Hill.

"New 'Plurinational' State Begins to Take Shape." 2010. *Latin American Andean Group Report*, June, 4.

Nobles, Melissa. 2000. *Shades of Citizenship: Race and the Census in Modern Politics*. Stanford, CA: Stanford University Press.

Norris, Pippa. 2004. *Electoral Engineering: Voting Rules and Political Behavior*. Cambridge, UK; New York: Cambridge University Press.

Núñez, Rogelio. 2011a. "Ollanta Humala, entre Chávez y Lula." *Infolatam*, 7 abril.

  2011b. "Perú: lo que Ollanta Humala esconde." *Infolatam*, 30 marzo.

Oakley, Peter. 2001. "Social Exclusion and Afro-Latinos: A Contemporary Review." Washington: Inter-American Development Bank.

Olmos, José. 2003. "Vargas Llosa dice que el indigenismo es un peligro democrático." *El Universo*.

Oppenheimer, Andres. 2003. "What Would Latin America Be Without Western Influence?" *The Miami Herald*, 16A.

Ordeshook, Peter C., and Olga V. Shvetsova. 1994. "Ethnic heterogeneity, district magnitude, and the number of parties." *American Journal of Political Science* 38 (1): 100–23.

Orellana, Patricia, Claudia Méndez Villaseñor, Francisco González Arrecis, and Jessica Osorio. 2007. "Arrecian ataques verbales en campaña." *Prensa Libre*, June 25.

Ortiz Loaiza, Paola, María Alejandra Erazo, Silvia Montepeque, and Sara Sapón. 2008. "22 años después: lo inédito del proceso electoral 2007." In *Cuadernos de información política*. Guatemala: FLACSO.

"Pachakutik pierde su fuerza urbana." 2005. *El Comercio*, December 14.

"Pachakutik se requesbraja por el indigenismo." 2005. *El Comercio*, December 15.

"Pachakutik va en alianza: Rafael Correa es su primera opción." 2006. *Kipu* 47: 289–90.

Pachano, Simón. 2007. *La trama de Penélope: Procesos políticos e instituciones en el Ecuador*. Quito: FLACSO, Sede Ecuador.

Pacheco, Diego. 1992. *El indianismo y los indios contemporáneos en Bolivia*. La Paz, Bolivia: HISBOL/MUSEF.

Pajuelo Teves, Ramón. 2006. *Participación política indígena en la sierra peruana: Una aproximación desde las dinámicas nacionales y locales*. Lima: Instituto de Estudios Peruanos.

  2007. *Reinventando comunidades imaginadas: Movimientos indígenas, nación y procesos sociopolíticos en los países centroandinos*. Lima: Instituto Francés de Estudios Andinos.

Palacín Quispe, Miguel. 2008. *Respuesta comunitaria a la invasión minera y la crisis política: CONACAMI para el mundo*. Lima: CONACAMI.

Pallares, Amalia. 2002. *From Peasant Struggles to Indian Resistance: The Ecuadorian Andes in the late 20th Century*. Norman: University of Oklahoma Press.

Panfichi, Aldo. 2006. "El comandante Ollanta Humala: ¿Outsider o insider?" *Coyuntura: Análisis Económico y Social de Actualidad* 2 (6): 15–17.

Panizza, Francisco, ed. 2005. *Populism and the Mirror of Democracy*. London: Verso.

Paredes Castro, Juan. 2006. "Comentario del editor: Cara y cruz en los atributos de los candidatos." *El Comercio*, March 4.

Paredes, Maritza. 2006. "Discurso indígena y conflicto minero en el Perú." In *Perú: El problema agrario en debate – SEPIA XI*, ed. J. Iguiñiz, J. Escobal and C. I. Degregori. Lima: SEPIA: 501–39.

———. 2007. "Fluid Identities: Exploring Ethnicity in Peru." *CRISE Working Paper* 40.

———. 2008. "Weak Indigenous Politics in Peru." *CRISE Working Paper* 33.

Paschel, Tianna S., and Mark Q. Sawyer. 2008. "Contesting Politics as Usual: Black Social Movements, Globalization, and Race Policy in Latin America." *Souls* 10 (3): 197–214.

Patiño, Ninfa. 1996. *El discurso de los políticos frente al otro*. Quito: Abya-Yala.

Patzi Paco, Félix. 1999. *Insurgencia y sumisión: Movimiento indigena-campesino (1983–1998)*. La Paz: Muela del Diablo Editores.

———. 2004. "De movimiento indígena al fracaso en la escena del parlamento." *Temas Sociales* 25: 77–109.

Payne, J. Mark, Daniel Zovatto G., Fernando Carrillo Flórez, and Andrés Allamand Zavala. 2002. *Democracies in Development: Politics and Reform in Latin America*. Washington: Inter-American Development Bank.

Pedraglio, Santiago, and Martín Paredes Oporto. 2003. "El poder alucinado: Una entrevista con Antauro Humala." *Quehacer* 144: 26–40.

"Perfil de los candidatos." 2002. *Cursor*, November 15, 7–8.

"Perú: carrera hacia la presidencia sigue incierta a días de los comicios." 2011. *Infolatam*, 30 mayo.

"Perú: Ollanta Humala y Keiko Fujimori compiten por moderar sus discursos." 2011. *Infolatam*, 27 abril.

Perz, Stephen G., Jonathan Warren, and David P. Kennedy. 2008. "Contributions of Racial-Ethnic Reclassification and Demographic Processes to Indigenous Population Resurgence: The Case of Brazil." *Latin American Research Review* 43 (2): 7–33.

Planas, Pedro. 2000. *La democracia volátil: Movimientos, partidos, líderes políticos y conductas electorales en el Perú contemporáneo*. Lima: Friedrich Ebert Stiftung.

"A political awakening." 2004. *The Economist*, February 21, 35–7.

Pontificia Universidad Católica del Perú – Instituto de Opinión Pública. 2006. "De cara a la segunda vuelta electoral." Lima: PUCP.

———. 2011. "Intención de voto presidencial 2011." *Estado de la Opinión Pública* 6.

Posner, Daniel N. 2005. *Institutions and Ethnic Politics in Africa*. Cambridge; New York: Cambridge University Press.

Postero, Nancy. 2004. "Articulation and Fragmentation: Indigenous Politics in Bolivia." In *The Struggle for Indigenous Rights in Latin America*, eds. N. Postero and L. Zamosc. Portland: Sussex Academic Press: 189–216.

Postero, Nancy and León Zamosc, eds. 2004. *The Struggle for Indigenous Rights in Latin America*. Portland: Sussex Academic Press.

Powell, G. Bingham. 1976. "Political Cleavage Structure, Cross-Pressure Processes, and Partisanship: An Empirical Test of the Theory." *American Journal of Political Science* 20 (1): 1–23.

Programa de las Naciones Unidas para el Desarrollo. 2004. *Interculturalismo y globalización: La Bolivia posible*. La Paz: PNUD.

Psacharopoulos, George, and Harry Anthony Patrinos, eds. 1994. *Indigenous People and Poverty in Latin America: An Empirical Analysis.* Washington: The World Bank.

Quintero López, Rafael. 1978. Los partidos políticos en el Ecuador y la clase terrateniente en las transformaciones del Estado. Dissertation, Dept. of Political Science, University of North Carolina, Chapel Hill.

2005. *Electores contra partidos en un sistema política de mandos.* Quito: Ediciones Abya-Yala.

Quispe Lázaro, Arturo. 2007. *La interculturalidad: Un debate necesario en el Perú,* [accessed July 13, 2008]. Available from http://www.eibsur.org/ver_entrevista.php?id= 2010006.

Rabushka, Alvin, and Kenneth Shepsle. 1972. *Politics in Plural Societies.* Columbus: Merrill Publishing.

Rae, Douglas. 1971. *The Political Consequences of Electoral Laws.* New Haven: Yale University Press.

Ramón Valarezo, Galo. 1993. *El regreso de los runas: La potencialidad del proyecto indio en el Ecuador contemporaneo.* Quito: COMUNIDEC-Fundación Interamericana.

Rasch, Elisabet Dueholm. 2011. "'The Root is Maya, the Practice is Pluralist': Xel-jú and Indigenous Political Mobilisation in Quetzaltenango, Guatemala." *Bulletin of Latin American Research* 30 (4): 1–15.

Recalde, Paulina. 2007. "Elecciones presidenciales 2006: Una aproximación a los actores del proceso." *Iconos* 27: 15–25.

"Regional Parties Make Gains at García's Expense." 2006. *Latin American Andean Group Report,* December, 13.

Reilly, Benjamin. 2001. *Democracy in Divided Societies: Electoral Engineering for Conflict Management.* New York: Cambridge University Press.

Relea, Francesca. 2000. "El 'fenómeno Toledo'." *El País,* April 4, 8.

Remy, María Isabel. 1995. "The Indigenous Population and the Construction of Democracy in Peru." In *Indigenous Peoples and Democracy in Latin America,* ed. D. L. Van Cott. New York: St. Martin's Press: 107–30.

"Reyes Villa demands that Morales resign." 2007. *Latin American Weekly Report,* September 6.

Reyna Izaguirre, Carlos, Martín Monsalve Zanatti, Carlota Casalino Sen, and Daniel Parodi Revoredo. 2004. *Los procesos electorales entre 1989–1995: Problemas y lecciones.* Lima: Oficina Nacional de Procesos Electorales.

Reynolds, Louise. 2007. "Participación política de indígenas sin cuotas de poder." *Inforpress Centroamericana,* August 17.

Ribando Seelke, Clare. 2008. "Afro-Latinos in Latin America and Considerations for U.S. Policy." In *CRS Report for Congress.* Washington: Congressional Research Service.

Rice, Roberta Lynne. 2006. From Peasants to Politicians: The Politicization of Ethnic Cleavages in Latin America. Dissertation, Dept. of Political Science, The University of New Mexico, Albuquerque.

Rice, Roberta Lynne, and Donna Lee Van Cott. 2006. "The Emergence and Performance of Indigenous People's Parties in South America: A Subnational Statistical Analysis." *Comparative Political Studies* 39 (6): 709–32.

Rivera Cusicanqui, Silvia. 1986. *Oprimidos pero no vencidos: Luchas del campesinado aymara y quechua de Bolivia, 1900–1980.* Ginebra: Instituto de Investigaciones de las Naciones Unidas para el Desarrollo Social.

Rivero Pinto, Wigberto. 2002. "Indígenas y campesinos en las elecciones: El poder de la Bolivia emergente." *Opiniones y Análisis* 60: 11–40.
Roberts, Kenneth M. 1995. "Neoliberalism and the Transformation of Populism in Latin America: The Peruvian Case." *World Politics* 48 (1): 82–116.
　2006. "Populism, Political Conflict, and Grass-Roots Organization in Latin America." *Comparative Politics* 38 (2): 127–48.
　2007. "Latin America's Populist Revival." *SAIS Review* 27 (1): 3–15.
Roberts, Kenneth M., and Moisés Arce. 1998. "Neoliberalism and Lower-class Voting Behavior in Peru" *Comparative Political Studies* 31 (2): 217–47.
Rocha, José Antonio. 1992. "Apuntes en torno al planteamiento político aymara." In *La cosmovisión aymara*. La Paz: Hisbol: 241–63.
Rojas Ortuste, Gonzalo. 2000. "La eleccion de alcaldes en los municipios del país en 1999–2000: Persistencia de la coalición nacional." *Opiniones y Análisis* 49: 83–113.
Rojas Ortuste, Gonzalo, and Luis Verdesoto Custode. 1997. *La Participación Popular como reforma de la política: Evidencias de una cultura democrática boliviana*. La Paz: Secretaría Nacional de Participación Popular (SNPP).
Romero Ballivián, Salvador. 1999. *Reformas, conflictos y consensos*. 1a ed. La Paz, Bolivia: Fundación Hanns-Seidel : Fundemos.
　2002. "La elección presidencial 2002: Una visión de conjunto." *Opiniones y Análisis* 57.
　2003. *Geografía electoral de Bolivia*. 3. ed. La Paz, Bolivia: Fundemos.
　2005. *En la bifurcación del camino: Análisis de los resultados de las elecciones municipales 2004*. La Paz: Corte Nacional Electoral.
　2006. *El tablero reordenado: Análisis de la elección presidencial de 2005*. 1. ed. La Paz: Corte Nacional Electoral.
Rosenblat, Angel. 1954. *La población indígena y el mestizaje en América Latina*. Buenos Aires: Editorial Nova.
Sachs, Jeffrey. 1989. *Social Conflict and Populist Policies in Latin America*. Cambridge, Mass.: National Bureau for Economic Research.
San Martín Arzabe, Hugo. 1991. *El Palenquismo: Movimiento social, populismo, informalidad política*. La Paz: Editorial Los Amigos del Libro.
Sánchez, Enrique, and Paola García. 2006. "Los Afrocolombianos." In *Más allá de los promedios: Afrodescendientes en América Latina*, eds. J. Stubbs and H. N. Reyes. Washington: The World Bank.
Sánchez López, Francisco, and Flavia Freidenberg. 1998. "El proceso de incorporación política de los sectores indígenas en el Ecuador: Pachakutik, un caso de estudio." *América Latina Hoy* 19: 65–79.
Sánchez-Parga, José. 1996. *Población y pobreza indígenas*. Quito: Centro Andino de Acción Popular.
　1999. "La campaña electoral: Ecuador 1998." In *Campañas electorales y medios de comunicación en América Latina*, eds. F. Priess and F. Tuesta Soldevilla. Buenos Aires: CIEDLA: 381–457.
　2007. *El movimiento indígena ecuatoriano*. Quito: Centro Andino de Acción Popular.
Sanjinés C., Javier. 2004. *Mestizaje Upside-Down: Aesthetic Politics in Modern Bolivia*. Pittsburgh: University of Pittsburgh Press.
Santana, Roberto. 1995. *Ciudadanos en la etnicidad: Los indios en la política o la política de los indios*. Quito: Ediciones Abya-Yala.

Santos, Aldo, and Paulo Vilca Arpasi. 2011. "Puno: En busca de perdedores y ganadores." *Revista Argumentos* 5 (2): 56–9.

Sartori, Giovanni. 1970. "Concept Misformation in Comparative Politics." *American Political Science Review* 64: 1033–53.

    1976. *Parties and Party Systems: A Framework for Analysis.* Cambridge: Cambridge University Press.

Schady, Norbert R. 2000. "The Political Economy of Expenditures by the Peruvian Social Fund (FONCODES), 1991–95." *American Political Science Review* 94 (2): 289–304.

Schmidt, Gregory D. 2000. "Delegative Democracy in Peru? Fujimori's Landslide and the Prospects for 2000." *Journal of Interamerican Studies and World Affairs* 42 (1): 99–132.

    2002. "The Presidential Election in Peru, April 2000." *Electoral Studies* 21: 339–63.

Secretaría Técnica del Frente Social. 2006. *Racismo y discriminación racial en Ecuador.* Quito: Secretaría Técnica del Frente Social.

Seligson, Mitchell A., Abby B. Cordova, Juan Carlos Donoso, Daniel Moreno, Diana Orcés, and Vivian Schwarz-Blum. 2006. *Democracy Audit: Bolivia 2006 Report.* Nashville: Latin American Public Opinion Project.

Seligson, Mitchell A., Daniel Moreno Morales, and Vivian Schwarz Blum. 2004. *Democracy Audit: Bolivia 2004 Report.* Nashville: Latin American Public Opinion Project.

Selverston-Scher, Melina. 2001. *Ethnopolitics in Ecuador: Indigenous Rights and the Strengthening of Democracy.* Miami: North-South Center Press.

Selverston, Melina. 1994. "The Politics of Culture: Indigenous Peoples and the State in Ecuador." In *Indigenous Peoples and Democracy in Latin America*, ed. D. L. Van Cott. New York: St. Martin's Press: 131–52.

Sheriff, Robin. 2001. *Dreaming Equality: Color, Race and Racism in Urban Brazil.* New Brunswick: Rutgers University Press.

Shugart, Matthew Soberg, and John M. Carey. 1992. *Presidents and Assemblies: Constitutional Design and Electoral Dynamics.* New York: Cambridge University Press.

Sidanius, Jim, Yesilernis Peña, and Mark Sawyer. 2001. "Inclusionary Discrimination: Pigmentocracy and Patriotism in the Dominican Republic." *Political Psychology* 22 (4): 827–51.

Sifuentes Alemán, Ítalo. 2006. "Ollanta Humala ofrece revisar la deuda externa." *El Comercio*, March 19.

Sisk, Timothy D. 1996. *Power Sharing and International Mediation in Ethnic Conflicts.* Washington: U.S. Institute of Peace Press.

Sistema Integrado de Indicadores Sociales del Ecuador. 2007a. "Cifras de la desigualdad y la etnicidad en Ecuador." *Indice* (10): 8.

    2007b. "Indígenas y afrodescendientes: Etnicidad y desigualdad (resultados de la ECV 2006)." *Indice* (10): 6–7.

Stefanoni, Pablo. 2004. "Algunas reflexiones sobre el MAS-IPSP." *Temas Sociales* 25: 15–43.

Stefanoni, Pablo, and Hervé Do Alto. 2006. *Evo Morales, de la coca al palacio : una opportunidad para la izquierda indígena.* 1. ed. La Paz: Malatesta.

Subramanian, Narendra. 1999. *Ethnicity and Populist Mobilization: Political Parties, Citizens, and Democracy in South India.* Delhi: Oxford University Press.

Sue, Christina. 2009. "An Assessment of the Latin Americanization Thesis." *Ethnic and Racial Studies.* 32 (6): 1058–70.

Sulmont Haak, David. 2005. *Encuesta nacional sobre exclusión y discriminación social: Informe final de análisis de resultados.* Lima: Estudio para la Defensa y los Derechos de la Mujer.

———. 2009. "Lineas de frontera y comportamiento electoral en el Perú." Lima: Pontificia Universidad Católica del Perú.

Tanaka, Martín. 1998. *Los espejismos de la democracia: El colapso del sistema de partidos en el Perú.* Lima: Instituto de Estudios Peruanos.

Tanaka, Martín, Rodrigo Barrenechea, and Sofía Vera. 2011. "Cambios y continuidades en las elecciones presidenciales de 2011." *Revista Argumentos* 5 (2): 3–10.

Tannenbaum, Frank. 1947. *Slave and Citizen, the Negro in the Americas.* New York,: A. A. Knopf.

Tapia, Luciano. 1995. *Ukhamawa jakawisaxa = Asi es nuestra vida: Autobiografía de un aymara.* La Paz: Hisbol.

Taylor, Lewis. 1987. "Agrarian Unrest and Political Conflict in Puno, 1985–1987." *Bulletin of Latin American Research* 6 (2): 135–62.

———. 2001. "Alberto Fujimori's Peripeteia: From 'Re-Reelección' to Regime Collapse." *Revista Europea de Estudios Latinoamericanos y del Caribe* (70): 3–24.

Telles, Edward E. 2004. *Race in Another America: The Significance of Skin Color in Brazil.* Princeton: Princeton University Press.

Ticona Alejo, Esteban, Gonzalo Rojas Ortuste, and Xavier Albó. 1995. *Votos y wiphalas: Campesinos y pueblos originarios en democracia.* La Paz: Fundación Milenio-Centro de Investigación y Promoción del Campesinado.

Tituaña, Auki. 1996. "Cotacachi: el reto de la minga cantonal." In *Por el camino del arco iris.* Quito: Agencia Latinoamericana de Información: 101–5.

Torres Guzmán, Alfredo. 1989. *Perfil del elector.* Lima: Editorial Apoyo.

Tribunal Supremo Electoral. 1981. *Principios ideológicos y planes de gobierno de los partidos políticos de la República del Ecuador.* Quito: Tribunal Supremo Electoral.

Trivelli, Carolina. 2005. *Los hogares indígenas y la pobreza en el Perú: Una mirada a partir de la información cuantitativa.* Lima: Instituto de Estudios Peruanos.

Tronconi, Filippo. 2005. "Ethnic Identity and Party Competition: An Analysis of the Electoral Performance of Ethnoregionalist Parties in Western Europe." *World Political Science Review* 2 (2): 137–63.

U.S. Department of State. 2007. "Country Reports on Human Rights Practices – 2006: Bolivia." Washington: U.S. Department of State.

United Nations. 1986. "Study of the Problem of Discrimination against Indigenous Populations." New York.

Urioste, Miguel. 2004. "Ninguno de los indígenas que está en el Parlamento hoy en día hubiera llegado a ese nivel si no era a través de la Participación Popular." In *Voces críticas de la descentralización*, ed. D. Ayo. La Paz: Friedrich Ebert Stiftung: 333–63.

Vaca, Marcos, and Gabriel Muñoz. 2006. "La fisura indígena afloró en las urnas." *Kipu* 48: 213.

Valladares de la Cruz, Laura. 2009. "La construcción de democracias indígenas desde abajo: Los caminos de la colonización del Estado en tiempos multiculturales." Paper delivered at Congress of the Latin American Studies Association, June 11–14, 2009, Rio de Janeiro.

Van Cott, Donna Lee. 2000. *The Friendly Liquidation of the Past: The Politics of Diversity in Latin America*. Pittsburgh: University of Pittsburgh Press.

2003a. "Andean Indigenous Movements and Constitutional Transformation: Venezuela in Comparative Perspective." *Latin American Perspectives* 30 (1): 49–69.

2003b. "From Exclusion to Inclusion: Bolivia's 2002 Elections." *Journal of Latin American Studies* 35 (4): 751–76.

2003c. "Institutional Change and Ethnic Parties in South America." *Latin American Politics and Society* 45 (2): 1–39.

2005. *From Movements to Parties in Latin America: The Evolution of Ethnic Politics*. New York: Cambridge University Press.

2007. "Country Report – Bolivia." In *Countries at the Crossroads 2007*. New York: Freedom House.

2009. *Radical Democracy in the Andes*. New York: Cambridge University Press.

Van Evera, Stephen. 2001. "Primordialism Lives!" *APSA-CP* 12 (1): 20–2.

Vargas Llosa, Mario. 1994. *A Fish in the Water: A Memoir*. New York: Farrar, Straus and Giroux.

Verdesoto Custode, Luis. 2005. *Instituciones y gobernabilidad en Ecuador: A un cuarto de siglo de democracia*. Quito: Ediciones Abya-Yala.

Vergara, Alberto. 2011. "El Perú tras la elección imposible." *Letras Libres* (Julio).

Wade, Peter. 1997. *Race and Ethnicity in Latin America*. Chicago, Ill.: Pluto Press.

Weismantel, Mary. 2001. *Cholas and Pishtacos: Stories of Race and Sex in the Andes*. Chicago: University of Chicago Press.

Weyland, Kurt. 1999. "Neoliberal Populism in Latin America and Eastern Europe." *Comparative Politics* 31 (4): 379–401.

2000. "A Paradox of Success? Determinants of Political Support for President Fujimori." *International Studies Quarterly* 44: 481–502.

2001. "Clarifying a Contested Concept: Populism in the Study of Latin American Politics." *Comparative Politics* 34 (1): 1–22.

Whitten, Norman, ed. 1981. *Cultural Transformations and Ethnicity in Modern Ecuador*. Champaign: University of Illinois Press.

Wilkinson, Steven. 2006. *Votes and Violence: Electoral Competition and Ethnic Riots in India*. Cambridge, UK; New York: Cambridge University Press.

Wray, Natalia. 1996. "Proyecto de investigación: Pueblos indígenas y participación electoral." Quito: CEPLAES.

Yashar, Deborah J. 2005. *Contesting Citizenship in Latin America: The Rise of Indigenous Movements and the Postliberal Challenge*. New York: Cambridge University Press.

Zamosc, Leon. 1994. "Agrarian Protest and the Indian Movement in the Ecuadorian Highlands." *Latin American Research Review* 29 (3): 37–68.

2004. "The Indian Movement in Ecuador: From Politics of Influence to Politics of Power." In *The Struggle for Indigenous Rights in Latin America*, eds. N. Postero and L. Zamosc. Brighton: Sussex Academic Press: 131–57.

Zeas, Santiago. 2006. "Pachakutik teme otro fracaso." *Kipu* 47: 224–5.

Zegada Claure, María Teresa. 2002. "Sorpresas de la elección: MNR, MAS, NFR y ADN." *Opiniones y Análisis* 57: 47–83.

Zimmerman, Yvonne. 2002. "Taking It from the Streets." *In These Times*, September 16, 8.

Index

Acción Democrática Nacionalista (ADN), 42n10, 46, 66–7
Acción Popular (AP), 24, 121
Acevedo, Angela, 128
activism, 12–14, 148
    Colombia and, 153
    Bolivia and, 53–4
    Ecuador and, 85
    Guatemala and, 150
    Peru and, 117
    Venezuela and, 155
affirmative action, 3, 121
Afro-Latinos. *See also* blacks; mulattos
    Andes and, 146–7, 159–61
    legal restrictions on, 21
    Nicaragua and, 146
    prejudice and, 160
    traditional populism and, 161
agrarian reform, 25, 47–8, 119n11, 151, 168, 176, 180
Aguilar, Josefina, 169
Aguinaga, Carlos, 76–7
Albó, Xavier, 9, 39n2, 42n10, 47, 48n23, 166, 167n3
Alcántara, Manuel Sáez, 3, 9–10, 13, 35, 86, 96
Alenda Mary, Stéphanie, 48
Alianza Democrática M-19, 152–3
Alianza Electoral Frente Popular Llapanchik, 111
Alianza Nueva Nación, 150
Alianza País, 102, 105, 107, 129
Alianza para la Alternative de la Humanidad (APHU), 110
Alianza Social Afrocolombiana, 160
Alianza Social Indígena (ASI), 2, 27, 33, 146n1, 153–4

Alonso, Sonia, 191
Alvarez, Michael R., 68n49
Amazon, 27
    Bolivia and, 51n29
    Colombia and, 153–4
    Ecuador and, 83–5, 92, 102, 106
    Peru and, 109–10, 114–19, 130–1, 139, 142, 144
    Venezuela and, 154–6
Andes
    activism and, 148, 150, 153, 155
    Afro-Latinos and, 146–7, 159–61
    Amazon and, 153–6
    anti–establishment approach and, 148, 153, 163, 178–9, 183–4
    Aymara and, 166
    blacks and, 159–60
    coca growers and, 180
    Colombia and, 152–4
    democracy and, 33, 148, 160, 162–5, 170n7, 171–4
    demonstrations and, 168
    discrimination and, 150–1, 161, 163, 175–6, 183
    disenchantment in, 161
    education and, 151, 154, 165, 167, 169, 176–7, 181
    electoral issues and, 146–58, 164, 168–70, 177–8, 182
    ethnic fluidity and, 164
    ethnic parties and, 162–5, 183
    ethnic polarization and, 163–5
    ethnic representation and, 165–8
    exclusionary strategies and, 158, 161–5, 183
    fragmented party systems and, 147, 159
    Guatemala and, 147–52
    inclusive strategies and, 148, 151, 161, 183